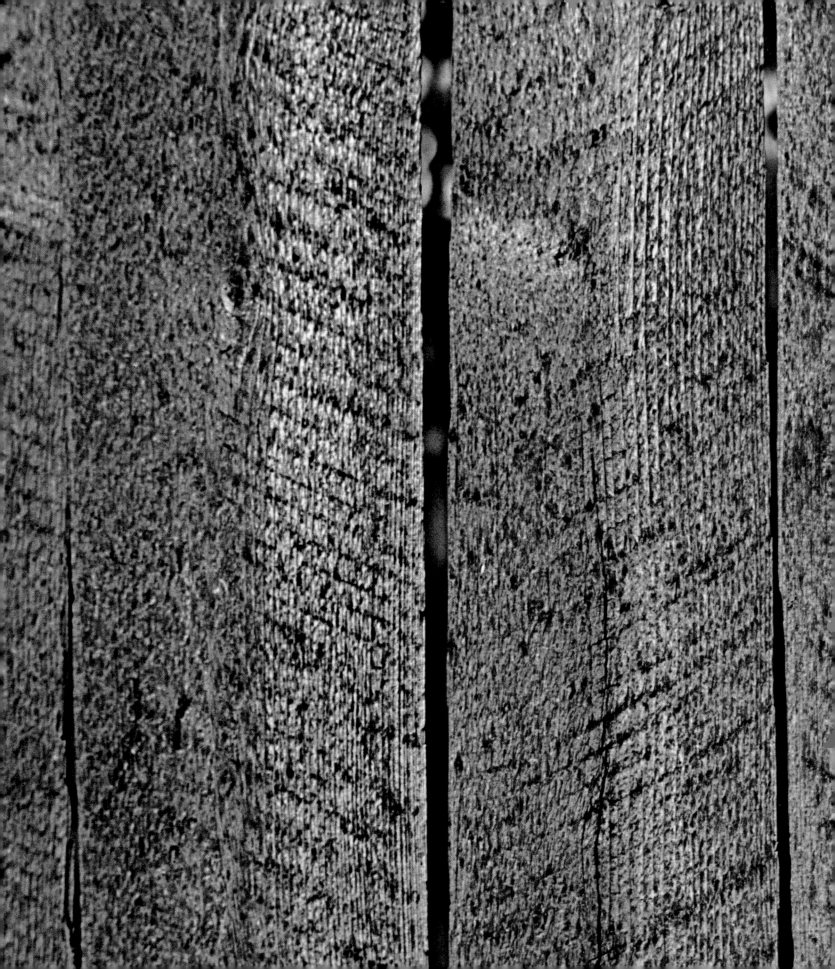

THE FAMILY CREATIVE WORKSHOP

7

Glass Working, Gold Leafing
Gold Panning, Granny Squares
Greenhouse Construction
Greeting Cards, Hammocks and Slings
Hardanger Embroidery
Heraldry, Herbs
Hibachi and Hot-Pot Cookery

Plenary Publications International, Inc.
New York and Amsterdam

Published by Plenary Publications
International Incorporated
300 East 40 Street, New York, N. Y.
10016, for the
Blue Mountain Crafts Council.

Library of Congress Catalog Card
Number: 73-89331.
Complete set International Standard
Book Number: 0-88459-021-6.
Volume 7 International Standard
Book Number: 0-88459-006-2.

Manufactured in the United States
of America. Printed and
bound by the W. A. Krueger
Company, Brookfield, Wisconsin.

Printing preparation
by Lanman Lithoplate Company.

Publishers:
Plenary Publications
International, Incorporated
300 East 40 Street
New York, New York 10016

Allen Davenport Bragdon
EDITOR-IN-CHIEF AND
PUBLISHER OF THE FAMILY
CREATIVE WORKSHOP

Nancy Jackson
ADMINISTRATIVE ASSISTANT

Jerry Curcio
PRODUCTION MANAGER

Editorial preparation:
Tree Communications, Inc.
250 Park Avenue South
New York, New York 10003

Rodney Friedman
EDITORIAL DIRECTOR

Ronald Gross
DESIGN DIRECTOR

Paul Levin
DIRECTOR OF PHOTOGRAPHY

Donal Dinwiddie
CONSULTING EDITOR

James Wyckoff
TEXT EDITOR

Sonja Douglas
ART DIRECTOR

Rochelle Lapidus
ASSOCIATE DESIGNER

Betty Friedman
ADMINISTRATIVE MANAGER

Barnet Friedman
COPYREADER

Editors for this volume:
Frank Cogan
GOLDLEAFING

Andrea DiNoto
GLASSWORKING
HERALDRY

Donal Dinwiddie
GOLD PANNING
HAMMOCKS AND SLINGS

Michael Donner
GREENHOUSE CONSTRUCTION

Linda Hetzer
GRANNY SQUARES
HARDANGER

Nancy Levine
GREETING CARDS

Marilyn Ratner
HERBS
HIBACHI AND
HOT-POT COOKERY

Contributing illustrators:
Sonja Douglas
Harry Fischman
Pat Lee
Nancy Levine
Ruth Nowakowski
Sally Shimizu

Contributing photographers:
Dick Anderson
Dick Frank
Ronald Gross
Paul Levin
Frank Lusk
Stephen McCarroll

Contributing editors:
Edward Claflin
Stuart James
Molli Nickell
Nona Remos
Lari Siler

Photo credits:
GLASS WORKING:
Egyptian Vase,
Corning Museum of Glass,
Corning, New York,
page 775. GREENHOUSE
CONSTRUCTION: Window
Greenhouse, Lord
Burham, Irvington, New
York, page 816.
HERALDRY: U.S. Seal,
Local History and
Genealogy Division, The
New York Public
Library, Astor, Lenox
and Tilden Foundation,
page 871.

Acknowledgements:
HERALDRY: Artwork on
pages 867, 870 (upper
left), and 872, 875
(lower right) are
reprinted from "Herald-
ry for the Designer"
by William Metzig by
courtesy of
Van Nostrand Reinhold
© 1969.

The Project-Evaluation
Symbols appearing in the
title heading at the
beginning of each project
have these meanings:

Range of approximate cost:

¢ Low: under $5 or free
and found natural materials

$ Medium: about $10

$$ High: above $15

**Estimated time to completion
for an unskilled adult:**

⧗ Hours

🕐 Days

Weeks

Suggested level of experience:
Child alone

Supervised child or
family project

Unskilled adult

Specialized prior training

Tools and equipment:
Small hand tools

Large hand
and household tools

Specialized
or powered equipment

On the cover:
Lampblown glass bottles
delicately formed in subtle and
vibrant colors by Suellen Fowler.
See entry "Glass Working,"
beginning on page 774.
Photograph by Paul Levin.

**Contents and
Craftspeople for Volume 7:**

GLASS WORKING
Forms by Hand and Flame

What flows like honey one moment, then stands rigid and brittle the next? What has no form of its own, yet takes any and all forms? Thousands of years ago, craftsmen became intrigued with the substance that posed such riddles: glass. Today, the methods of glass working that they evolved are still used in refined forms, as in the simple projects described on pages 776 through 779 and in the more advanced lampwork techniques shown on pages 780 through 787. The small opaque-glass ewer at right was made by a sand-core technique invented by the ancient Egyptians. This process involved immersing a vessel-shaped mold into a crucible of molten glass. The glass adhering to the mold was then shaped and ornamented. When the glass had cooled, the core was chipped out. This early glass was melted in ceramic crucibles heated with oil lamps, hence the derivation of the term "lampwork" to designate advanced work with glass and flame. In the First Century A.D., the blowpipe was invented, probably by a Syrian, and the techniques of glass working were revolutionized. That craftsman's method of blowing glass into a mold is still used, but differs from what is now called "off-hand" glassblowing or freeblown glass.

Off-Hand Glassblowing
Visitors to the famous glass factories throughout the world have seen spectacular demonstrations of off-hand glassblowing. The master glassblower raises a "gather" of molten glass from the mouth of the furnace, called the glory hole, and blows a magnificent bubble in the air, free of any mold. Crystal goblets, vases and art objects are made by this method; but mass-produced glass (such as the world's most ubiquitous soda bottles) is made by machines that reproduce the ancient mold-blowing technique on a grand scale.

Lampwork
Because the heavy metal blowpipes and blazing furnaces were unsuited to the crafting of delicate precision apparatus for laboratory and optical use, a method was devised in the nineteenth century for using small burners to heat and shape pre-blown glass. The result was the development of lampwork as a highly skilled craft. Today, lampwork is still used primarily for this purpose, but glass craftsmen are now applying the techniques to the creation of a great variety of art glass objects. Anyone who has taken a chemistry class in high school will have bent glass tubes and rods in a small flame. This simple demonstration of the properties of glass is also a good prelude to lampworking, or flameworking, as it is sometimes called.

Kinds of Glass
The chemistry of glass deserves study by any glass worker who wishes to delve more deeply into the nature of his medium. In simple terms, glass is formed by the fusion of three major oxides (oxides are elements that have combined with oxygen to form compounds): silica (sand), or silicon dioxide (SiO_2), is the most important in forming glass, imparting viscosity; soda, or sodium dioxide (NaO_2), speeds fluidity during melting; and lime, or calcium oxide (CaO), sometimes called calcia, adds durability to glass by protecting it against the corrosive effects of water. All of these elements occur abundantly in nature. Other kinds of oxides (lead is the most widely used, but there are many), when added in varying amounts to the basic combination, produce different kinds of glass varying in hardness, softness, heat resistance and color (see Craftnotes, page 783). The projects on the following pages use two basically different kinds of glasses, soft and hard. In the first three simple projects, the glass objects are hand-formed rather than blown.

Glass bottles blown by Suellen Fowler (see page 780) demonstrate what can be done with a craftsman's skilled and experienced hand. The balanced forms and subtle colorings result when advanced technique joins imagination to produce original design variations.

Carl H. Betz is a master glassblower and engineer whose varied career began 30 years ago as a glass worker in atomic research. Over the years, he has developed experimental glass laboratory equipment for both research and industrial projects, meanwhile pursuing artistic glass working as a hobby and avocation. He is the president of Glass Creations, a company specializing in hand-crafted fused-glass products. Mr. Betz lives in a suburb of Philadelphia.

Three thousand years ago, an Egyptian craftsman made this opaque glass ewer, which may have held the perfume and unguents of a queen. It was created during Egypt's eighteenth dynasty in the reign of Amenhotep II. Decorated with "snake threads" of colored glass, it is 4½ inches tall, approximately the size of the contemporary glass bottles opposite.

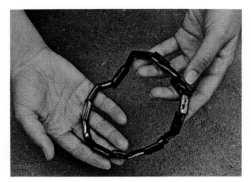

Iridescent gray-blue beads of lead glass can be made quickly and simply even by someone beginning to acquire glass-working skills.

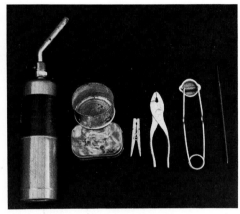

1: All of the soft-glass beginner projects described here can be made with these simple tools: propane torch, tunafish can, sardine can, spring clothespin, pliers, spark lighter and three-cornered file.

Glass and Plastics
Creations from soft glass $ ▯ 👥 ✈

Glasses with a high lead or soda-lime content are called soft because they have a low melting point. Soft glass is also called spun or knit glass and may be used to create small decorative objects. Lead glass tubing, used to make the iridescent beads pictured (left) is the same as that used in neon signs.

Since I have worked most of my life as a master glassblower in research and industry, I am familiar with the properties of all kinds of glasses. Over the years I have developed a special interest in the properties of soft glass and its advantages for the beginning craftsman. First, soft glass will melt in an ordinary propane-torch flame, unlike the hard Pyrex glass used by artists, which requires a much hotter, oxygen-enriched flame. This means that a beginner can work with glass without needing a complex heat source. Second, since no special tools are required, the over-all cost is small.

The techniques demonstrated in the three simple projects that follow evolved as the result of an invitation I received to create an introductory course in glass working for young people at a local arts center. There were no funds with which to purchase expensive glass working equipment; and the center did not wish to ask young students to make a large expenditure for materials. My ingenuity was put to the test and I accepted the challenge. I found that with adequate adult supervision, children between the ages of nine and thirteen were able to handle the torch and complete many satisfying projects in soft glass. The time required for each of the soft-glass projects is less than an hour. The lead glass beads are ready to be strung as soon as they have cooled, and the swizzle sticks may be plunged into tall, cool drinks soon after their colorful tops have been fire-polished.

Tools, Supplies and Materials
The few simple tools needed for the projects that follow are pictured (left). The propane torch with a pencil-burner tip (also called hot tip or jet tip), is manufactured under several brand names and is available at almost any hardware store. I usually work in my basement on a table surfaced with laminated plastic. You may wish to take the precaution of covering your work surface with asbestos padding to prevent scorch marks.

A supply of soft glass (lead and soda-lime) rods and tubing can be obtained from laboratory and neon-sign suppliers listed in the Yellow Pages. Though glass is usually sold by the pound, some suppliers prefer to sell small quantities of rods and tubes by the 4-foot length. You will need several lengths of 5-mm. and 3-mm. or 2-mm. solid rods (not tubing) of soda-lime glass. One length of 10-mm. lead glass tubing will make several of the iridescent necklaces. Lead glass discolors to a luminous blend of gray, blue and gold when heated. Soda-lime glass tubing will not discolor, but you may want to use it to make clear glass beads, then color them with lacquer, glass stain (available in hobby shops), or even nail polish. Any glass object can also be sprayed with gold or silver.

Iridescent Glass Beads
Select a length of 10-mm. lead glass tubing. Using the notched tin can (photograph 1) and the three-cornered file, break the rod first into more manageable 12-inch lengths, then into bead-sized pieces. Make your first cut by laying the tubing across the top of the notched can so that it rests in the notch (photograph 2), with 12 inches extending beyond the notch. Place the edge of the file on the tubing above the notch and draw it across, scraping sharply (photograph 3). Rap the tube sharply on the extended end and it will break cleanly (photograph 4). When you have made several 12-inch lengths in this manner, you can make bead-sized pieces (15 to 20 beads for a necklace). The edges of the beads can be made irregular by varying the position of the notched glass on the can before rapping (photograph 5). If you align the glass notch over the tin can notch, the break will be even. By varying the position of the glass notch, either inside or beyond the rim of the can, you can make the break become irregular.

2: Cut a notch into the rim of the tunafish can with a three-cornered file. This will serve as a holder on which to cut rods and tubes.

3: Rest the tubing in the notch and score the glass by drawing the edge of the file sharply across the glass, directly above the notch.

4: Rap the end of the tube good and hard with the three-cornered file. It will break off evenly and cleanly at the can's rim.

Fractures in individual beads do not mean that the bead must be discarded. As long as the bead is still intact, fractures can be fused in the flame of the torch. When you have cut enough beads for a necklace, ignite the torch with the spark lighter. Do not allow anyone to stand near the flame, do not wear loose clothing, and be sure to direct the flame away from you at all times. Place the sardine can, bottom side up, on the tuna can and set one bead on top. Adjust the flame so the inner cone is approximately 1 inch high. When you hold the ignited torch upside down, the flame may get larger, so you will have to allow for this when adjusting it. The bead must be heated first on both ends and then in the middle; the point of the inner cone of the flame must touch the glass. The flame is aimed at an angle (photograph 7) so that it penetrates the bead while heating the upper edge of one side to incandescence. When you have fire-polished both ends, bring the tip of the cone down close and direct it steadily at the very center of the bead (photograph 9) until it becomes incandescent and the color appears. The tin cans heat up during this process, so do not touch them with your hands at any time. Take the flame away and turn the bead over with the file. It may stick to the surface of the can but a slight tap with the file will loosen it.

5: These bead-sized pieces have been rapped from 12-inch lengths of glass rod.

Repeat the same firing process on the other side of the bead. The underside of the bead will not melt, as the tin can conducts heat away from the glass. For added decoration, you can press the tip of the file into the soft hot glass on one side to make indentations. But if you press too hard, or if you fire-polish the bead too long, the center will flatten and the bead will not be usable. You will learn how to time your firing by trial and error.

As each bead is finished, push it off the sardine can with the file into an aluminum foil saucer. Give the beads several minutes to cool; then they will be ready to be strung into necklaces like the one pictured opposite, or bracelets. Using thin round elastic eliminates the need for jewelry clasps; the elastic becomes invisible after the knot has been tied and trimmed. Glass beads can also be strung with other kinds of beads—wooden or metal—or added to leather fringe on bags and jackets.

6: Irregular edges and variations in length give an interesting effect in the finished beads.

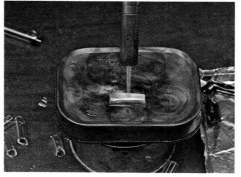

7: Using the bottom of a sardine can as a work surface, heat the open ends of bead segments, first one and then the other, to incandescence.

8: As you heat the second opening, you will see discoloration begin to transform the bead from clear to a gray-blue-gold iridescence.

9: To bring out the maximum iridescence of the lead glass, hold the torch steady and direct the flame's cone at the center of the bead.

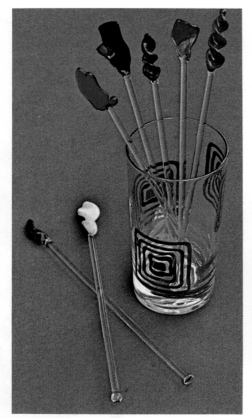

Garnish a glass of lemonade or a mint julep with a handmade swizzle stick. Colorful tops are made from scraps of ordinary bottle and cathedral glass, fused, twisted and swirled in a flame.

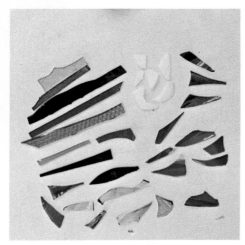

10: For swizzle sticks, choose glass fragments shaped somewhat like these. Avoid thick shards from large bottles, like gallon jugs.

Glass and Plastics
Swizzle sticks

The colorful twisted glass plumes atop the swizzle sticks at left were made from fragments of ordinary bottle and cathedral glass. The rods are 5-mm. soda-lime glass. Lead glass is not suggested for this project as the discoloration would not be desirable on swizzle sticks. Glass fragments of suitable shapes and sizes are also pictured (photograph 10). Scraps of cathedral glass can be bought at hobby shops (less than $1 a pound) or you can break up small colored glass bottles by wrapping them thickly in newspapers and smashing them with a hammer. Do not use large, heavy bottles because large pieces of thick glass might explode in the flame. Be

11: Hold a glass fragment and a rod of 5-mm. glass in the flame in a V formation and heat both until they start to melt. When both are drippy, press together, remove from flame and straighten.

12: Allow joint to set and return to flame. Heat the first ¼ inch of the fragment, turning it back and forth, from edge to edge, until the glass is soft enough to begin the twist.

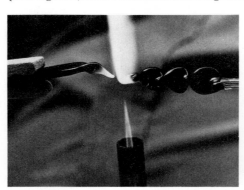

13: When the spiral is about 1½ inches long, sever the excess in the flame and fire polish the tip for a final shaping.

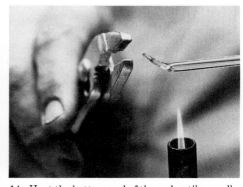

14: Heat the bottom end of the rod until a small glob of glass forms; then squeeze it with pliers and bend it up slightly to form a paddle.

15: To make a flat end, simply press the molten glob on a flat surface, such as the top of the tin can.

16: A tear-drop end is formed by rotating the glob at an angle in the flame until it droops slightly.

careful when selecting fragments to use as edges and points will be razor-sharp. It is best to pick up the ones you want with a spring-type wooden clothespin. Pieces chosen should be wedge-shaped and not less than 2 inches long or ½-inch wide. Excess length can be severed easily in the flame. Fragments should not be more than 3/16-inch thick. Use a clip-type wooden clothespin to hold the pieces of glass in the flame. Metal pliers should not be used as the metal would conduct heat away from the glass, causing it to crack.

Attach the fragment to the rod (photographs 11 and 12). Hold the clothespin steady and begin the spiral by twisting the rod (photograph 13). After you have severed the excess length (photograph 14) put the rod in a tin can and let the tip cool in the air. Methods for making three types of bottom ends are described in photographs 14, 15, and 16. In each case, give the end plenty of time to air-cool.

The glass tops need not always be twisted into spirals. If the fragment is an interesting shape, it can simply be attached to the rod and fire-polished.

Glass and Plastics
Form-a-loop sculpture

$ ⧖ 👪 ✈

The delicate free-form glass sculptures shown at right are made from lengths of 2-mm. solid glass rod. The basic rules for making form-a-loops are simple: (1) never use hollow tubing of any kind; and (2) except for the first loop (see photograph 18, below), never terminate a loop upon itself, but only upon the one preceding it. You will quickly find that a third hand is necessary if you break the latter rule. Use pieces of rod of uniform lengths to get the best results. Sculptures here were made from 9-inch lengths. Because of the thinness of the rod you will be able to use either

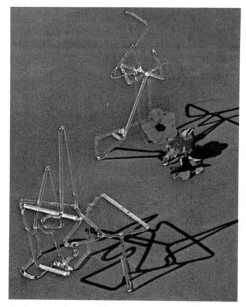

As long as glass and imagination hold out, form-a-loop sculptures like these can be built up and worked into fascinating light-catching forms.

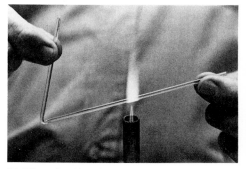

17: The second bend closes the initial triangle. Before bending, rotate the rod in the flame to allow the rod to become equally soft all around.

18: If a bit of rod extends when the triangle is closed, heat it, pull it off with pliers, then fire polish the joint all around.

19: Bend the second loop in the same way as the first, but terminate it on the first loop instead of on itself. Use a clothespin to help you join loops.

soda-lime glass (not lead) or Pyrex. But do not try to mix the two, since glasses of different consistencies do not melt at the same rate and will not adhere to one another. If different kinds of glasses get mixed up, it is impossible to tell the difference between them until you put them in the flame. Pyrex melts more slowly than soft glass.

Your first loop is actually a triangle. The bends are made by heating the rod at points that divide the rod into thirds. Allow each bend to cool before proceeding to the next one. After the first bend, you will have a wide V with one leg longer than the other. Bend the long leg back to join the short leg (photograph 17) and fuse the joint in the flame. If a piece of rod extends beyond the joint, trim it off (photograph 18). Turn each joint in the flame so that all sides fuse evenly. Lay the first loop on the table to cool for a few minutes.

The sculpture is made by simply joining loop to loop. Joining the second loop to the first is the only awkward moment. I use a clothespin (photograph 19) to help bend and join the last leg of the second loop to the joint of the first. As you begin to build the sculpture, it actually becomes easier to handle though it looks more and more complex (photograph 20). Finished sculptures may look like humorous abstractions of familiar forms and objects.

20: Carl Betz creates complex forms by simply attaching and bending rods in all shapes and directions. Mount or suspend finished sculptures.

Lampblown glass

Suellen Fowler studied lampwork glassblowing with Margaret Youd at Pepperdine University, Los Angeles, and later worked with a master glassblower, John Burton. Her work has been exhibited at New York's Fairtree Gallery and in California at the Galeria del Sol, Santa Barbara; Tarbox Gallery, La Jolla; Griswold's Foothill Gallery, Claremont; and Gallery 8, University of California at San Diego. She participated in the N.E.T. television documentary, "Harvest of Creative Hands."

As a lampworker I work on a rather small scale, but I am always aware of the mysteries inherent in this strange, ductile substance from which I coax such endlessly varied forms. My love of glass work is related, I know, to a craving for form and color that I've had since childhood. One of my most vivid memories is of receiving a huge box of lovely oil pastel crayons in one hundred different shades, and the excitement and enjoyment I got from using them. Glass offers me an even larger, almost infinite, range of colors, brilliant and subtle, with an unlimited horizon for design. I can work very formally within the classic structure of a bottle, like the one at left, or with complete freedom in three-dimensional sculpture.

Lampwork is a highly individual form of glass working, since, unlike off-hand glassblowing, it takes only one person to execute a design. This appeals to an independent streak in my nature. When I have created a design, the finished piece is completely my own. Anyone beginning in lampwork quickly learns to find his own style at his own pace. But a glass craftsman must develop quickness and great manual dexterity before he can claim control of his unusual medium.

Costs and Supplies

In different parts of the country, the costs of equipment and materials may vary, sometimes drastically, but I can tell you that setting up shop as a lampworker is not inexpensive. I have several hundred dollars invested in tools and supplies. I always keep a stock of 5-mm. rod, ½-inch rod, and ½-inch medium wall tubing. My most costly items are my blowtorch (3A National) and No. 5 Ox Torch tip, torch holder, oxygen and fuel gas regulators, and hose set. Since my oxygen supply continually needs replenishing, I maintain a small running cost for replacement of cylinders.

A Suitable Workspace

When I first began working with glass, I realized that a garage or shed with good ventilation, but free from drafts, away from the house, is an ideal space for lampwork (especially since the tanks of oxygen and fuel-gas that feed the blowtorch must be kept outdoors to conform to state fire codes). A check of my fire insurance further convinced me that this was not a craft to be practiced in an apartment or in any cramped space where leaking gases could possibly accumulate.

I work in a shed on a sturdy old wooden table, about 24 by 36 inches, large enough to accommodate my blowpipe, tools, and several lengths of Pyrex tubes and rods. As you will see from the photographs, the table's surface has become covered with char marks. But the danger of igniting the table is small, since the blowtorch is always secured in a stationary position by its holder (Figure A), and hot glass is not

This lampblown perfume bottle and stopper demonstrates the lovely symmetry that can be achieved with the glassblower's art.

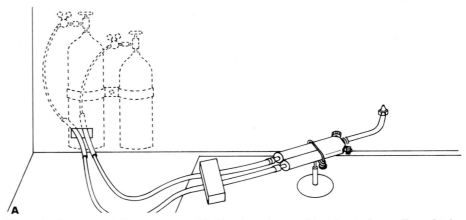

Figure A: A set-up to deliver oxygenated fuel gas to a glass-working shop is shown. For safety's sake, the blowtorch is fixed in place on the workbench. Fire codes in most states require that the pressurized oxygen and fuel-gas tanks be stored outside at all times. Each tank has its own pressure regulator. Copper tubing carries the gases through the wall of the workshop.

hot enough to ignite wood. To be on the safe side, many lampworkers cover their work surface with asbestos sheeting.

One of the major hazards in any work area is clutter, so I banish all rags, papers and other free-floating debris to the garbage pail immediately. I never wear floppy clothes that might inhibit the movement of my arms and hands or swing into the flame, or any fabric known to be especially flammable. And I have a fire extinguisher on hand at all times.

Oxygen-Fuel Gas Equipment

The Pyrex glass used by lampworkers has a high melting point. In order to create a flame with enough concentrated heat to melt this glass, fuels such as natural gas or liquefied petroleum gases (propane or butane) must be burned in the presence of oxygen. When the fuel gas and oxygen are fed simultaneously into the blowtorch, an extremely hot, oxygen-enriched flame is produced. Both the oxygen tank and the fuel gas tank are pressurized and must be used with regulators. Manufacturers provide excellent instructions for attaching such regulators and the connecting hoses. One particularly good guide on the handling and setting up of this equipment, "Precautions and Safe Practices in Welding and Cutting with Oxygen-Fuel Gas Equipment," Form F-2035-DD, may be obtained from Union Carbide, Linde Division, Marketing Communications Department, 270 Park Ave., N.Y.C. 10017.

Lighting the Blowtorch

Didymium glasses shield my eyes from the glaring yellow flare-off that occurs during the interaction between flame and glass. I put them on before lighting the blowtorch. The blowtorch comes fully assembled from the manufacturer, but the oxygen tip must be purchased and attached separately.

I adjust the oxygen pressure to between 5 and 7 pounds, and the gas pressure to between 2 and 4 pounds at the most. To light the torch, I first turn the red (gas) knob on the torch one half-turn counterclockwise and ignite it with a spark lighter. The pure gas flame is yellow. As the oxygen is added, it turns the flame blue. I turn the oxygen (green) knob slowly clockwise until a steady, light blue inner cone, ½ to ⅓ inch high, is achieved. The outer dark blue flame is 6 or 7 inches high. To turn off the torch, I switch the oxygen off first, then the gas. Both are turned off at the tank source if I stop work for more than ten minutes. The larger the inner cone, the hotter the flame becomes, and the hotter the flame, the louder is the noise the burner makes, a kind of low roar that you may have heard in welding shops. The blowtorch tip is constructed so that it directs the flame up and away from me at a slight angle (Figure A). From time to time, I must adjust the flame, however, making it either smaller and more of a pinpoint for heating tiny areas, or larger and hotter when an entire object needs to be warmed, for example.

Making a Blowpipe

When I made my own blowpipe for the first time from a piece of ½-inch tubing, I learned some basic things about the properties of Pyrex glass. The molten glass has the consistency and flow of cold, thick honey. Because glass is a poor conductor (and, conversely, a good insulator) of heat, only the part that is held in the flame melts. It is possible for me to hold a glass rod or tube in my fingers at one end while heating it at the other with no fear of burning myself. An object that has been heated, however, retains heat long after it loses its incandescence, from 10 minutes for something like a bead, to as much as six hours for a bottle (see "Annealing," page 782).

What keeps the molten glass from drooping down into an unworkable mass? The answer is rotation, a basic technique requiring much dexterity—but one that must be mastered by a lampworker to insure the successful forming of his objects. (It often takes several months for a lampworker or off-hand glassblower to learn how to rotate the blowpipe while blowing a perfectly rounded bubble.)

Glass must be rotated steadily in the flame to melt and fuse thoroughly and counteract the downward pull of gravity. As a beginner, I found it difficult to melt and fuse because my rotation technique was jerky. But gradually, as I became familiar with and could anticipate the melt and flow, I gained confidence and a steadier hand. I practiced first with a piece of ½-inch tubing, holding it horizontally between thumbs and fingertips. The thumbs roll it up and over alternately, one

21: Small hand tools used by a lampworker include, left to right: metal tongs, shears, small brass flaring tool and larger flaring tools used to shape openings, marver (also called a carbon flat) used as a leveling surface, small-nosed pliers; top, Didymium protective glasses.

An old engraving shows the proud stance of an off-hand glassblower. His craft links him with ancient Egyptian and Syrian craftsmen.

22: The central portion of a piece of half-inch Pyrex tubing is rotated and pulled apart in the flame as the first step in making a blowpipe.

23: The mouthpiece is fire polished by rotating it in the flame until the rough edges melt. It is then pressed and evened on the marver.

24: To start a basic bubble, a wrap of 5-mm. rod is coiled around the blowpipe. The flame does not touch the blowpipe wall but heats only the small area of rod being coiled.

25: The bubble is ready to be blown when it is whitish-pink as seen through Didymium lenses. Hanging the tube between thumb, index and ring finger, the bubble is blown out, but never while the glass is in the flame.

beginning where the other leaves off so a continuous rotation cycle is maintained. The tube is severed in the middle by being rotated just above the inner blue cone of the flame (photograph 22). As a general rule, if the glass starts to droop I know I am rotating it too slowly; if it becomes lopsided, I am not rotating at an even rate. The glass becomes incandescent and melts in about 30 seconds. As the center melts, I pull the tube apart. The melted glass on both ends contracts back into the tubes and fuses the ends closed. I now have made two blowpipes, each about 2 feet long. Next, I smooth, by fire polishing, the open end of one of the blowpipes (photograph 23). The blowpipe is ready to use as soon as the open mouthpiece has cooled.

The Basic Bubble

In lampwork, a part of the blowpipe itself, the first 1½ inches of the closed end, becomes part of the basic bubble. Because the walls of the blowpipe are quite thin, however, there is not enough glass in that first 1½ inches to be melted and blown into a completed bubble, so extra glass must be added to the outer wall. When this is done the glass will be of sufficient thickness to be heated and blown. It is impossible for molten glass to fuse with cold glass, so all pieces that are to be joined must first be warmed briefly in the flame. First I cut a piece of 5-mm. rod in half in the flame, like the blowpipe tubing. Then I warm the sealed end of the blowpipe in the flame, heat the tip of the 5-mm. rod, and touch rod to tubing about 1½ inches from the end. The rod will attach itself to the warmed tubing. With my left hand (I am right-handed) I hold the blowpipe next to but just outside the flame, so it won't melt. I heat the rod just in front of the point of joining and begin to turn the blowpipe slowly, feeding the rod in with my left hand (photograph 24). When the rod has been coiled all the way to the tip of the blowpipe, I sever it with the flame and pull it off. It is important never to force glass for fear of needlessly cracking it during a crucial stage of work. If a coil is not going on smoothly and I have to tug on it, that means the glass is not hot enough.

Blowing Out the Bubble

Holding the blowpipe horizontally in both hands (photograph 29 on page 784), I introduce the tip of the coils into the flame and rotate the tubing until the coils melt and fuse. Continuing to rotate the blowpipe, I gradually introduce more of the unmelted coils until they are all melted and fused into each other. The fused tip is then taken out of the flame and held vertically with the bubble hanging down (photograph 30, page 785). Next I blow it out gently to a diameter of about 1½ inches. I hold the suspended bubble in this position until it sets (about 30 seconds), then I rest it gently on the marver to cool. Only after this technique of forming a symmetrically-shaped bubble is mastered can a glass worker attempt other projects since, in lampwork, the bubble is the basis for almost all objects.

Annealing. Stopping and Restarting

In lampwork, because the pieces we work with are small and the wall of the bubble fairly thin, the annealing process is much shorter than it would be for large-scale, off-hand glassblowing. Still, all glass is subjected to a great deal of stress during the cooling process. This occurs because the outer wall of the bubble cools and contracts more quickly than the inner wall where the heat is more confined. Because of its chemical composition, Pyrex glass is able to withstand more extreme cooling stresses than soft glass. Small pieces, like a bead or Christmas ornament (page 787), are allowed to air-cool on the marver, while a bottle must be buried in vermiculite as it cools (page 785) to slow the annealing process. Before laying a piece down to cool, however, I make sure it has lost its incandescence and air-cooled for at least 30 seconds. Then I turn off the oxygen and rotate it in the gas flame for a few seconds to bring the temperature down gradually. After that it can be set down on a surface, such as the work table or marver, to continue cooling.

To continue working on a halted piece, I turn on the gas flame and hold the piece in the flame for two or three minutes until it is blackened with carbon. Then I turn on the oxygen slowly to make the flame hotter and proceed with the project. This insures an even rise in temperature throughout the piece I am working on and keeps the glass from cracking because it has contracted or expanded too rapidly in one spot. Once a blown piece has cracked, it is impossible to fix it.

Reinforcing the Basic Bubble

To make a glass bottle, additional coils of colored glass (see Craftnotes below) must be wound on to the basic bubble. But even before adding these colored coils, I reinforce the neck of the basic bubble by laying on short strips of 5-mm. rod at intervals around the blowpipe. The reinforcement supports the weight of added coils. Figure B, below, illustrates in three steps, the methods I use to add these strengthening strips.

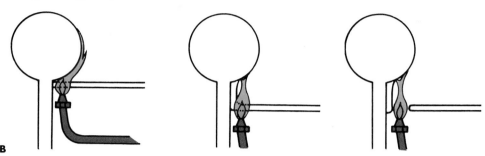

B

Figure B: The neck of the basic bubble is reinforced by first heating the tip of a 5-mm. rod and attaching it to the base of the bubble. The rod is then drawn through the flame and fused along ½ inch of blowpipe. The rod is severed by pulling off through the flame.

CRAFTNOTES: MAKING COLORED GLASS RODS

Lampblown objects are colored by means of colored glass rods that are made by the glassblower. It is difficult, and sometimes impossible, to find colored Pyrex rods ready-made. One of the obvious benefits of making my own is that I can experiment with variations in color by mixing the oxides as I please. The coloring agents are various metallic oxides that come in powder form and can be purchased by the pound (prices vary according to color) at ceramic and scientific supply outlets. Cobalt oxide makes a deep blue; tin oxide makes milk-white; chromium oxide makes green; copper oxide makes red. Silver oxide makes yellow, but this is often difficult to find outside of chemical suppliers. Tints of color are achieved by combining three parts of one oxide, such as cobalt, with one part tin oxide. The result is a pastel of the primary color (light blue).

To make a blue rod, I start by cutting a 4-inch section of ½-inch tubing in the flame, as in making a blowpipe. If both ends seal, I crack one end to let the air escape. Then I attach a 12-inch piece of ½-inch rod, reserving one more piece of rod of the same length. As shown above, I place ⅛ teaspoon of cobalt oxide in the

tubing; then I attach a second piece of ½-inch rod onto the bottom lip of the open end, leaving a space for air to escape while the tube is being heated.

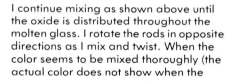

Holding the tube by the rods on either side, I heat the 4-inch tube segment until it softens (above), then I collapse the tube inward, pushing and kneading the glass into a ball with the rods. I twist and turn the glass ball in the flame to mix the oxide with the molten glass.

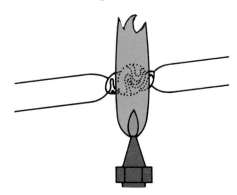

I continue mixing as shown above until the oxide is distributed throughout the molten glass. I rotate the rods in opposite directions as I mix and twist. When the color seems to be mixed thoroughly (the actual color does not show when the

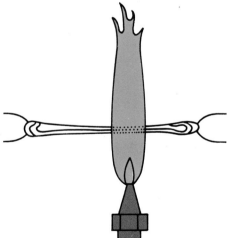

glass is incandescent), I take the ball out of the flame and begin to pull the mixing rods apart, drawing the colored glass into a thin 2- or 3-mm. rod about 12 inches long. Then I detach one mixing rod from the end of the colored stick by severing it in the flame and hold the colored rod with pliers to detach the other rod in the same way. To make the blue glass bottle on page 780, I used two dark blue rods and one light blue rod.

A Second Wrap of Colored Coils

Using the light and dark cobalt blue rods, the second wrap of coils is now added. I turn up the oxygen about a quarter turn to produce a very hot flame (as I did when making a basic bubble) and use this to warm the bubble. Then I warm the tip of a light blue rod and begin to coil it around the bubble, starting at the base (photograph 26) and winding continuously three times around. The rings are overlapped slightly to prevent gaps in color. I lay two dark blue coils next to the light blue ones (photograph 27), then finish covering the bubble in the same way coiling on more light blue rods to the tip. The coils are fused and blown out a little.

26: The second wrap of light blue coils is started at the base of the bubble, just above the reinforcements that were added to the neck.

27: At the halfway point, the light blue rod is severed and two coils of dark blue are added; then the rest is covered with light blue coils.

28: A blue rod is used to "comb" the colored coils into a scallop design around the neck of the bubble before the coils are fused together.

29: The artist demonstrates the hand positions she uses for rotating the blowpipe when she is fusing the coils in the blowtorch flame.

Combing a Design

To shape the design, the coils must be combed while they are still soft and warm, so it is essential that I work quickly at this point. To avoid distortion of the bubble, I adjust the flame to a pinpoint that will heat only a small area at one time. I select a blue rod, heat the tip, and catch it on the bubble's side at the edge of the dark rings. Next I drag, or comb, the hot glass down (photograph 28), in a straight line to the neck of the bubble. The flame heats only the point where the tip of the rod and the coils touch. As I do this, I make the colored rings describe a continuous scallop design around the neck of the bubble.

When the scallop is completed, I pull the combing rod off in the flame. If a small knob of glass is left on the bubble, I can remove it by heating the knob, taking the bubble out of the flame and, with small-nosed pliers, pulling the knob off. Now the coils are ready to be fused. The flame is turned up again to 6 or 7 inches. Holding the blowpipe in both hands again (as in making the basic bubble), I put the coils in the flame and fuse them (photograph 29), rotating steadily. Smooth fusion depends upon good heat and smooth rotation, not on the way the coils are wrapped. Minor irregularities in the colored rods or overlapping in the coiling will be fused smooth when rotated in the flame.

Drooping the Neck of the Bottle

When the coils have fused, I stand and raise the blowpipe to a 45-degree angle to the flame. The mouthpiece is the high end and the bubble is in the flame. The flame is concentrated just below the upper third of the bubble. When rotated in this position, the neck of the bottle begins to elongate and droop. The moment this begins to happen, I remove the bubble from the flame and hold it vertically (photograph 30), until the neck straightens and sets. The body of the bubble is then rewarmed in the flame, removed, and blown out to its final shape and size: approximately 2½ inches high by 3 inches wide. (Blowing is done only when the glass is *not* in the flame.) I give the bottle a flat base by pressing it gently onto the surface of the marver, anneal it in a gas flame for a few moments, then push it into a bucket of vermiculite (photograph 31) to cool for several hours.

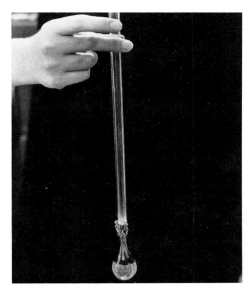

30: The bottle is blown out to its actual finished size as the blowpipe is held in a vertical position between thumb and two fingers.

31: With the blowpipe still attached, the bottle is buried in a bucket of vermiculite, where it is left to cool for several hours.

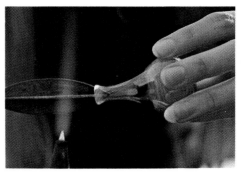

34: A flaring tool is inserted into the neck and turned gently. If the lip will not flare, the glass is too cool and needs still more heating.

32: The bottle is severed from the blowpipe in the flame just below the reinforced area and pulled off with a sealed end in the flame.

33: The sealed tip of the bottle is cracked off with small-nosed pliers. The edges left will be jagged, so the open tip is reheated in the flame.

35: After the mouth of the bottle has been flared to the desired size, it is pressed gently on the marver and evened.

The Mouth of the Bottle and Stopper

When the bottle has cooled to air temperature, I sever it from the blowpipe using the flame to make a mouth and lip, as shown in photographs 32 through 35.

The first step in making the glass stopper is, again, much the same as making a basic bubble. The tip of a piece of half-inch clear, solid rod (not tubing) is wrapped with a quarter-inch of cobalt blue coils. The coiled tip is then rotated in the flame and fused into a ball. When fused, the ball is removed from the flame and the heated end held down vertically until it sets. The tip of any easily handled length of 5-mm. rod is then heated and joined to the top of this ball. As the half-inch rod is held vertically, the 5-mm. rod will align and set. This rod serves temporarily as a handle. This method is often used instead of pliers when working with small pieces (beads, Figure C, page 786).

The section of half-inch rod (photograph 36) just below the ball is rotated in the flame until soft. It is then taken out of the flame and held vertically so the half-inch rod, blue ball and 5-mm. rod are all in alignment. The 5-mm. rod is pulled gently downward, causing the stopper's tail to be pulled out of the clear rod.

At this point, the blue ball is about 1 inch long and ¾ inch around; the tail is about ⅛ inch wide and 1 inch long. When the tail has set, the 5-mm. rod is severed in the flame and pulled off. The knob is then rotated and fire polished in the flame. Then I take it out of the flame, hold it ball-downward, and let it set. I hold the ball with tongs and sever the tail in the flame. The completed stopper is held in the tongs for a moment, just long enough to let the delicate tail set. It can then be placed on the marver to cool.

36: Before the stopper's tail is pulled out, the ½-inch tubing is heated at the point where it extends from the ball.

You'd be smiling too if you were wearing a string of multi-colored hand-blown glass beads.

Glass and Plastics
Glass beads

The blue glass bead pictured below was made by using the basic bubble technique as a starting point. Any of the colored glass rods could be used to vary this design. I begin by warming the sealed end of my blowpipe and the tip of a colored rod at the same time. Starting ½ inch from the blowpipe tip, I wind on colored coils until they reach the tip. I sever the colored rod in the flame, then rotate and fuse the coils (photograph 29, page 784). When coils have fused, I remove the tip from the flame and blow gently to form an elongated bubble, approximately ½ inch long and ¼ inch in diameter. The tip of the bubble is then heated again (photograph 37). When it is hot, I remove it quickly from the flame and blow hard into the pipe. This creates a thin-shelled bubble (photograph 38). I knock this bubble gently on a hard surface to break it off. A rough edge results, which I trim off with shears (photograph 39),

37: The extreme tip of the bead bubble is heated to incandescence in the flame.

38: By blowing into the pipe hard and quickly after heating the tip, this thin-shelled, easily-shattered bubble is produced, then cracked off.

39: Shears are used to trim the jagged edge of the broken bubble, leaving a bead to be finished by flaring, marvering and fire-polishing.

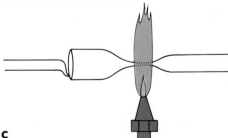

C

Figure C: A 5-mm. rod, attached to a bit of the bead lip, serves as a handle for pulling the bead from the blowpipe.

40: In this blue bead, the white stripe has been combed (see page 784) into a scallop design.

then flare slightly and press gently on the marver. To remove the bead from the blowpipe, I attach a handle of 5-mm. rod to one part of the finished bead lip (Figure C). This I do exactly the same way as for the bottle stopper (page 785). When this rod has set, I heat the blowpipe just below the blown-out bead and pull the bead out of but not off the pipe, using the 5-mm. rod as a handle. I then sever the bead from the pipe in the flame, leaving a sealed end, as was done with the neck of the bottle (photograph 32, page 785). I crack the sealed end off the bead with pliers and finish the opening by heating, trimming, flaring and marvering as I did the other side. Still holding it by the rod, I let it set. The rod is removed by holding the bead with pliers and heating the spot where it joins the bead lip in a small needlepoint flame. The rod can then be severed and pulled off. If a glob of glass is left on the bead lip, the spot can be melted off by fire-polishing. The finished bead is placed on the marver to cool.

Design Variations
Bead designs can be varied by coiling several colors on one bead, by varying the combing technique to create more irregular lines, or by adding hobnails of contrasting color to a finished bead. I also love to experiment by varying the sizes of the beads although the shapes are always slightly irregular. A string of beads for a special friend can be one of the most personal gifts I have to offer.

Glass and Plastics
Hanging ornament   💲 ⬛ 👤 ⚗️

To create ornaments like the one at right, I begin once again with the basic bubble. I reinforce the neck and enlarge the bubble with a second wrap of coils. Using any combination of colored rods, I lay stripes of glass radiating from the tip of the bubble to 1 inch along the neck of the blowpipe. I turn the torch down to a small pinpoint flame, warming the bubble and 1 inch of neck tubing, select a colored rod, heat the tip, and attach it to the tip of the bubble (photograph 41). As I heat the section of rod just ahead of the part that has been attached, I curve it around the bubble and down to the neck and along 1 inch of tubing. I lay on three more stripes at quarter turns around the bubble in the same way, then rotate and fuse the stripes in the flame but leave the neck stripes unfused, in relief. Holding the blowpipe horizontally (photograph 42), I blow the bubble out to a diameter of about 3 inches. When the bubble is blown in this position instead of downwards, I must blow and rotate the blowpipe at the same time maintaining an even rhythm. The result is a less pear-shaped and more rounded bubble. It requires practice and coordination to keep the pull of gravity from distorting the bubble. I allow the bubble to set, then attach a piece of 5-mm. rod, about 6 inches long, to the top of the bubble and allow this rod to set in line with the blowpipe. Then, holding the bubble in the flame by tube and rod, I rotate the striped neck of the bubble until it softens. Then I take it out of the flame, hold it vertically by the blowpipe, and pull down gently on the rod, pulling out the ornament's neck to about 2 inches but leaving it attached to the blowpipe. Then I allow the neck to set.

The Corkscrew Tail and Hook
I next adjust the flame so the cone is about ¼ inch high, and heat the point where the rod joins the bubble. Holding the blowpipe in my right hand, I bend the rod at a 90-degree angle to the blowpipe; then, with the rod in my left hand, I slowly turn the blowpipe away from me, drawing the rod into a corkscrew tail (photograph 43), continuously heating the rod just ahead of the section being curled. The corkscrew is 3 or 4 inches long. When this is completed, I straighten the uncurled portion of rod left at the base of the corkscrew by warming the bend and hanging it down between my fingers. It resets in line with the blowpipe once again.

Now I sever the blowpipe from the ornament. The technique is basically the same one I used to sever the neck of the bottle from the blowpipe (page 785, photograph 32). I hold the ornament by the straightened piece of rod at the end of the corkscrew tail and put the base of the pulled-out neck in the flame, then sever the neck in the flame with a sealed tip. I snip off the tip of the sealed tubing with pliers, fire-polish the open tip without closing the hole; then heat and attach another 5-mm. rod to the open end, sealing it again. I heat and bend this rod into a C-curved hook (photograph 43), then sever the rod from the hook in the flame. Holding the body of the ornament gently with tongs, I sever the straightened end of the corkscrew in the flame and place the finished ornament on the marver to cool. In about ten minutes it is cool enough to touch and hang.

41: A colored rod is attached to the tip of the warmed bubble then wrapped around and down along 1½ inches of the neck of the blowpipe.

42: A bubble blown and rotated simultaneously in this position is more rounded than the pear-shaped vertically-blown bubble.

The finished ornament is ready to hang in a sunny window or on a Christmas tree.

43: A rod attached to the tip of the bubble is heated just ahead of the part being coiled, beginning the corkscrew.

44: A hook is formed by bending a second piece of ½-inch rod attached at the blowpipe end and severing it in the flame.

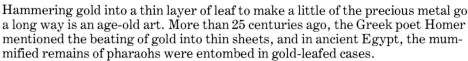

GOLD LEAFING
Much from Little

Walter Methner, like most people who gild professionally, is a sign painter. He operates a sign and display studio in Newport Beach, California.

Hammering gold into a thin layer of leaf to make a little of the precious metal go a long way is an age-old art. More than 25 centuries ago, the Greek poet Homer mentioned the beating of gold into thin sheets, and in ancient Egypt, the mummified remains of pharaohs were entombed in gold-leafed cases.

From those early times until this century, artisans hammered gold into leaf by hand. Now, gold is beaten by machine into sheets 3⅜ inches square and less than 1/250,000 of an inch thick. Gold leaf is so thin that one ounce contains enough to cover 175 to 200 square feet. The chair in the photograph opposite cost less than $15 to gild when the world market price for gold bullion was $165 an ounce.

Suitable Surfaces

You can apply gold leaf to almost any smooth, hard, non-porous surface—painted or varnished wood, for example, or glass. There are also paints, pastes and powders that simulate gold, but none of these have its brilliance or its resistance to tarnish, although they are less expensive.

Even though the gold substitutes do not contain real gold, they are included in the broad meaning of the term "gilding." However, gold leafing means one thing only: the covering of a surface with gossamer-thin sheets of real gold.

Candidates for Gold Leafing

Gold leaf, which can be used in a number of ways, is particularly effective in gilding furniture. The chair shown here was gold-leafed to accentuate the carving on the back; and the method used (see page 792) can be applied to many furnishings, including picture or mirror frames. Gold leaf is also widely used for lettering signs—you can see gold signs in almost any business district on store windows, in offices and even on truck panels. If you wish to make a gold-leafed sign of your own, see the instructions on page 795.

Like store windows, glassware can be gilded with leaf. Instructions for this and other projects follow.

An Inexpensive Experiment

For experimenting with the way gold leaf looks and to get used to some of the techniques, you may want to use an imitation called composition leaf or German metal. This is an inexpensive alloy of copper and nickel which resembles gold, but will tarnish quickly unless it has a protective coating of varnish. I chose composition leaf to gild the outer edges of a shadow box (page 790) because it is an easy, inexpensive way to get started working with leaf.

Kinds of Gold Leaf

Gold leaf is packed in cardboard folders called books. Each of the 25 leaves in a book is separated from its neighbor by a sheet of tissue paper. If the tissue and leaf are packed loosely together, the gold is called loose gold or loose leaf. This type of gold should be used for the chair (page 792) and the dish (page 793). If each sheet of gold is adhered to a sheet of tissue paper, it is called patent gold. This, used on the sign (page 796), is not quite as shiny as loose gold, but it is easier to handle because the tissue reinforces the material until it is applied to a surface and the tissue removed.

Which Leaf to Order

When ordering gold leaf for the projects here, specify Deep XX 23 karat. This is the purest and most deeply toned gold leaf available. The 23 karat means that the metal is 23/24 gold and 1/24 some other metal, usually silver. Leaf with lesser concentrations of gold is also available, but as the concentration of gold decreases, the risk of tarnish increases. In addition to gold, other metals, such as bronze, silver and aluminum, are also available in leaf form.

A microscopically thin layer of 23-karat gold leaf accentuates the carving on the back of the chair (opposite) with a luster that cannot be achieved with gold-like paints, pastes or powders.

Loose gold leaf is sold in two grades, surface gold and glass gold. Glass gold has fewer imperfections than surface gold and costs slightly more. It is so named because sign painters use it for gilding glass, where pinholes or other flaws would be particularly noticeable. Both types, however, can be applied to any suitable surface with equal ease. The wooden chair (page 792) and the glass dish (page 793) were both gilded with glass gold.

The adhesive that holds the gold leaf to a surface is called size. There are several types of size, but for the projects here you will need only two, quick gold size, for the chair, sign and shadow box, and water size for the glass dish. You can purchase quick gold size ready made (see sources listed below), but water size must be mixed fresh for each use by dissolving an empty gelatin capsule (available in drugstores) in hot water (see page 794).

An Array of Brushes

Gilding requires an assortment of brushes. You will need one known as a gilding tip to pick up the fragile leaves of loose gold and lay them on the prepared surface. This brush—once fashioned from the tip of a squirrel's tail—is now made by mounting a broad, thin row of camel-hair bristles between two pieces of cardboard. Its use is explained on page 794. You will also need a 2- or 3-inch wide household paint brush, for applying water size, and several camel-hair or sable artist's brushes. These should include a No. 8 and No. 16 flat and a No. 2 and No. 12 round for coating smaller areas with size or varnish. When deciding which brush to use, choose the largest practical for the area you are coating. When lettering, for example, you would want one slightly narrower than the narrowest line. You may also want to try a French quill—a brush widely used by sign painters for lettering and striping which has a long round tip of camel or greyhound hair. Another aid is a mahlstick that you can use to steady your hand when lettering or doing other fine work (see photograph 14, page 797). Other materials you will need are listed with each project. Sources of hard-to-find materials are given below.

Where to Find Supplies

Gilding materials are available at large painting and decorating stores as well as sign-painting supply houses that may be listed in the yellow pages of your telephone directory. If you have difficulty locating a source nearby, small paint stores will often order the necessary supplies for you. Or, you can purchase them by mail from: Kurz-Hastings, Inc., Dutton Roads, Philadelphia, Pa. 19154; or Carson and Ellis, 1153 Warwick Avenue, Warwick, R. I. 02889.

Furniture and Finishes
Gilt-edge shadow-box

Gilding the outside edges of a shadow box (see photograph, left) creates a bright frame for the objects displayed in the box's compartments. The box I used was purchased unfinished for less than $10, but the method outlined here can be used to gild the rim of a finished box you already own.

I chose composition leaf (see page 788) for the shadow box because it costs less than genuine gold leaf and makes this project an inexpensive introduction to the art of applying leaf to a surface.

Materials Needed

In addition to the shadow box, you will need one book of composition leaf; 2 ounces of quick gold size; yellow pigment; a flat camel-hair brush, slightly narrower than the rim of the box; a roll of absorbent cotton (the drugstore variety); 180- and 240-grit sandpaper; clear, glossy polyurethane varnish; and solvents for the varnish and gold size. (Different manufacturers recommend different solvents; see the labels on the containers.)

Work in a well ventilated room that is free of drafts and dust. Dust can spoil a gilding job, and the vapors of some solvents, varnishes and sizes can make you feel ill if you are exposed to them for too long.

The gilt edging framing the objects in this shadow box was created by applying imitation gold leaf to the rim. This is an easy, low-cost way to familiarize yourself with gilding.

Preparing the Box

I started the shadow box by removing one side, sliding out the glass, replacing the side and smoothing the face of the rim with first 180- and then 240-grit sandpaper. Then I painted the sanded edge with two coats of polyurethane varnish (see Furniture Refinishing, Volume Six). If the shadow box you are gilding has already been finished, sand and varnish the face of the edge anyway to be certain that it is smooth and non-porous.

When the last coat of varnish has dried—allow at least a week for this to make sure any trace of tackiness has disappeared—sand the surface lightly with 240-grit sandpaper (photograph 1) and wipe it free of dust with a tack cloth or a rag moistened with the varnish solvent.

Sizing the Edge

Mix ¼ cup of quick gold size with 1½ teaspoons of yellow pigment. The pigment makes the size easy to see so you will know where you have painted, and a light rather than a dark surface beneath the leaf adds brilliance to the leaf.

Paint the edge of the box with size, covering only the area you want to gild. The leaf will follow the size exactly: If you miss an area with the size, you will have a bare spot when you lay on the leaf. If the size runs over an edge, so will the leaf. The size will take from 1 to 2 hours to set. While you are waiting, use scissors to cut the leaf into strips about ¼ inch wider than the width of the edge you intend to gild. Do not peel off the tissue backing that adheres to each leaf. This will be removed later.

Testing the Size

Start testing the size about 1 hour after you apply it. Making sure your hands are clean, touch the knuckle of your first finger to the size. If the size is ready for gilding, it will feel dry to the touch, but you will feel a slight suction when you pull your hand away. (Your knuckle is less likely than your finger to leave a mark.)

1: Smooth varnished edge of shadow box with 240-grit sandpaper. Wipe away any dust with a tack cloth or rag moistened with varnish solvent and paint the edge with quick gold size.

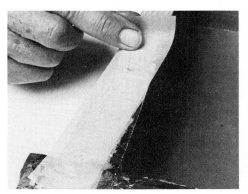

2: Lay strips of composition leaf on the edge so that each strip overlaps the previous strip by at least ⅛ inch. Remove tissue from each strip of leaf after it is in place.

3: Strike the leaf firmly with the edge of your hand to smooth it into the size. This will also knock away some excess leaf. The rest will tear away when you polish it with a pad of absorbent cotton.

Laying the Leaf

When the "knuckle test" indicates that the size is ready, pick up a strip of leaf by the tissue attached to it and lay the exposed leaf along the edge of the box, so that the leaf extends over the edge on both sides. Press it firmly against the size with your fingers. This will loosen the tissue backing, which should now be removed. Pick up another strip of leaf by the tissue, lay it lengthwise on the same edge, overlapping one end of the first strip by at least ⅛ inch (photograph 2). Continue laying overlapping strips of leaf around the edge of the box until it is completely covered.

Don't worry about wrinkles. When the edge is entirely covered, hit the surface of the gold lightly with the edge of your hand along its length (see photograph 3). Do this all the way around the box to smooth and flatten the leaf into the size. Next, rub leaf lightly but briskly with a 2-inch wad of cotton to polish the surface and remove excess leaf. Wait 24 hours, then varnish the leaf to prevent tarnishing. When the varnish dries, fill the box (see "Framing," Volume Six) and replace the glass cover.

4: Carefully coat the area you want to gild with quick size, placing the chair on its back on a box or table while you work.

5: With the top cover of the book of gold leaf folded back and under the book, hold the tissue away from the leaf and sweep the book gently over the sized surface so the free edge of leaf touches the size. As your hand continues its sweep, the leaf will be pulled from the book and will adhere to the sized surface.

6: Polish the leaf with absorbent cotton after the sized area is totally covered. The leaf is so fragile that the excess will crumble away as you rub.

Furniture and Finishes
Gold leafing a carved chair

Gold leaf can be used to enhance the carving on wooden furniture, as in the chair shown on page 789. The procedure for gilding the chair can be used to gold-leaf almost any surface that is hard, smooth and non-porous and does not have complex carving. This technique requires relatively flat, accessible areas, such as those on the chair back. It is not satisfactory for use on deep, complex carvings filled with fine detail.

Before starting, make sure the surface you are gilding is sound. If you are refinishing the chair, complete this first, and then wait a week to let the finish dry.

In addition to the piece of furniture to be gilded you will need 4/0 steel wool, 4 ounces of quick gold size; yellow pigment; a roll of absorbent cotton; flat and round camel-hair brushes of the right size for the work (see page 790); solvents suitable for the size and varnish (check container labels); two books of Deep XX 23-karat glass-grade gold leaf; and polyurethane varnish.

Preparing the Surface

Rub the area you are gilding with 4/0 steel wool and wipe away any dust with a soft tack cloth or a large piece of cotton moistened with solvent. Mix 4 ounces of quick gold size with one tablespoon of yellow pigment and coat the areas you will gild with a camel-hair brush. Paint only the areas to be gold-leafed (photograph 4).

Applying Loose Gold Leaf

When the size on the chair is dry but tacky—use the "knuckle test" (page 791)—start applying leaf to the surface. Loose gold leaf is so fragile that even a brisk puff of air can disintegrate it. Don't try to lift it with your fingers. Pick up the whole book instead and fold the cover back so it creases about ½ inch from the spine. Press it back under the bottom cover.

Holding the book at the spine between your thumb and forefinger, fold the tissue covering the first leaf of gold back and under, just as you did the cover of the book. Next, sweep the whole book gently over the sized area of the chair so that the free edge of the exposed leaf touches the size. This edge will stick to the size and as your hand sweeps past, the leaf will tear from the book and fall into place. Fold back the next tissue and repeat this procedure, overlapping the first section by at least ⅛ inch. Continue applying and overlapping leaf in this manner until the sized surface is covered.

Now, using a clean, flat camel-hair brush, pat the leaf into any corners in the carving. Tap the gold very lightly with the flat side of the tip of the brush. Do not use a brushing motion.

Correcting Flaws

Polish the gold-leafed surface by rubbing it briskly but lightly with a 2-inch pad of cotton (photograph 6) to burnish the gold and remove excess leaf. Some gilders discard flakes of excess gold. Others save them in a clean, tightly capped jar for patching small imperfections. To do this, just breathe on the tip of a small, round camel-hair brush, pick up a flake with it and place it on the spot to be covered.

Another way of correcting flaws is to hold the book as you did to cover the size originally and pat the entire gilded area with the exposed leaf. Wherever a bare spot of size shows through the gold, a bit of leaf will tear off and cover it. When surface is fully covered, polish it again with a fresh piece of cotton.

Finishing Touches

Chair backs are subject to abrasion that will wear away the gold over the years. Giving the leaf a coat of polyurethane varnish will protect the finish and is a good idea, even though the varnish will dull the luster of the gold slightly. On the other hand the 23-karat gold leaf does not tarnish or discolor, so if the article is one that is touched infrequently, such as a picture frame, this step is unnecessary.

This dish was embellished with bands of gold leaf held to the underside with water size. The texture of the center band was created by stippling a layer of varnish before gilding.

Glass and Plastics

Gold on glassware

If you want to gild a dish like the one above, choose one of clear glass with a smooth, even underside where the gold will be applied. The one I selected is 8 inches in diameter. The center disk is 4 inches in diameter with a fish design etched in the bottom.. The outer band is 2 inches wide.

The gold leaf, applied to the bottom of the dish, shows through the glass when the dish is placed right-side-up. The design was achieved by gilding a ½ inch stripe of plain gold around the rim, another stripe—¼ inch wide—around the center disk, and gilding the area between them with stippled gold.

To gild a dish like this one, you will need one book of Deep XX 23-karat glass gold; two 2/0 gelatin capsules (available in drugstores); a gilding tip (see page 794 and photographs 9 to 12); flat camel-hair brushes; a 2- to 3-inch wide household paint brush for applying size; a pint of rubbing varnish (if you cannot find rubbing varnish, use a slow-drying synthetic varnish); absorbent cotton; Bon Ami glass cleaner; a fine felt-tipped pen; a 1-gallon paint can; and 1 tablespoon of Japan black (a finish sign painters mix with varnish and use to back up gold leaf; you can substitute black enamel for the Japan black/varnish mix.) You also need 2 ounces of damar varnish used for the stippling on the plate that is later gilded.

About two weeks before you gild the dish, open the damar varnish and leave it uncapped until it has the consistency of honey. Now you can begin. Wash the dish with detergent and water and dry it. Using the felt pen, draw two circles on the front of the dish around the band to be stippled, thus marking the edges of the inner and outer stripes of plain gold. The outer circle should be ½ inch in from the rim and the inner circle should be ¼ inch away from the center disk (Figure A). Draw these circles by holding the dish face-up in one hand and bracing one finger of the pen hand against the rim of the dish. Holding the pen steady, rotate the dish with the fingers of the other hand. This provides an accurate circle.

Place the dish upside-down on the paint can. From this point on, avoid touching the bottom of the dish with your fingers since any oil or grease on the surface will prevent the leaf from adhering to the glass. When you move the dish, slide your

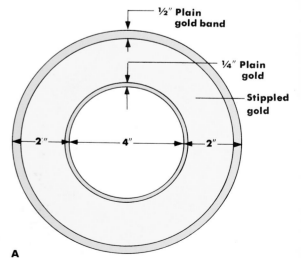

A

Figure A: The inner and outer stripes on the band of the dish are gilded with plain gold, the space between them stippled. The dish's central disk is not gilded.

fingers beneath the rim and lift the dish, slipping your hand underneath it so it rests upside down on your hand. Reverse this procedure to put the dish back on the can.

With the dish in position, scrub it with cotton moistened with Bon Ami and wipe off any residue. If you need to steady the dish while doing this, hold it down with your fingers on the center disk, where you will not apply any gold leaf.

Preparing Water Size

Next prepare the water size that will hold the gold to the glass. Heat one cup of water until it comes to a boil. Reduce the heat until the boiling stops, and while the water is still hot, drop one gelatin capsule into it and stir until the capsule is completely dissolved. With a 2- or 3-inch wide household paint brush, cover the inner and outer bands of the dish with size.

7: With the cover of the gold-leaf book folded back and creased, press back the top tissue. Use a sheet of cardboard as a pallet for the book.

8: Cut the gold leaf with your fingernail, using very light pressure. If it wrinkles when you touch it, blow on it very gently to straighten it.

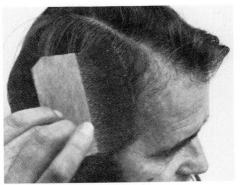

9: Stroke the gilding tip through your hair several times. This will make the gold leaf stick to the brush so you can pick it up.

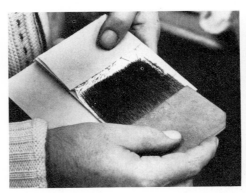

10: Touch the gilding tip to the leaf and pull. The gold will snap away from the book at the cut you made with your fingernail.

11: Holding the leaf almost parallel to the surface, touch it to the dish at its free edge. The water size will pull it from the brush.

Using a Gilding Tip

After sizing the bands of the dish, use a gilding tip to pick up a gold leaf from the book and transfer it to the band. Begin by placing the book of leaf on a 5-inch square of heavy cardboard. Fold back the top cover of the book to within about 1 inch of the spine of the book. Bend back the tissue covering the first sheet of gold (photograph 7), and cut the leaf by running your fingernail lightly across it next to the crease in the tissue (photograph 8).

Brush the gilding tip through your hair a few times (photograph 9); this will make the leaf stick to the brush. Some gilders say that the static electricity thus generated holds the leaf to the brush; others claim that the oil in your hair makes the brush slightly sticky. All agree the method works.

Touch the side of the brush to the exposed leaf of gold (photograph 10) and pull it, removing the leaf from the book. Touch the end of the leaf to the prepared surface (photograph 11); the wet size will pull the leaf from the gilding tip as you withdraw it. Do not allow the brush itself to touch the size.

Keep laying leaves of gold on the bands of the dish, overlapping all edges by at least ⅛ inch, until both the inner and outer stripes are completely covered and overlapped. Wait for about an hour for the size to dry, at which point the gold will have become bright. Polish the surface with a 2-inch pad of cotton to remove any gold that is not held in place by size. Inspect the surface for cracks or holes. If you find one or two, re-size the flawed areas—working very lightly to avoid softening the size already beneath the gold. Then apply leaf over the flaws with the gilding tip. If there are many flaws, you may find it is easier to apply another complete layer of leaf over the entire area.

Again, wait for the size to dry and polish the surface with cotton. Then rinse the size brush in warm water and use it to wash gilt surface with hot water and a light touch. This will increase the brightness of the gold, help conceal the joints between pieces of leaf and prevent cloudiness in the size. When the surface is dry, give it a final polishing with cotton.

Backing Up the Gold

When you look at the bottom of the plate at this stage, you will see a general gilded area, but no sharply defined inner and outer stripes. These you can create by "backing up the gold"—painting stripes directly over the gold leaf with a mixture of varnish and Japan black, then scrubbing the surface after the paint dries to remove excess gold. The gold leaf that is not backed up by paint will be scrubbed away, the gold under the paint will remain in place. When the dish is right-side-up, you see two crisp gold stripes.

Start by mixing 1 tablespoon of Japan black with 4 ounces of rubbing varnish. Using flat camel-hair brushes, paint the inner and outer stripes (photograph 12) with the mixture. The circles originally drawn on the front of the dish will show faintly through the gold and serve as guides as you paint. Let the varnish dry for at least 24 hours; then scrub away the excess gold with Bon Ami on a moistened cotton wad. Use additional wads of cotton to remove the Bon Ami.

Creating a Stippled Effect

When the back of the dish is dry, brush the thickened damar varnish into the area between the inner and outer stripes. Wait until the varnish becomes firm—this will take about 20 minutes to an hour. Test it by drawing a design with a dull point, such as the end of a brush handle. If the varnish returns to a smooth surface, wait and try again. If it holds the design, stipple the whole area between the bands with any desired pattern.

Put the dish aside for a week to allow the varnish to dry thoroughly. Once the varnish is set, mix a fresh batch of water size and gild the stippled area exactly as you did the inner and outer bands. Finally, give the whole gilded area a coat of rubbing varnish, overlapping the ungilded glass slightly at the outer and inner edges. When the final coat of varnish is dry, the dish is complete. It can be washed by hand with mild detergent and lukewarm water. Do not put it in a dishwasher, let it soak in a dishpan or rub the back with a scouring pad.

12: Use your free arm as a brace to support your brush hand while you paint a mixture of Japan black and varnish over the gold that is to remain in the inner and outer stripes. When the mixture is dry, scrub the back of the dish with glass cleaner. The unprotected gold will be scrubbed away.

Graphic Arts
Lettering a sign in gold $ ☒ ⚆ ⚶

To gild a sign you will need one book of patent gold leaf; 4 ounces of clear, glossy polyurethane varnish; 4 ounces of quick gold size; yellow pigment; round and flat camel-hair brushes; a prepared signboard or a piece of 1-inch clear white pine; 180- and 240-grit sandpaper; a saber saw or jigsaw; heavy paper; a pounce wheel (a toothed wheel for perforating patterns, such as is used in sewing); an 18-inch square of closely woven fabric (a worn out dress shirt would be a good source); talcum powder; pushpins; stiff paper or cardboard; and pattern paper (brown wrapping paper will do).

For lettering your sign, you can use the alphabet in Figure B on the next page. If you want a type style you feel is better suited to the sign you have in mind, art supply stores stock alphabets in a myriad of styles and sizes.

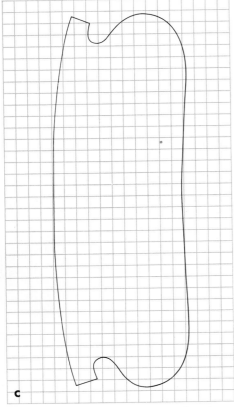

Figure C: This signboard pattern can be enlarged to any size. Measure the width of the board you need for your sign in inches and divide by 32. The resulting figure will be the width in inches of the grid square needed to enlarge the pattern (see page 57, Volume One).

Figure B: Enlarge the letters to be used in your sign on a piece of heavy paper or cardboard and cut them out. Instructions for enlarging are in the Craftnotes on page 57, Volume One.

Making a Pattern

Trace each letter you will need for your sign or enlarge it on a piece of stiff paper or cardboard, using the method described on page 57, Volume One. Cut the letters out of the paper or cardboard, making one copy of each letter for every time it appears in the sign.

Use a ruler to draw a straight line on the pattern paper and, aligning the cut out letters on the line, arrange them just as you want them to appear on the finished sign. Tack the letters into place with two or three pushpins each. Then trace each letter on the pattern paper and remove the cardboard cutouts.

Now sketch the shape of the sign on the pattern paper. The lettering should fill the space comfortably without looking crowded. If you select a simple rectangle for the sign, measure the width and depth of the outline sketched on the pattern and order a prepared signboard from a sign company. If you prefer starting from scratch, cut the sign from a length of 1-inch clear white pine that has no imperfections. Finish it according to the instructions that follow.

Cutting and Finishing a Signboard

If you wish to make a signboard like the one shown in Figure C, decide the width of the sign you plan in inches and divide this figure by 32. The result will be the grid width needed to enlarge the pattern according to the instructions on page 57, Volume One.

Cut out the signboard pattern, trace it on the piece of white pine, and cut the shape out with a saber saw or jigsaw. (I molded the edge of the sign I made with a router, but you can round the edges with sandpaper.)

Sand the signboard to a smooth surface, using 180-grit paper and then 240-grit paper. Wipe away dust with a tack cloth or a rag moistened with turpentine or paint thinner. The sign can now be stained (see Furniture Refinishing). I chose to use dark walnut. Follow the stain with three coats of clear, glossy polyurethane varnish, allowing 24 hours between coats. Rub the finish lightly with 4/0 steel wool between coats and wipe it free of dust with a rag moistened with thinner.

Put the sign aside for a week to let the varnish dry completely. Different varnishes have different drying times, and although most varnishes feel dry to the touch and can be smoothed and recoated in less than 24 hours, some remain faintly tacky for much longer.

Transferring the Pattern

While the signboard is drying, the pounce bag can be made. Pour about a cup of talcum powder onto the center of an 18-inch square of closely woven fabric, placing a handful of absorbent cotton on top of the talc and gathering up the edges of the fabric to form a bag. Fasten the neck of the bag closed with five or six turns of masking tape.

Next, spread a thick towel or blanket on your work table and place the letter pattern over it. Hold the pattern steady with one hand and with the other, roll the toothed edge of the pounce wheel over the outlines of the letters. When you are finished, hold the pattern up to the light to make sure that all the lines have been perforated. Put the pattern down and retrace any lines you have missed.

When the varnished signboard has dried thoroughly, center the perforated pattern on it and tack it in place with pushpins. Now tap the pounce bag on the pattern wherever there are tracings for the lettering (photograph 13). The talcum powder in the bag will fall through the perforations in the pattern and form the letter outlines on the sign in a series of white dots. Make sure the letters have been completely transferred by lifting a corner of the pattern, then remove the pushpins and pattern carefully so the pattern does not slide against the talcum dots and smear them.

Painting the Letters

The next step is to paint the letters on the sign with quick gold size. Position the signboard on your work table and run a length of masking tape along the bottom of the lettering, outlined on the board so that the top of the strip of tape forms the bottom edge of each letter. Do the same at the top of the letters. These two strips of tape will keep the tops and bottoms of the letters evenly aligned.

Mix 4 ounces of quick gold size with 1 tablespoon of yellow pigment and paint in the letters using a flat camel-hair brush slightly narrower than the width of the lines you are painting. A round brush will fill in corners and other areas with fine detail.

Steady your hand with a mahlstick as you paint (photograph 14). You can buy one in a paint store or make one by nailing a large cork to one end of a dowel 2 feet long and 1 inch in diameter. When you paint, hold the mahlstick in your free hand, resting the cork against your work table. Brace your brush hand against the stick to steady it as you paint.

Painting the letters neatly is the most difficult part of making a sign, and it helps to practice beforehand. Pounce the design on a sheet of blank paper, tack it down and paint in the letters, using paint left over from some other job. Do this several times until you feel you can paint the sign easily.

When you do paint the sign, work at a comfortable pace. Do not rush, but do avoid going so slowly that your hand shakes or hesitates and produces a ragged line. Don't worry about mistakes: If your hand slips while painting, clean the area with some cotton moistened with thinner and paint it again.

Applying the Leaf

When all the letters are covered with size, wait about 1¼ hours, then use your knuckle to test the tackiness of the last letter you painted. When the size is ready (see page 791), begin applying patent gold to the letters.

Pick up a leaf of patent gold by the tissue and lay it over the first sized letter of the sign. Cover the letter completely, but do not let the leaf touch the next letter. This will prevent seams from appearing within the letters. Peel the tissue from the gold. Pick up a second leaf of gold in the same way and apply it to the second letter, taking care not to let it touch the third letter. If it overlaps the first letter that is already gilded, it doesn't matter. Continue in this manner until every letter is covered with a leaf of gold. Then polish the surface with a pad of cotton.

After the surface is polished, pick up a leaf of gold by the tissue and pat the whole gilded surface with it to cover any bare spots in the leaf. Polish the surface once again with cotton and let the size dry for 24 hours. Finally, give the sign a finishing coat of clear, glossy polyurethane varnish.

For related projects and crafts, see "Antiquing Furniture," "Bookbinding," "Framing," "Marquetry and Inlays."

13: With the letter pattern tacked to the sign, pat the surface with the talc-filled pounce bag.

14: Steady your hand with a mahlstick when you paint the letters with quick gold size. Tape at top and bottom of letters helps keep them even.

GOLD PANNING
Bright Prospects Underfoot

Stuart James has been at home with outdoor sports and adventures since early boyhood. An accomplished fisherman, hunter, boatsman, camper, and scuba diver, Stuart has also broken ground as an explorer of new outdoor skills. He first wrote about the art of gold panning in 1963 while outdoors editor of Popular Mechanics. *Since then he has been executive editor of* True, *the editor of* Rudder *and the author of numerous freelance articles on a variety of topics.*

It has been years since there was a genuine, stampeding gold rush in the United States. But the "fever" that can set a man to delving all day in a creek bed, when he might be taking his ease, has never been more rampant.

Today's prospectors are not the grizzled old storybook "sourdoughs," however, but families spending weekends and vacations panning for gold. The rush of recent years has been for fun rather than gain, for the most part, but it has set the old diggings from North Carolina's Rowan County to the Mother Lode of Northern California aswarm with vacationers searching for gold.

"Times haven't changed all that much," said the owner of a hardware store in Nevada City, Cal. "Folks still dream of striking it rich, and the man selling the equipment—" he paused to total the cost of pan, tools and guidebook being bought by a vacationer—"he usually gets the gold."

Gold has lured adventurers ever since it was discovered in North Carolina in 1799. This was the first find in the United States, and while legend has it that most gold came from California, more than $50 millions' worth was taken out of the eastern and southern states, and some $500 millions' worth from Colorado. South Dakota's Homestake Mine alone has yielded more than $600 million in gold and is still producing. Placer gold—the loose ore deposits to be found in the dirt and gravel at the bottom of riverbeds and streams—is an excellent starting point for the neophyte prospector, because it is easy to find with simple, inexpensive equipment. These deposits are the result of erosion. Gold-bearing rock is worn away from a lode (a mineral vein or mass of ore embedded in rock) by a natural force, such as running water. As the rock is carried downstream, it begins to fragment, and gold flakes and nuggets are freed. The largest and heaviest mater-

1: Rick Anderson, son of expert prospector Dick Anderson, demonstrates the first step in panning for gold: Place a pan containing the gravel and dirt to be worked in a shallow stream that has just enough current to carry away loose material. The steps that follow are on page 801.

Underwater prospector Jack Huber inspects a gold nugget retrieved from a rock crevice in the Yuba River in California's High Sierras. This technique is described on pages 804 and 805.

A

Figure A: The yellow areas on this map, drawn from one prepared by the U.S. Bureau of Mines, indicate major placer, or loose ore, gold deposits in the U.S. Gold can still be found in stream beds in these areas.

ial, including the gold, sinks, gradually sifting down through layers of soil, sand, loose rock, and gravel, until it reaches bedrock, the solid rock layer that lies at the bottom.

The excitement of finding these deposits and separating the gold from the gravel and sand is what today's gold rush is all about. The lucky gold seeker may also make some money. At the current market price for gold being paid by rock shops, metal refiners and jewelers, your hunt just may pay for itself. Working for one day in the Yuba River in California, prospector Jack Huber gleaned 10 ounces of gold from a single rock crevice. It more than paid for his weekend in the High Sierras.

Where to Look for Placer Gold

Colorado, Montana, and, of course, California are the best-known source areas for placer gold. The Carolinas and certain regions in Georgia, Tennessee, Nevada, Arizona, New Mexico and Texas (see map above) are also good hunting grounds. Many other areas may yield pay dirt: Wherever there was a major placer strike in the past, there is gold remaining in the streams. Don't lose interest in a stream if you are told that it has been panned out—spring floods shift tons of silt and gravel, stirring everything up and carrying gold from one hiding place to bury it in another. Search the dry riverbeds in late spring and early summer—here, where the flood waters rushed through, there is gold to be found. These deposits are too meager to interest a mining company or a professional prospector, but can pay off in fun— and, occasionally, profit—for the hobbyist.

Finding a good place to pan is like finding a good place to fish. The best help is local information. Any history of gold discoveries includes specific locations of placer gold, such as Virginia City, Mont.; Telluride, Colo.; Downieville, Cal., to name just three. The surrounding waters are good sources of gold. You will find small local museums that emphasize the gold rush in these places, along with hardware stores that sell panning equipment, and mineral shops. People there, including local guides, have a great deal of information and enjoy talking about gold. You will hear dozens of tall tales, but the facts to be gleaned from them could lead you to streams that have produced in the past and will produce again. You then have to do what prospectors have been doing for centuries—find the gold.

There are no absolute rules about prospecting, but most placer gold is found close to bedrock, that is, the solid rock that lies under the soil or loose gravel. Try to discover where two streams formerly converged; the eddies created where the two currents joined may have let the heavy gold drop down to bedrock. For the same reason, you are more likely to find gold in the slow-moving side of a river. Work the curves and bends, getting right down to the rock.

Don't Be a Claim-Jumper

If you are going to pan for gold on public land, be sure you won't be working on someone else's claim without his permission. A claim is almost always well-marked with the owner's name and the boundaries, so, in general, you needn't worry about making a mistake. However, should there be any question, ask someone. If the stream is on private land, get the owner's permission before you begin prospecting.

The Art of Sniping

The easiest method for the weekend prospector to use in looking for gold is that known as crevicing or sniping.

When a stream bed is shifted during the turmoil of flooding, small nuggets and flakes of gold are lifted, carried downstream and deposited in crevices between rocks. These deposits are gradually covered by mud and sand. As a sniper, you look for crevices hidden from view. When you find one, scoop it out, saving the material and panning it for gold.

On dry banks of a creek, you usually can see how high flood waters rose, so you know how far to look for gold on either side. A large obstruction like a boulder would slow flood waters, allowing the gold to drop to the bottom. If you dig around such obstacles, you might come upon a profitable crevice. Rock fissures in the creek bed, often extending many yards onto the bank, may have been exposed during a flood and are well worth exploring.

To begin panning, you will need the tools shown in Figure B. The heavy pry bar is optional, but it is useful for prying crevices open.

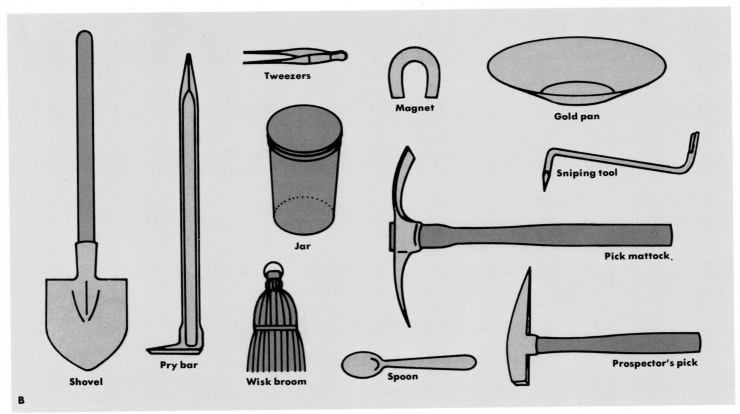

Tweezers

Magnet

Gold pan

Jar

Sniping tool

Pick mattock.

Shovel

Pry bar

Wisk broom

Spoon

Prospector's pick

B

Figure B: Above are the basic tools you will need for placer gold prospecting and panning. The wide-mouthed jar is used to carry black sand containing tiny flakes of gold to the local assay service.

2: The first step in sniping, or scraping crevices for gold, is locating the crevice and clearing away loose debris with a whiskbroom.

3: Use a prospector's hammer and a sniping tool to work material loose from the bottom of the crevice, cleaning it out thoroughly.

4: Transfer the dirt and gravel from the bottom of the crevice to your pan with a large spoon. The next step is to pan the material (Figure C).

Digging away the loose topsoil with pick and shovel, work down to the rock. When you find a crevice, clean it out carefully, using the prospector's pick and a sniping tool to loosen the material and then transferring it to your gold pan with a large spoon (photographs 2 to 4). Fill the pan about two-thirds full, leaving roots and moss in the potential pay dirt. (They often hold small flakes of gold.)

How to Pan

Locate a shallow spot in the stream—one where you can rest the pan in water just deep enough to cover it and with a strong enough current to carry away the loose material you will discard (photograph 1, page 798). Stir the material with one hand, letting the water carry away the light matter. Carefully wash and clean all rocks and pebbles, moss and roots *over the pan* before discarding them. It is important to break everything down over and over and to continuously stir and turn the material. The gold is heavy (heavier than lead, actually) and will sink to the bottom.

C
Figure C: To pan for gold, barely immerse the pan in water and stir to let the water remove lighter material. Lift the pan slowly, spill off some water and, with the pan held level, shake it back and forth to mix the material. Spill off additional water.

D
Figure D: After working pan back and forth to shake loose the larger material, change to a gentle swirling motion to help dissolve finer dirt and clay, gradually spilling more water and dissolved dirt over the edge of the pan.

The next process is known as sloughing off. To do this, hold the pan firmly, one hand on each side, and lift it slowly from the water. Tilt the pan slightly forward to spill some water off, and then level the pan and work it back and forth to mix the material with the water (Figure C). Once a mixture is achieved, carefully spill off more water. Now change from the back-and-forth shaking motion to a gentle swirling movement (Figure D) gradually sloughing additional water over the edge. The revolving motion helps dissolve the remaining dirt and clay and swirl it out of the pan. In this way, you work the material in the pan down to gravel and sand.

801

Stop at this point and search through the material with your fingers or tweezers. If there are any sizeable gold flakes or small nuggets, you should be able to spot them by their characteristic dull yellow gleam. The color photographs shown below illustrate the difference between real gold and the more commonplace "fool's gold" or pyrites.

The next step is to add some water and pan the remaining material down to black sand—the heavier, finer concentrate at the bottom that frequently contains both magnetic iron minerals and tiny flakes or flecks of gold—known as flourgold. Pan for this by repeating the initial shaking and swirling motions, but use a gentler touch to make sure you do not inadvertently discard any black sand and flourgold. If you have a plastic pan, apply a magnet to its underside, and, tilting the pan slightly, gently swivel it. This will help separate the gold particles from the

5: Below are enlarged photographs of real gold and of the pyrites known as "fool's gold," frequently mistaken for the real thing. (If you guessed that the real gold is on the left, you will make a good prospector.) Real gold is heavier, more malleable, and usually less brassy in appearance than "fool's gold." As in the photograph at left, gold is frequently embedded in quartz, though the roiling action of water in streambeds may separate the gold nuggets from the crystals.

magnetic black sand as the gold is not attracted to the magnet. Even after these operations there is often a residue of fine gold particles left in the sand, so you may want to take the remaining mix to a miner's assay service. (A wide-mouthed jar is useful for this.) There, centrifugal separators and concentrating tables will separate the flourgold from the remaining sand. Local newspapers and phone books are good sources of information about such assay services, as is *The California Mining Journal*, published in Santa Cruz, California.

Winnowing Dry Placers

Dry placers may exist wherever there once were gold-bearing streams. Arizona and New Mexico are ideal hunting grounds for dry placers. When you find an old stream bed, or even an annually flooded arroyo, in what is known to be a gold area, dig down to expose dirt and gravel near bedrock. Search this for "color," the tiny flakes of gold that mean a place is worth prospecting.

The common method used to get to "color" is called winnowing. For this, you need a wool blanket and a sieve—the latter is easily made with some window screening framed with 2-by-4s. Place the sieve on the outspread blanket, shovel dirt into it and sift the dirt through the screening. Remove the sieve, and then, with the help of a friend, hold the blanket by the corners and repeatedly toss the

Practice Panning at Home

With a washtub full of water, a pan of dirt and a handful of birdshot, you can simulate the panning process. Mix the birdshot into the dirt, then wash it and slough off. When you have finished, there should be nothing but birdshot in the pan. Once you feel proficient at this, test yourself by counting the number of pieces of birdshot left. If you start with 20, you should end with 20.

E

Figure E: This artist's rendering, which appeared long ago in *Harper's Weekly*, shows how gold was winnowed in the old West. After the gravel pay dirt was shoveled on a sieve and sifted onto a blanket, the blanket was tossed lightly by the two people holding it. Wind carried off lighter dirt and gravel, leaving the heavier gold and black sand on the blanket. You can use the same technique today if you work dry streambeds with no water handy for panning.

material into the air (Figure E). The wind will carry off the light dirt, leaving the gravel and other heavy particles on the blanket. Put this material into a bucket for later panning with water. If there was gold "color" present, there is an excellent chance you will find it caught on the blanket.

A note of caution about dry panning: In western Texas, New Mexico, and Arizona, there may be flash floods to be reckoned with. If you are digging in a dry riverbed in the middle of a desert and you hear what sounds like a million tons of water coming at you, move to higher ground quickly. If this precaution is followed, the floods do not present any great danger.

Diving for Gold

Underwater prospecting is relatively new and remarkably productive. Crevices on river banks or in the shallows may be worked again and again by weekend gold-seekers, but those at the bottom of a cold, deep, flowing stream are much harder to get at.

If you plan to dive for gold and are an experienced snorkeler, you can try this technique in relatively calm water. Working the gold out of underwater crevices takes time and patience, however, and it is generally more effective to use a wet-suit, face-mask, and a mouthpiece with a built-in breathing regulator and an air-hose connection, as in scuba diving. Rather than the bulky tanks used in the latter, however, an air compressor driven by a small gasoline engine is your air source. An air hose connects the compressor to your breathing regulator, and both compressor and engine can be mounted on an inner tube that floats on the water (color photograph, opposite). For information on this equipment, send for the free catalog, *Prospecting and Mining Supplies*, listed opposite.

If you will be prospecting in a swift-flowing stream, you will need a weight belt with sufficient lead weights to secure you against the force of the current. Unless you are an experienced scuba diver, it is best to stay in water no more than 6 or 7 feet deep and to go no more than 15 or 20 feet away from your air supply unit. And —experienced or not—one should never prospect underwater without a companion to keep a watchful eye on both prospector and air supply equipment.

What you look for underwater are cracks or crevices that form natural catch pockets in the solid bedrock of the stream or river. These, like the "riffles" of a miner's sluice box, are grooves in the surface of the bedrock where gold tends to settle. Work these crevices as you would those on the surface, cleaning rocks and gravel from them with a sniping tool (as illustrated below) until you get to the bottom. If you are lucky, gold nuggets will be there.

Rick Anderson is pleased with these gold nuggets he took from the Yuba River, using the underwater sniping technique described in the text.

6: Working gravel from an underwater crevice with a sniping tool, Rick has on a wet-suit, face-mask, and mouthpiece with breathing regulator. His air hose is connected to an air compressor.

This diver uses a homemade dredge operated by a compressor, water pump and small engine mounted on a large inner tube. The dredge sucks sand, water and gravel from the bottom and discharges it through a "riffle" box, used to trap gold particles, built into the wide end of piping.

Serious underwater prospectors use either a surface or submersible dredge operated by a gasoline engine and water pump as shown above. The dredge works much like a large vacuum cleaner, sucking from the bottom of the stream through a pipe or large hose. On the surface, this matter is run through a sluice or riffle box. These dredges are relatively costly and rarely used by the weekend prospector, but the sluice or riffle box is economical and this can be bought and used as a separate unit. It consists of a metal chute lined with removable riffles (the slats shown in Figure F, below). These riffles catch the heavier particles, causing them to fall through a mesh screen onto matting whence they may be recovered (Figure F). Setting the sluice box in the water, tilt it so that the riffles are at the lower end. Then shovel gravel into the upper end and let it work its way down over the riffles.

For related projects and entries, see "Mineralogy," "Pathfinding and Maps," "Scuba and Snorkeling."

Books on Gold Panning

Summer Gold, by John N. Dwyer, North Star Press, St. Cloud, Minn. 56301.

Gold Finding Secrets, by Edwin P. Morgan. The Old Prospector, Box 20094, Sacramento, Cal. 95820.

Prospecting and Operating Small Gold Placers, by William F. Boericke. John Wiley & Sons, 605 Third Avenue, New York, N.Y. 10016.

Montana Paydirt, A Guide to the Mining Camps of the Treasure State, by M. S. Wolle. Swallow Press, 1130 South Wabash Avenue, Chicago, Ill. 60605.

Gold Rush Country, by the Editors of Sunset Magazine. Lane Book Co., Menlo Park, Cal. 94025.

Government Pamphlets

Placer Mining Methods. U.S. Bureau of Mines, Report No. 2315.

Principal Gold Producing Districts of the United States, edited by Koschmann and Bergendahl. U.S. Geological Survey, Professional Papers No. 610.

Catalog

Prospecting and Mining Supplies. Keene Engineering Co., 11483 Vanowen Street, North Hollywood, Cal. 91605. Everything for the amateur or professional, from a pair of tweezers to a surface dredge.

Monthly Magazine

California Mining Journal. P. O. Drawer 628, Santa Cruz, Cal. 95061. Reports on mining activities. The advertisements cover a variety of equipment for the amateur.

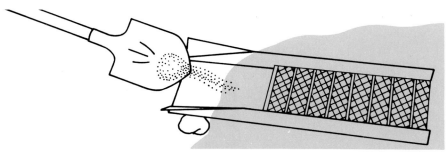

F

Figure F: To use a riffle box, position it so water flows over the series of slats at the lower end, then shovel in gravel and let it wash down over the slats, called riffles. Heavier particles like gold will drop through the wide mesh onto a mat below.

GRANNY SQUARES
Patchwork Crochet

For everyone who likes to crochet, granny squares provide a good way to use odd pieces of yarn left over from other projects. A granny square is a crocheted shape that starts with chain stitches slip-stitched into a ring. The first round is worked into the ring, the second round into the first round; five such rounds make the traditional granny square. Each round is made of groups of double crochet stitches separated by chain stitches. (Directions for making these basic stitches may be found in Crochet Craftnotes, pages 30-31, Volume One.)

The traditional square was usually made with 4-ply knitting worsted, and its dimensions varied slightly according to the size of the hook used. I remember my grandmother making hundreds of small squares that she sewed together into afghans. When I was seven years old, she started me by teaching me to crochet a potholder in a traditional granny-square pattern.

Today's granny squares may differ in several ways from the ones our grandmothers made. They now can include any stitch or combination of stitches used in crocheting. And squares are no longer used only for afghans. They can be made into clothing such as the cap and scarf on page 812, or accessories such as the roomy tote bag on page 814. Knitting worsted is still the yarn most often used, but any weight yarn, jute, or even string can be made into a granny square. The place mat on page 810 is made with string.

You can crochet granny squares in the specific color combinations suggested in the directions for each project, or you can arrange leftover yarn to create your own designs. The number of colors used and the way they are arranged make the work interesting. Since you crochet only one square at a time, you can carry the work with you wherever you go. In addition to information on the basic crochet stitches, you will find advice on crochet hooks and a method for testing the gauge in the entries "Afghan Stitch" in Volume One and "Crochet" in Volume Five.

Connie Kuznekoff grew up on a farm in Oklahoma where she was active in 4-H clubs for nine years and won many prizes for her sewing and embroidery. She majored in clothing, textiles and merchandising at Oklahoma State University. She is also adept at knitting, needlepoint, embroidery and rug-making.

Needlecrafts
Traditional afghan

Sixty-three granny squares in two harmonious color combinations are used in this traditional afghan (far left in the photograph opposite). The squares are simple to make because you use only the chain stitch, slip stitch, and double crochet stitch (see Crochet Craftnotes, pages 30-31, Volume One). To adapt the directions to your scrap yarn, vary the colors for Rounds 1 through 4, but use only one color for Round 5 on all the squares.

Size: About 36 by 46 inches.
Materials: 4-ply knitting worsted (4-ounce skein), 1 each of dark turquoise, peach, light blue, aqua, dark rose, 2 each of violet and green. Crochet hook size G or size needed to obtain gauge. No. 18 tapestry needle.
Gauge: Each square is 5 by 5 inches.
Main square: With dark turquoise, ch 5 and join with sl st to form ring. Round 1: Ch 3, 2 dc in ring, *ch 1, 3 dc in ring. Repeat from * twice more. Ch 1

and join with sl st to top of ch-3. Fasten off. Round 2: Join peach in any ch-1 space. Ch 3, 2 dc in same sp. *Ch 1, in next sp 3 dc, ch 1, 3 dc. Repeat from * twice more, ch 1, 3 dc in same sp as first ch-3, ch 1, and join with sl st to top of ch-3. Fasten off. Round 3: Join violet in any ch-1 corner sp, ch 3, 2 dc in same sp. *Ch 1, 3 dc in next sp, ch 1; in corner sp work (3 dc, ch 1, 3 dc). Repeat from * twice more; ch 1, 3 dc in next sp, ch 1, 3 dc in same corner sp as ch-3, ch 1 and

Abbreviations used in crochet directions:

ch	chain
dc	double crochet
*****	repeat from
rnd	round
sc	single crochet
sl st	slip stitch
sp	space
st(s)	stitch(es)
tr	treble crochet
yo	yarn over

The three afghans opposite show the diversity possible with granny squares. The traditional granny-square afghan (far left) has a muted, harmonious color scheme. The afghan in shades of blue (center left) uses a pattern with a floral center. The bright red-and-white afghan (near left) is made with a raised stitch called the popcorn stitch.

The look of the traditional granny square changes with different color emphasis. The contrasting squares above are used as a border on two sides, and the outer edge is a row of double crochet.

join with sl st to top of ch-3. Fasten off. Round 4: Join light blue and work as rnd 3 except there will be 2 groups of 3 dc alternating with 1 ch between each corner. Fasten off. Round 5: Join green and work as for rnd 3 except there will be 3 groups of 3 dc alternating with 1 ch between each corner. Fasten off. Make 49 squares.

Contrasting square: Follow directions for main square using peach for ring and rnd 1, aqua for rnd 2, violet for rnd 3, dark rose for rnd 4, and green

for rnd 5. Make 14 squares.

Joining: Join main squares together so afghan is 7 squares by 7 squares. Join contrasting squares into 2 strips of 7 squares each; sew strips to each end of afghan. See Craftnotes below and opposite for details on joining and blocking.

Border: Join dark turquoise in any dc and ch 3, * 1 dc in each st and 1 dc in each seam until the corner. Work 2 dc in the corner ch and 2 dc in the next dc. Repeat from * around entire afghan. Join with sl st to top of ch-3 and fasten off.

CRAFTNOTES: BLOCKING

The blocking of articles made of granny squares—the process whereby the squares are squared up—can be done in one of two ways. The granny squares can be blocked individually, but this is extremely time-consuming and should be done only if a square seems very distorted. To ready such a square for blocking, pin it wrong side up to a flat surface —measuring to make sure the dimensions of the square are the same as those given in the directions—and proceed as described at right for blocking assembled articles.

For most granny-square projects, blocking can be done after the squares are joined and borders completed. This is the quick way. Pin the assembled unit securely to an ironing board, bed or work table, measuring so the article is same size as dimensions given in directions.

With an iron set on "wool" and using a dampened pressing cloth, lightly pass the iron over the granny squares. Do not rest the full weight of the iron on the article. Let the work become completely dry before unpinning it.

CRAFTNOTES: JOINING SQUARES

To complete any granny square project, individual squares must be joined. First, all yarn ends should be woven into the back of each square and trimmed. With experience, you will find it easy to conceal yarn ends on one round when crocheting the next round. This requires placing the yarn end along the stitch into which you are crocheting so the stitch you are working will conceal both the top of the stitch on the previous row and the yarn end. (See "Fastening Yarn" in Crochet Craftnotes, "Afghan Stitch," Volume One, page 31).

Squares may be sewn or crocheted together. Sewing provides a flat finish and works better when you are easing or fitting a larger square to a smaller one. Always work on the wrong side of the squares and use matching yarn (contrasting yarn is shown in the photographs only for clarity). The best way to assemble a number of squares for an afghan is to sew them together into strips of the desired length and then join the strips to the width you want. Sewing strips is easier than sewing squares because you don't have to knot and cut the yarn so often, and strips keep the granny squares better organized. When joining multicolor squares, arrange them on a table until you have achieved a pleasing effect, then join them as they are positioned.

After you have threaded a No. 18 tapestry needle with an 18-inch length of yarn and tied a slip knot in one end, slip needle through the bottom two loops of corner chain (left above). Insert needle into bottom two loops of second square (right) and through the slip knot, pulling to tighten knot.

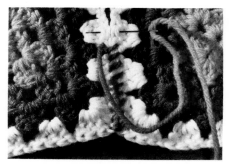

Working from the lower edge toward upper edge and right to left, insert needle through bottom two loops of last round in right square and the adjacent two loops of the last round in left square. Sew in this manner, matching squares stitch for stitch and concealing any yarn end in with stitches.

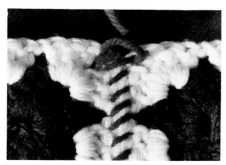

To fasten yarn at upper edge, take two stitches at corner chains, and before pulling second stitch tight, insert needle through stitch as shown above. Finish by pulling tight and weaving yarn end into square for a few inches before cutting.

When sewing strips together, use a cross stitch formed by stitching a second stitch over first one, as shown, to reinforce corners so they will match more evenly. Except at the corners, use the same procedure for sewing strips as you do for sewing squares together.

To crochet squares together, place them with right sides together, attach yarn to the top loop of each corner, then slip stitch for the length of squares as shown. To finish, fasten off at end of squares and weave yarn end in on the back.

Needlecrafts
Place mat

Ordinary household string (cable cord No. K-106) was used to make the durable, 12-by-15-inch place mat shown below. The center is a traditional granny square enlarged to 10 rows. To make the square into a rectangle, three rows of double crochet were added to the two opposite sides.

Size: 12 by 15 inches.

Materials: Cable cord (No. K-106), approximately 2½ balls of 200 feet each for one place mat. Crochet hook size H or size needed to obtain gauge.

Gauge: Square is 10½ by 10½ inches. Double crochet sides: 4 st = 1 inch.

Square: Follow directions for traditional granny square (page 807) but enlarge it by making 10 rows. The last row has eight groups of 3 dc plus the corner st for each side.

Side: Row 1: Attach the string to one corner, ch 3, 1 dc in each dc and 1 dc in each sp. At end of row, ch 3, turn. Row 2: 1 dc in each dc, ch 3 and turn. Row 3: Repeat row 2, fasten off. Repeat rows 1 through 3 for the opposite side. Do not fasten off.

Border: Starting at end of last row of dc, 1 dc in each dc, 3 dc in corner. Continuing along side of original square, 1 dc in each dc and 1 dc in each sp, 3 dc in corner. Repeat for remaining 2 sides. 2 dc in last corner and join with sl st to 1st dc. Fasten off.

This place mat is one large granny square with three rows of double crochet added to two opposite sides to make a rectangle. The natural color of the string is attractive in this setting.

Light blue floral centers stand out against the darker blue background colors of the squares in this afghan. The scalloped border adds an unusual finishing touch.

Needlecrafts
Floral granny-square afghan $ 🎞 🚶 🧶

Although 180 squares are required for the 50-by-62-inch afghan (above and center in the photograph on page 806), the 4-inch squares and the scalloped border work up quickly as you gain experience. I can finish a square in only 10 minutes. Use scrap yarn or your three favorite colors for this project. The design also makes a lovely baby afghan if worked in a smaller size such as 9 squares by 15 squares.

Size: About 50 by 62 inches.

Materials: 4-ply knitting worsted (4-ounce skeins), 3 light blue, 4 robin blue, 5 medium blue. Crochet hook size G or size needed to obtain gauge. No. 18 tapestry needle.

Gauge: Each square is 4 by 4 inches.

Squares: With light blue, ch 4, join with sl st to form ring. Round 1: *1 sc in ring, ch 10. Repeat from * 7 times. Join with sl st to first sc and fasten off. Round 2: With robin blue, join yarn in any ch-10 loop. Ch 3, 2 dc in same sp. *In next loop work (3 dc, ch 2, 3 dc) for corner; 3 dc in next loop. Repeat from * twice more. Work (3 dc, ch 2, 3 dc) in next loop for corner. Join with sl st to top of ch-3. Fasten off. Round 3: With medium blue, join yarn in any ch-2 corner sp; ch 3 and work 2 dc in same sp. *1 dc in each dc to next ch-2 corner sp; 3 dc in corner sp. Repeat from * twice

more. Work 1 dc in each dc of last side, join with sl st to top of ch-3 and fasten off. Make 180 squares.

Joining: Sew squares together so afghan is 12 squares by 15 squares. See Craftnotes on page 809 for details.

Border: With robin blue, join yarn in the center dc of any corner and ch 1, 2 sc in same st. Work 1 sc in each dc of squares with 1 sc in seam between squares. Continue around afghan in this manner, working 3 sc in each corner dc. Join with sl st to top of ch-1 of first corner and fasten off. With light blue, join yarn in center sc of 3-sc corner, * sl st in next sc, sc in next sc, dc in next sc, 3 tr in next sc, dc in next sc, sc in next sc. Repeat from * around entire afghan, working 2 or 3 sl sts as needed at corners to even the design. Join with sl st to first sl st and fasten off. This border is distinctive yet simple to do.

811

Cap and scarf were coordinated with the navy coat by working the last row of each square and the scalloped border on the scarf in navy. Inner rows of the squares use six bright colors in various combinations.

Needlecrafts
Cap-and-scarf set

$ ⏱ 👫 🧶

The squares used to make the bright cap and scarf pictured (left) are the same kind of squares as those used in the floral afghan (page 811), but each square has an additional row of double crochet stitches to make it larger. The cap is made with four of these 5-inch squares sewn together with one smaller 4-inch square for the crown. The scarf is made with 24 of the larger squares. You could use scrap yarn for the squares or harmonize the colors with your winter coat.

Size: Cap fits head sizes 20 to 25 inches (for sizes 16 to 20 inches use only 4-inch squares). Scarf is 12 by 62 inches.

Materials: 4-ply knitting worsted (4-ounce skein), 1 each of light blue, pink, rose, lime, green, and purple, 2 of navy. Crochet hook size G or size needed to obtain gauge. No. 18 tapestry needle.

Gauge: Large square is 5 by 5 inches. Small square is 4 by 4 inches.

Large square: Follow crochet directions for floral afghan square on page 811 for rnds 1 and 2. Round 3: With desired color, join yarn in any ch-2 corner sp, ch 3, 2 dc in same sp. *In next sp between 3-dc group, work 3 dc. Re-peat once. For corner, in ch-2 sp work (3 dc, ch 2, 3 dc). Repeat from * twice. Work 3 dc in next 2 sp. In beginning corner sp, work 3 dc, ch 2, join to top of first ch-3 with sl st and fasten off. Round 4: Same as rnd 3 of floral afghan square. When making large squares, alternate colors as desired for rnds 1, 2, and 3. Use navy for rnd 4. Make 28 squares: 24 for the scarf and 4 for the cap.

Small square: Follow directions for floral afghan square; use desired colors for rnds 1 and 2, navy for rnd 3.

Blocking: For cap, block squares before joining. Scarf is blocked after it is completed. See Craftnotes on page 808.

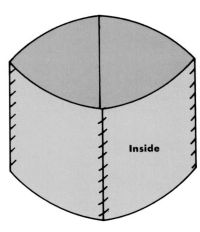

A

Figure A: To make the body of the cap, join the sides of four large granny squares so they form a circle. Make sure that the seams are on the inside so they will not show when cap is completed.

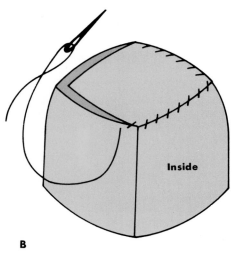

B

Figure B: To make the crown, sew a small square to one end of the circle, easing or fitting large squares to the small one so the corners of small squares match seams between the larger squares.

Joining cap: For 20- to 25-inch head size, join sides of large squares together in a circle (Figure A). Sew small square to one end for top of cap, easing large squares to smaller one so corners of small square are matched to seams of large square (Figure B). For 16-to-20-inch head size, join 4 small squares together in a circle (Figure A) and sew another small square on top for the crown, matching the corners.

Border: Attach navy to any dc along edge of cap, ch 1. Work 1 sc in each dc of squares and in each seam. Join with sl st to first sc. *Ch 1, work 1 sc in each sc around cap. Join with sl st to first sc. Repeat from * once more and fasten off.

Joining scarf: Sew squares together, 12 squares long by 2 squares wide, alternating colors for pleasing effect.

Border: Follow directions for floral afghan border using navy for both rows.

A granny-square afghan can look modern rather than old-fashioned. The bold geometric look of this design is due to the use of only two colors, with their sequence reversed in the border squares.

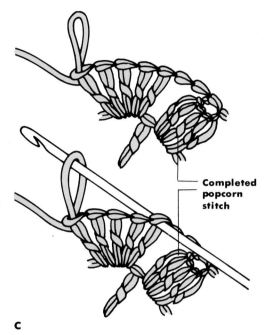

C

Figure C: To make a popcorn, work five double crochet stitches in the space between double crochet stitches in the previous row, and drop the loop (top). Insert the hook in top of the first double crochet, pick up the loop (bottom), and pull through. The stitch on the right of the stitch being worked is a completed popcorn stitch.

Completed popcorn stitch

Needlecrafts
Popcorn granny-square afghan $ 🎲 🚶 🧵

The circles within the squares of this afghan (above and far right in the photograph on page 806) use a raised design called the popcorn stitch for a textured effect. The popcorn stitch, made of five double crochet stitches (Figure C), is easy to master. I chose to use only two colors for the afghan, with the color sequence reversed in the squares used as a border, to create a dramatic design.

Size: About 42 by 47 inches.

Materials: 4-ply knitting worsted (4-ounce skein) 5 each of red and white. Crochet hook size G or size needed to obtain gauge. No. 18 tapestry needle.

Gauge: Square is 5 by 5 inches.

Main square: With white, ch 4, join with sl st to form ring. Round 1: Ch 3 (count as 1 dc), work 15 dc in ring and join with sl st to top of ch-3 (16 dc in ring). Round 2: Ch 4, *1 dc in next dc, ch 1; repeat from * 14 times. Join with sl st to 3rd ch of ch-4. Fasten off. Round 3: Join red in any ch-1 sp, ch 3, 4 dc in same sp. Drop loop from hook, insert hook in top of ch-3, pick up loop and pull through, ch 2 (popcorn made). *5 dc in next sp, drop loop, insert hook in top of 1st dc, pick up loop and pull through, ch 2. Repeat from * 14 times (16 popcorns) and join with sl st to top of ch-3 of first popcorn. Fasten off. Round 4: Join white in any ch-2 sp, ch 3, 2 dc in same sp. *(3 dc in next ch-2 sp) 3 times, in next sp work (3 dc, ch 2, 3 dc) for corner. Repeat from * twice. Work 3 dc in each ch-2 space of last side, 3 dc in corner, ch 2 and join with sl st to top of 1st ch-3.

Fasten off. Round 5: Join red in any ch-2 corner sp, ch 1, 2 sc in same sp. Work 1 sc in each dc with 3 sc in corner sp. Join with sl st to ch-1 and fasten off. Make 42 squares.

Contrasting square: Follow crochet directions for main squares, reversing color sequence: work ring, rnds 1, 2 and 4 in red, and rnds 3 and 5 in white. Make 30 squares.

Joining: Join main squares together so afghan is 6 squares by 7 squares. Join contrasting squares so there are 2 strips of 6 squares and 2 strips of 9 squares. Sew shorter contrasting strips to ends of afghan and longer strips to sides (Figure D).

Border: With red, join yarn to center sc of 3-sc group in corner of afghan, ch 3, 1 dc in same sc. Work 1 dc in each sc and 1 dc in seam between squares. Continue in this manner, working 2 dc in each center sc of corner. Join with sl st to first ch-3. Ch 4, dc in same dc, *ch 1, skip 1 dc, dc in next dc. Repeat from *around afghan, working 1 dc, ch 1, 1 dc in corner st. Join with sl st to 3rd ch of ch-4. Fasten off.

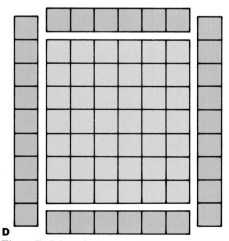

D

Figure D: Join main squares of the popcorn afghan so the body is 6 squares by 7 squares. Then join contrasting squares into two strips of 6 squares (for the top and bottom) and two strips of 9 squares (for the sides).

The combination of geometric shapes and a bold color scheme gives a look of contemporary fashion to this commodious carryall.

Shoulder tote bag

Earthy tones of brown, gold and orange were used for the soft-sided shoulder tote bag shown in the photograph at left. Its 15-by-15-by-2½ inch dimensions give it a generous capacity. Each side is made of nine 5-inch squares; the band joining the sides and the handle is made of a continuous strip of double crochet.

Size: 15 by 15 by 2½ inches deep. Handle portion is 34½ inches long.

Materials: 4-ply knitting worsted (4-ounce skein), 1 each of orange, beige, gold, and rust, 2 each of dark brown. Crochet hook size G or size needed to obtain gauge. No. 18 tapestry needle. 2¼ yards of 2¼-inch-wide brown grosgrain ribbon, 1 yard of 1-inch-wide brown grosgrain ribbon. ½ yard of 45-inch-wide heavy-weight brown lining, brown thread, sewing needle.

Gauge: Squares are 5 by 5 inches. Handle gauge is 4 st=1 inch, 2 rows of dc=1 inch.

Squares: Follow crochet directions for popcorn afghan squares, alternating colors for rnds 1, 2, 3 and 4. Use dark brown for rnd 5 only. Make 18 squares.

Joining: Join squares for sides, 3 squares by 3 squares. Alternate squares to vary colors. From right side, along what will be upper edge of tote, join dark brown yarn in center sc of corner, ch 1. Work sc in each sc of square and sc in seam between squares. Fasten off yarn in center sc of left corner. Block sides of tote after squares are joined.

The handle/band: Join dark brown yarn at center of middle square at lower edge, ch 1. Work 1 sc in each sc of square and 1 sc in seam between squares. Do not increase at corner. At upper edge of side, work 2 sc in side of sc edging to secure it. Then ch 134. Join chain to other side of upper edge with 2 sc in side of sc edging. Work 1 sc along side and bottom of tote, joining to first ch-1 with sl st. *Ch 3, work 1 dc in each sc and ch around entire bag and handle. Join to top of ch-3 with sl st. Repeat from * 3 more times. Ch 1 and work final row of sc in each dc. Join with sl st; fasten off.

The under handle: With dark brown, ch 140. Insert hook in 4th ch from hook and work 1 dc in each ch. *At end, ch 3, turn, work 1 row dc. Repeat from * twice more. Ch 1, turn and work final row of sc. Fasten off.

Assembling tote: Each side of the tote bag is made of nine squares sewn together to make a larger square. The 2-inch-wide band between the sides and the 2-inch-wide handle, called a handle/band, is one continuous strip of double crochet that is crocheted directly on to one of the granny-square sides (see directions for the handle/band above). Working on the inside of the tote, sew second granny-square

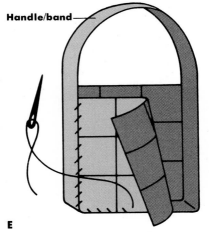

E

Figure E: Crochet the handle/band, one continuous strip, to one of the granny-square sides. Working from the inside, sew the second side to the handle/band along three sides, using yarn and a tapestry needle.

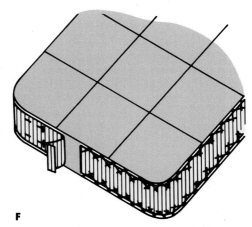

F

Figure F: Sew a 2¼-inch-wide ribbon reinforcement all around the inside of the double-crochet handle/band, using small stitches. Lap the ends where they meet.

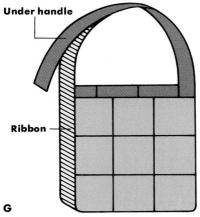

G

Figure G: With the bag turned inside out, place the crocheted under handle over the ribbon reinforcement on the handle (as shown) but not along the band between the granny-square sides.

H

Figure H: With the bag right side out, attach the three layers of the handle—the handle, the ribbon reinforcement, and the under handle—with a row of single crochet on each edge of the crocheted pieces, sandwiching the ribbon between them.

side to outside of handle/band (Figure E), along sides and bottom.

The handle/band is reinforced with grosgrain ribbon. With the tote inside out and starting at center bottom, pin 2¼-inch-wide ribbon to the inside of the entire handle/band. Lap ends and secure ribbon in place with catch stitches (Figure F). To finish the handle, the crocheted under handle (see directions on opposite page) is placed over the grosgrain ribbon along the handle (but not along the band between granny-square sides) (Figure G). The three layers of the handle, two layers of double crochet with a ribbon reinforcement between them, must be crocheted together. To do this, turn tote right side out. From right side of upper handle, join dark brown yarn to top loop of upper handle above sides and top loop of 2nd stitch of the under handle. Ch 1 and work 1 row of sc through one loop of each handle section (Figure H). Fasten off at other granny-square side. Join other edge of crocheted handles in same manner, sandwiching the ribbon between handle sections. Lightly steam the under handle to shrink any fullness. Let dry before attaching lining.

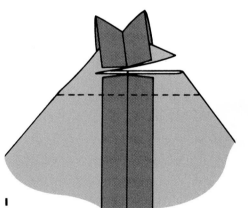

I

Figure I: Stitch seams of lining and press open, then fold corner into a triangle, stitch across the corner 1⅛ inch from point of triangle, and trim corner to ½ inch.

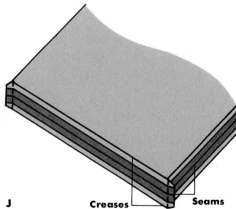

J   **Creases**   **Seams**

Figure J: Press a crease along either side of the seams of the lining from one end of the corner stitching to the other. This will make the lining fit the shape of the crocheted tote.

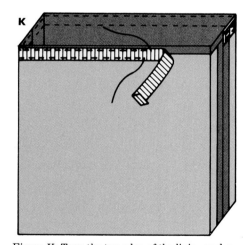

K

Figure K: Turn the top edge of the lining under ½ inch and press, then stitch 1-inch-wide ribbon along the top as a reinforcement before you stitch the lining into the bag.

Lining: Cut two pieces of lining each 18½ inches wide by 17½ inches long. One-half inch seams are allowed. With right sides together, machine stitch along one side of lining, across bottom, and along other side. Press seams open. Fold into triangle at corner and stitch across corner 1⅛ inch from end. Trim corner to ½ inch (Figure I). Press crease along either side of lining from one end of stitching to the other (Figure J). Turn under ½ inch at top of lining and press. Stitch 1-inch-wide ribbon just inside pressed edge of lining (Figure K), and overlap edges of ribbon where they meet. Insert lining into bag, aligning side seam of lining with center of bands and hand sew in place just below edge along sides. Secure lining to lower edge of tote at corners with several small stitches.

For related crafts and projects see "Afghan Stitch," "Crochet," "Patchwork."

815

GREENHOUSE CONSTRUCTION
Room to Grow

Greenhouse designer William A. Roberts, who has been chief engineer of Lord & Burnham, Irvington, New York, since 1954, is a graduate of Rensselaer Polytechnic Institute, Troy, New York. A licensed engineer, he is also a captain in the Civil Engineer Corps of the U.S. Naval Reserve.

A typical reach-in window greenhouse made of aluminum and glass can be assembled with only a screwdriver in single units or tandem arrangements. The top can be opened for ventilation.

Greenhouses make it possible for gardeners to grow-and-show on a year-round basis. A wealth of exotic flowers—orchids, camellias, lilies and anemones among them—thrive in the controlled environment.

A conventional walk-in greenhouse built of glass is expensive, but there are less costly alternatives that will let you try this kind of gardening. To start, you do not even need one big enough to walk inside, since the simplest kind of gardening-under-glass is done in either a cold frame or a hotbed—essentially glass-topped boxes that serve to extend the gardening season. Only a bit more complex is the pit greenhouse, sunk in the earth to tap its warmth during winter. Instructions for building all of these are on the pages that follow. In addition, I have designed a walk-in, lean-to greenhouse of fiberglass and aluminum that you can build for one-third the cost of a comparable glass structure (sketch, opposite).

Gardening-Under-Glass Fundamentals

Your goal in gardening under glass will be to duplicate, insofar as possible, the conditions of light, temperature and humidity under which the plants you select would normally grow. As far as lighting is concerned, if you do not plan to use artificial lighting, your greenhouse, cold frame or hotbed should face south or southeast to take maximum advantage of sunlight. The sun is the primary source of natural heat as well, but supplemental heat, provided with electrical cables, as in a hotbed, hot-water or steam pipes, space heaters, or tapped from an adjacent building, will let you raise delicate plants in cold climates. Depending on the plants you choose, you can let winter temperatures drop as low as 40 degrees Fahrenheit.

How well the structure holds heat is important. The earth itself has long been used as an insulator, and three of the projects here—cold frame, hotbed and pit greenhouse—rely on this factor. Mulches or commercial insulation and weather stripping can be used to help in this regard. Windbreaks, too, are a good defense against heat loss, so advantage should be taken of existing structures and hills.

Overheating and under-ventilation can be hazardous to plants under glass. Thus, the structure, even a simple cold frame, must have windows that open. In a large greenhouse an exhaust fan triggered by a thermostat, combined with an opening that will admit fresh air, will eliminate any danger of overheating, and, as an added precaution, the glass can be shaded with blinds or covered with whitewash.

Plants must be watered, of course, and a handy source of water is a great convenience. Plants also benefit from high humidity and this they can create for themselves—with a little help. In a greenhouse or pit, a floor of gravel, bark mulch or loose bricks laid in sand can be kept damp without getting muddy; a commercial humidifier will maintain an even more precise balance.

Any of these structures will have a moist atmosphere, so any wood used should be a rot-resistant variety such as cedar or cypress, and metal fasteners should be rust-proof—galvanized or made of aluminum or brass. Beneath the soil of plant benches in pit or greenhouse, panels of asbestos cement will prove long-lasting. Such plant benches give the gardener maximum control of soil and drainage conditions plus the advantage of being able to work without having to stoop. Make them 2 or 3 feet wide and 6 or 8 inches deep, and support them on cinder blocks.

As an introduction to greenhouse gardening, you might want to try a prefabricated window greenhouse (photograph, left). They protrude about 16 inches and are available in sizes ranging from 3 by 4 feet to 4 by 6 feet. Even more down-to-earth beginning alternatives, however, are the cold frame and the hotbed.

Artist's sketch opposite shows a corrugated fiberglass lean-to greenhouse that you can build in only a few days. Framed with aluminum and wood, the greenhouse is designed to be built against an existing house or garage wall. Detailed blueprint plans appear on pages 824–825, and building instructions with how-to-do-it diagrams start on page 822.

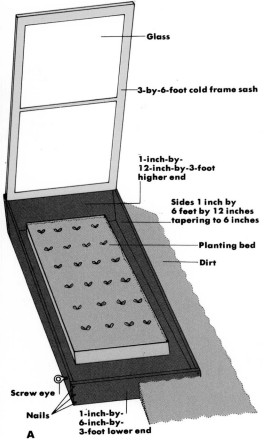

Figure A: To construct the cold frame, glue and nail the ends to the sides. The sash is hinged to the top of the frame and can be opened on warm days to permit ventilation—a necessity since overheating is hazardous to young plants. Clothesline, run through hook eyes on either side of the frame, will keep the sash from being lifted by wind.

The cold frame

The most primitive kind of "greenhouse" is the cold frame, a bottomless wooden box higher on the north end than the south, covered with glass, and heated only by the sun (Figure A). It is used for storing tender bulbs and plants during winter, for starting seedlings in advance of their normal outdoor growing season, for propagating plants started from cuttings, and as a way-station for plants started indoors that need toughening to withstand the shock of being moved to the garden. Plants may be grown in the soil beneath the cold frame, or in flats and pots placed inside the frame and/or recessed into the ground.

The drawing at left shows a cold frame covered with a single 3-by-6-foot storm sash; larger units can be of any desired multiple. The sash is hinged to a wooden header strip across the high end (Figure B), both to make the inside of the frame accessible and to permit ventilation on warm days.

The box itself, made of rot-resistant wood, has a 3-foot-long piece of 1-by-12-inch lumber across the high end, two 6-foot-long side pieces of 1-by-12-inch lumber cut diagonally to provide a slope to a 6-inch height at the lower end, and a 3-foot-long piece of 1-by-6-inch lumber across the low end. The corners are joined with waterproof glue and galvanized screws or box nails.

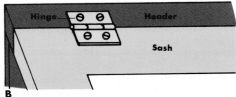

B
Figure B: Use butt hinges to fasten the sash to the header strip, which extends across the width of the frame at its highest point.

C
Figure C: A ventilating block, made from scraps of 1-by-6-inch rot-resistant wood, props the sash open at variable heights.

Choose a sunny, well-drained location, sheltered from the wind, and position the frame with the high end to the north, so the glass top traps a maximum amount of sunlight and heat. If you intend to plant the soil beneath the frame, spade it in the fall before you put the frame in place.

The ventilating block (Figure C), used to hold the sash ajar when the inside temperature exceeds 70 degrees Fahrenheit, has steps so the amount of ventilation can be adjusted. To retain the day's heat during cold winter nights, cover the frame with a heavy tarpaulin and be sure to bank the sides with dirt.

The hotbed

The hotbed is similar to the cold frame in design and function, but is heated so it can be used earlier and later in the year, and the glass-topped box is often set on a masonry foundation extending below soil level (Figure D).

To build a hotbed, first excavate a 4-by-7-foot pit to a depth of 24 inches, lining the excavation with three layers of cinder blocks laid without mortar. Space these block walls so the box frame, built as described above, will sit comfortably on the top edge at ground level.

In the past, hotbeds were warmed by fermenting manure, but today they are usually heated with insulated electrical cables coiled under the planting bed and connected to the house wiring by a heavy-duty extension cord. The cable, along with a thermostat, is available at most garden supply centers.

Fill the bottom 12 inches of the pit with cinders or fine gravel to provide insulation and drainage, and add a 2-inch layer of sand as a bed for the cable. Loop the cable back and forth across the bed, 3 inches in from the cinder block walls and with lines 6 inches apart (Figure E). Cover the cable with a layer of ¼-inch-mesh

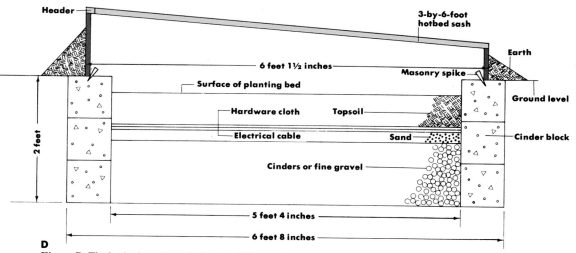

D

Figure D: The hotbed consists of a basic cold frame (Figure A) above a pit heated by insulated electrical cable. The cable, coiled under the planting bed and connected to house wiring, is activated by a thermostat when the temperature drops low enough to endanger plants, and the frame is insulated with tightly packed earth on all four sides.

hardware cloth to serve as a heat conductor and to shield the cable from your digging tools. Finally, add 6 inches of good top soil for the plants to grow in, and position the box frame and sash on top of the cinder block foundation. Mount the cable switch box and thermostat in a shaded corner of the wooden frame.

For added insulation, you can pour vermiculite into the hollows of the cinder blocks and pack the space outside the blocks and around the frame with earth. To anchor the top structure more firmly, drive masonry spikes or cut nails into the cinder block at 1-foot intervals (Figure D).

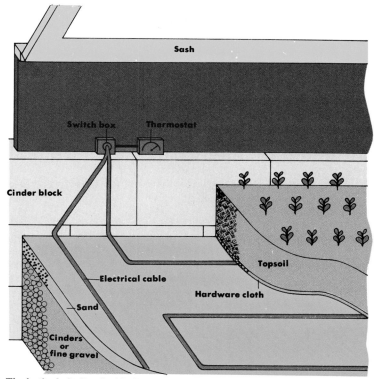

E

Figure E: The hotbed pit, lined with three layers of cinder block, contains a 12-inch insulation-and-drainage layer of cinders or fine gravel, a 2-inch bed of sand for the cable, the cable coils—covered by a ¼-inch-mesh hardware cloth—and 6 inches of rich topsoil. Masonry spikes are used to hold the frame in place on the cinder block foundation.

Cold Frame Tools and Materials

1 Standard 3-by-6 foot cold frame or hotbed sash

2 Rot-resistant side-boards 1 inch by 12 inches by 6 feet (nominal)

1 Rot-resistant end-board 1 inch by 12 inches by 3 feet (nominal)

1 Rot-resistant end-board 1 inch by 6 inches by 3 feet (nominal)

1 Rot-resistant hinge-board 1 inch by 1½ inches by 3 feet (nominal)

Waterproof glue

30 8-penny galvanized box nails or 1½-inch No. 8 screws

Thermometer

Hammer

Crosscut saw

Rule

2 3-by-1½-inch butt hinges with screws

Screwdriver

2 screw eyes

4 feet of clothesline

Hotbed Tools and Materials

Same materials as cold frame, above, plus:

Shovel

42 8-by-8-by-16-inch cinder blocks

Insulated electrical heating cable with heavy-duty extension cord and thermostat

28 cubic feet of cinders or fine gravel

3 by 6 feet of ¼-inch-mesh hardware cloth

5 cubic feet of sand

14 cubic feet of topsoil

22 1½-inch masonry spikes

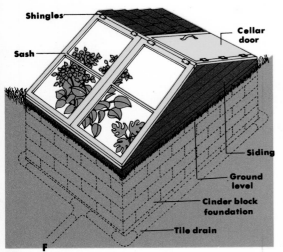

Figure F: The pit greenhouse consists of a gable roof set directly on a cinder block foundation. Storm sashes comprise the south roof, and a cellar door is built into the north roof. The remainder of the roof is shingled and the gable ends are then covered with siding.

Environmental Projects

The pit greenhouse

Should you decide to settle for nothing less than a walk-in greenhouse, the pit greenhouse is a simple and inexpensive structure that you can build with standard, readily available materials. (A good deal of useful information on pit greenhouses, with construction advice and bibliography, is given by Kathryn S. Taylor and Edith W. Gregg in *Winter Flowers in Greenhouse and Sun-Heated Pit.*)

Early American colonists made their greenhouses by digging into the ground to tap the natural warmth of the earth below the frost line. They made insulated pits that required no artificial heating and used a minimum amount of scarce and costly glass. Like the cold frame, the pit needed only to be covered with glass. Sometimes, however, it was made with a gable roof that had glass built into its south slope, which faced the sun, with insulation covering its north slope and gable ends. This type of greenhouse retained enough of the day's heat to let the plants inside survive even a heavy frost at night. Hay, leaves and manure were common insulating materials, and some pit greenhouses were built with the north side against an existing building, to take advantage of the added heat and wind protection this would provide. The pit was entered from the cellar of the adjacent building, or—if it did not adjoin one—through a small door in one gable end.

A simple variation of the pit greenhouse that you can make with modern materials is shown in Figures F and G. This model has no walls above ground level and is made with two standard hotbed sashes. Access is via a roof-top cellar door.

Building Instructions

Start by excavating a rectangular pit 10 feet 4 inches long, 7 feet wide and 4 feet deep. Working on high ground, orient the pit so that the window side of the roof will face south or southeast. Run tile drain, 6 inches in diameter, around the bottom of the pit and dig a trench for additional drain tile, leading to lower ground or to a dry well—a smaller, deeper pit filled with rocks. Inside the rectangle made by the drain tile, build your foundation wall, using 8-by-8-by-16-inch cinder blocks stacked six deep. The inner dimensions of the walls should be 8 feet by 4 feet 8 inches. Bed each block in enough mortar to assure a strong joint. Keep each layer level and plumb, checking frequently with a mason's level and a plumb bob. Depending on the thickness of the joints, the top of this wall will be 2 to 4 inches above ground level. Fill in the holes in the top layer with mortar mixed with gravel, and insert galvanized anchor bolts into this mixture before it hardens, spacing them at 2-foot intervals, keeping them 3 inches in from the outer face of the blocks so they project 2½ inches above the blocks. Fill the excavated area outside the wall with earth, tamping it in. Inside, make a floor with a 10-inch layer of coarse gravel topped with a 2-inch layer of bark mulch.

To make the sill that will fasten on the block wall cut two 9 foot-4-inch lengths and two 5-foot-8¾-inch lengths from a rot-resistant two-by-six. Drill holes in the sill pieces for the anchor bolts, then fasten it in place (Figure G) with nuts and washers so its outer edge is flush with the outside face of the blocks.

To assemble the roof frame that will be nailed to the sill, cut three pairs of rafters from two-by-four lumber, each piece 6 feet 2⅝ inches long. Miter the ends so they will fit flush against the face of the ridge board and against the top of the sill (Figure G). Using galvanized 10-penny nails, fasten the rafters to the side faces of a one-by-four ridgepole, 6 feet long, placing the gable-end rafters 1 inch in from the ends and centering the middle pair (Figure G). Then fasten the entire frame assembly in place by nailing the rafter ends to the sill.

Cut four two-by-four studs to run vertically from sill to gable rafters, two to each gable. These will be placed 2 feet 9 inches in from the corners. (To measure for length hold the stud in position and cut it at the point where it intersects the rafter.) Do not miter the tops; cut them square. On top of each pair, insert a two-by-four crossbeam, mitered to slip into the V between the stud and rafter (Figure G). Nail studs and crossbeams to sill and rafters, keeping the studs perpendicular and all outside edges flush. In gable ends, nail a third stud cut to fit crossbeam and sill. Cap

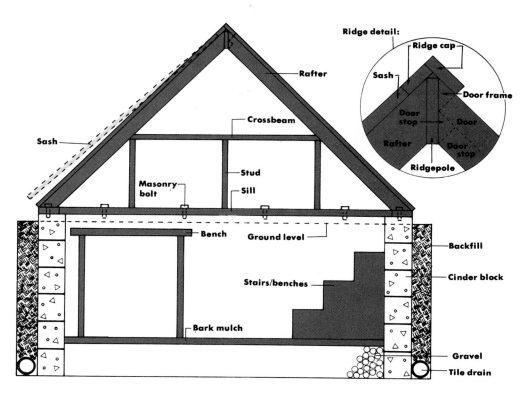

G

Figure G: The pit is surrounded with a tile drain and six-course cinder-block wall, then filled with gravel, 10 inches deep, topped by a 2-inch layer of bark mulch. The sill, fitted to cinder blocks, is secured with masonry bolts, and rafters, rising directly from sill to ridge, are braced with studs and crossbeam on each gable end. A ridge cap and doorstop complete the basic frame.

the ridgepole by nailing two 6-foot boards along the tops of the rafters, a one-by-four on one face lapping a board 1-by-2¾-inches on the other.

Roof one of the 3-by-6-foot openings on the north slope with boards and asbestos shingles (Figure F), covering the center rafter and extending 1 inch beyond the gable rafters. To build a recessed door frame in the other north opening, span the two rafters that frame it with a two-by-two crossbeam positioned under the ridge cap flush with its lower edge and mitered at its meeting with the ridgepole. Then nail two-by-twos to the part of the ridgepole that extends below this crossbeam and to the adjacent rafters so they are flush with the lower edges of the two-by-fours. Put a door 2 feet 8 inches wide and 6 feet high into this opening, resting on the two-by-twos. This size allows a small space all around for weather-stripping. Use three 3-by-1½-inch brass butt hinges to fasten the door to the gable rafter, a brass barrel bolt to latch it to the opposite rafter.

On the south roof, hinge two 3-by-6-foot greenhouse sashes to the ridge cap, using two 3-by-1½-inch brass butt hinges on each (Figure F). Both sashes will overlap the end rafter by 1 inch and extend to the center of the middle rafter. Use hook-and-eye latches to fasten the sashes to the sill inside the greenhouse.

Before putting siding on the gables, nail a one-by-two to the outside of the door jamb, with its face against the rafter and its upper edge flush with that of the rafter. Extend it from ridge to sill. Then cut and nail 8-inch-wide siding to cover both gable ends, starting at the bottom. Staple insulation to the gable ends and north roof, from ridge to sill, inside the greenhouse. If you like, you can cover this with paneling. Sheet metal flashing along the top of the ridge and removable weatherstripping between the sashes are optional. (You will need to open these sashes for ventilation on warm days, even in winter.)

Stairs leading from the door down to the greenhouse floor, each 9 inches high and wide, can be extended along the entire north wall to create plant shelves where the winter sunlight will be strongest. A higher bench is used for the south wall. In most areas, the temperature in this pit will not drop below freezing at night, but you might want to add a small electric heater to maintain a warmer temperature.

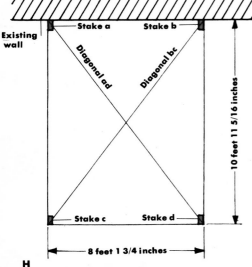

H

Figure H: To locate the corner stakes, mark off the width of greenhouse against your existing wall with stakes *a* and *b*. Then measure out from the wall the distance shown and set corner stakes *c* and *d*. Make sure corners are square.

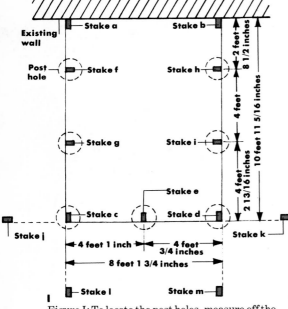

I

Figure I: To locate the post holes, measure off the distances shown and set stakes *e*, *f*, *g*, *h* and *i*. Set stakes *j*, *k*, *l* and *m* 1 foot or more beyond the corners of the plot and in alignment with the strings that connect the corner stakes. Holes for aluminum angle posts will be dug later at stakes *c*, *d* and *e*, and for two-by-four wooden posts at stakes *f*, *g*, *h* and *i*; stakes *a*, *b*, *j*, *k*, *l* and *m* will be connected with string and used to determine the locations of the posts after the other stakes have been removed in digging the post holes.

Environmental Projects
Curved fiberglass greenhouse $●⚒⚗

This unusual structure, sketched on page 817, has a rugged, translucent fiberglass covering and a rot-proof aluminum frame instead of the glass and wood of the traditional greenhouse. In addition to lowering the cost, these elements add to the life-span of the greenhouse, so it is, indeed, as hardy as any of the perennials it might house. In many places, buildings like this do not require a building permit, but check your regulations before you start construction.

The lean-to measures 8 feet 1¾ inches wide by 10 feet 11 5/16 inches deep, and is 9 feet 8 inches tall on the side that adjoins your house or garage. Select a site with a southern or southeastern exposure for the curved fiberglass side, so your plants will get maximum winter sunlight. You will need a clear, level space that is 9 feet wide and extends 12 feet out from the building. If no such area exists, look for a slope that you can level by moving dirt from the high to the low side. To insure good drainage, indispensable in a greenhouse, the site should be slightly higher rather than lower than the surrounding area.

The greenhouse needs a water supply—a house hose faucet inside the greenhouse will do—and a separate electrical circuit to run the exhaust fan and the 1650-watt heater. You could carry water from the house to the greenhouse, even in cold weather, but if you do not have the needed electric circuit, have your electrician install one. Do not attempt to operate the fan and heater on an extension cord.

Every greenhouse needs an outside door. The blueprint on pages 824 and 825 shows this door on the right-hand side of the greenhouse; it could just as well be on the left. Many other modifications are possible, so the building can, in effect, be tailored to your own personal specifications.

Establishing the Boundaries
Cut four 6-inch stakes to mark the corners of the greenhouse. With a 16-foot steel measuring tape, mark off an 8-foot-1¾-inch width along the building wall you will use (Post Plan, page 824). Drive a stake at each end of this span (*a* and *b*, Figure H) 3 or 4 inches into the ground. Measure out from stakes, at right angles to the wall, a distance of 10 feet 11 5/16 inches (Post Plan, page 824), and mark these points (*c* and *d*, Figure H) with the stakes. You can sight by eye to get approximate right angles, or use a framing square. Once the stakes are in, however, the angles should be checked. If the distance between *c* and *d* is the same as that between *a* and *b* (8 feet 1¾ inches), and diagonals *ad* and *bc* (Figure H) are equal in length, the corners are square. If necessary, reset the stakes until corners are square. Connect stake *a* with *c*, *c* with *d*, and *d* with *b*, using string tied to each stake. Cut nine additional stakes and use five to mark the locations of the post holes at points *e*, *f*, *g*, *h* and *i* (Figure I). Drive the remaining four stakes at positions *j*, *k*, *l* and *m* (Figure I), a foot or more outside the boundaries for future use in aligning angle posts. Then remove the strings to facilitate digging.

Using a post-hole digger, which you may be able to rent, dig holes at points marked by stakes *c* through *i*, going down 2 feet 9 inches. The stakes, of course, will be removed in the process. The diameter of the holes need be no greater than the post-hole digger itself, but make them slightly wider at the bottom than at the top, to insure good holding action for the concrete anchors you will pour. To re-establish the boundaries, connect stake *a* with *l*, *b* with *m*, and *j* with *k*, using string tied to each stake.

Installing the Angle Posts
At this point, you are ready to install the aluminum angle posts that will secure the rafters to the foundation (Post Plan and Typical Section, page 824, and list of materials, page 825). These posts come with pre-drilled bolt and screw holes to insure correct alignment with the rafters.

In post holes *c*, *d* and *e* (Figure I), set the angle posts so that their shorter (1¼-inch) faces are parallel with the building wall and the edge of their longer (1½-inch) faces points toward the wall from the left-hand edge of the post as you

(Text continues on page 826)

CRAFTNOTES: HOW TO READ A BLUEPRINT

Architectural drawings make use of a special—but quite simple—language, one you can begin to understand within minutes From an original pencil drawing on white paper, a special machine copies (and can mass-produce) a photographic image on blue paper so that the pencil lines appear in white. These reproductions, called blueprints, are representations of what a structure will be like when it is completed, and they serve as pictorial building instructions. They tell the builder what materials to use, the precise dimensions of all parts, and other important details. For example, from the blueprints for this greenhouse (pages 824 and 825), you can learn the location of the door, fan and jalousie ventilator, as well as the locations and types of weathersealers, nuts and bolts.

Since the drawings have to be of a size that can be easily handled, they are usually much smaller than the objects they represent. Many things such as lights, doors and windows are too small to be clearly indicated except by the use of standard symbols. If a structure is to be 8 by 11 feet, as is the greenhouse, the architect might decide to depict it in a picture that is only about 3 by 4 inches, using what is called a scale. In this case, the scale would be written on the drawings as 3/16" = 1'0", meaning 3/16 inch on the drawing is equal to 1 foot in the actual structure. If you know the scale of a drawing, you can measure any line on it with an ordinary ruler and multiply this dimension by the appropriate ratio (here it is 64) to determine the length of the full-size line. A line 1 1/2 inches long, multiplied by 64, translates into 96 inches, or 8 feet. Special rulers based on common architects' scales are available to do such calculating automatically.

These scales are used on the most common type of architectural drawing, the floor plan, which shows the configuration of rooms and walls as if they were being viewed from directly above through an open roof. The drawing labeled "Post Plan" on page 824 is such a view. But close-up views of details, showing how structural parts, trim and special fixtures are to be assembled, are usually drawn on a much larger scale, sometimes full size. The details on pages 824 and 825 are one-fourth full size.

Elevation views show the exterior of the building as seen head-on, as in the drawing labeled "Gable End Elevation." These are often made up in a set of four true-to-life but two-dimensional drawings, one for each compass direction. Section views, such as the one labeled "Typical Section" on page 824, depict interior construction, providing a cross-section view as though the structure had been cut apart and opened up. Finally, there are the drawings known as isometric views, that give a three-dimensional effect. The drawing labeled "Perspective End View" on page 824 is an isometric drawing.

Architectural drawings are usually accompanied by written instructions, called specifications, that clarify aspects of construction that cannot be communicated graphically, such as what materials to use, how to assemble them, or what standards of quality need to be maintained. The list of materials next to the greenhouse blueprints partly fills this function.

The dimensions of all parts and of the spaces separating them are given on the blueprint (in full size, not to scale) by a system of lines, arrowheads and figures. Beside each line in the drawing that indicates a length, width or height is a two-headed arrow, accompanied, and sometimes broken in the middle, by a figure that gives the measurement of that particular span. Sometimes two or more lines of the same length, such as the opposite ends of a rectangle, are marked by a single arrow, but only when it is obvious that the arrow refers to both lines. The tips of the arrow-heads end at what are called extension lines—short lines that extend out from the end points of the span that is being defined. The dimensions could just as well have been given directly on the drawing—in fact, they often are—but placing them to one side often increases clarity. For very small dimensions, two single-headed arrows are sometimes used, pointing toward each other from opposite sides of the extension lines which sandwich the dimension between them. Occasionally the space represented is so very small that the dimension must be given alongside the arrow at one end.

The way a line is drawn gives additional information. The unbroken lines indicate the edges of surfaces that would be visible from whatever viewing point the drawing assumes. Lines made up of a series of short dashes indicate the edges of surfaces that would be invisible from the assumed viewing point, but exist behind or beneath the visible surface so they would show up in an X-ray view. (In the greenhouse blueprints, construction details that would be hidden below the surface of the ground are indicated this way.) Light lines of alternately long and short dashes, on the other hand, indicate the center of something (such as a bolt).

A line with a wavy break in it at intervals indicates the full length of a structural element is not shown. A two-headed arrow with matching letters at each end indicates an area that is shown in more detail elsewhere, perhaps as a section view. In the greenhouse blueprints, the area labeled C-C in the perspective end view matches the detail labeled "Section C-C."

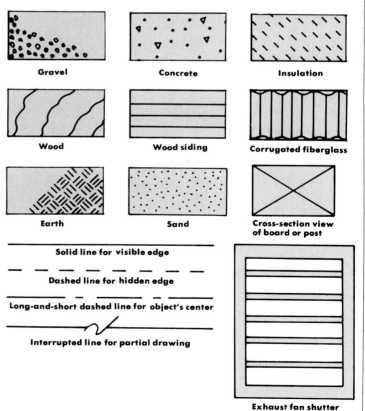

Gravel

Concrete

Insulation

Wood

Wood siding

Corrugated fiberglass

Earth

Sand

Cross-section view of board or post

———————— Solid line for visible edge

— — — — — Dashed line for hidden edge

—— — —— — —— Long-and-short dashed line for object's center

Interrupted line for partial drawing

Exhaust fan shutter

Above are a few of the many symbols used in architectural drawings.

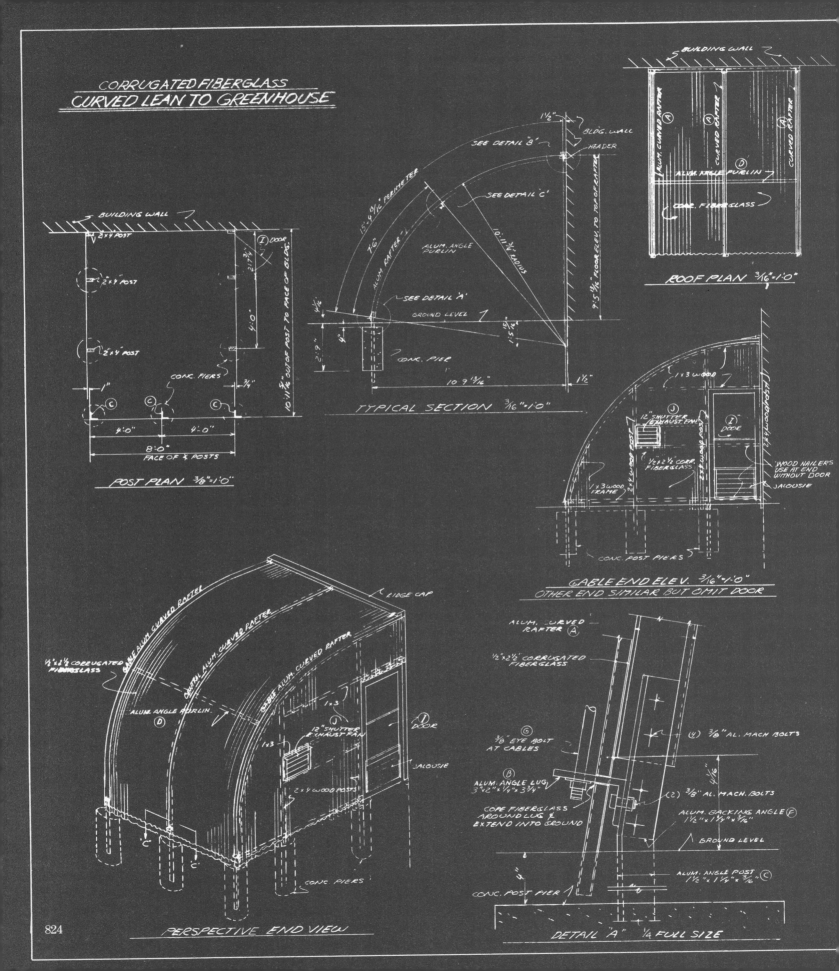

CORRUGATED FIBERGLASS
CURVED LEAN TO GREENHOUSE

ROOF PLAN 3/16"=1'0"

TYPICAL SECTION 3/16"=1'0"

POST PLAN 3/16"=1'0"

GABLE END ELEV. 3/16"=1'0"
OTHER END SIMILAR BUT OMIT DOOR

PERSPECTIVE END VIEW

DETAIL "A" 1/4 FULL SIZE

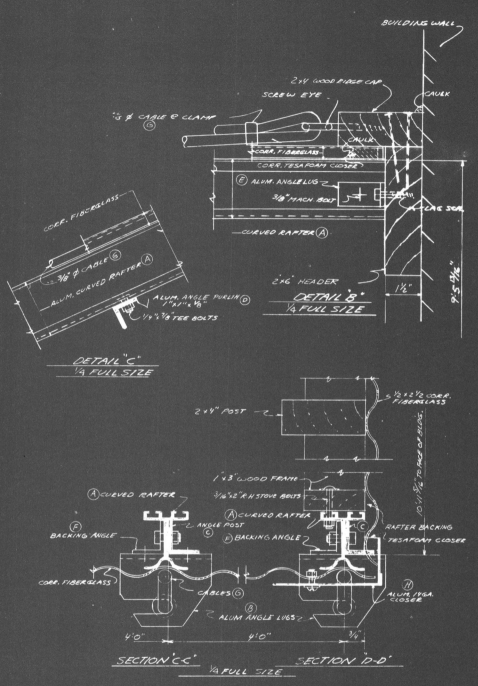

DETAIL "B"
¼ FULL SIZE

DETAIL "C"
¼ FULL SIZE

SECTION "C-C"
¼ FULL SIZE

SECTION "D-D"
¼ FULL SIZE

	PART NO.	DESCRIPTION
A	5181-22	ALUM. CURVED RAFTER
B	OL-511	ALUM. CABLE SILL LUGS
C	5506-491R	ALUM. ANGLE POST
D	5500-2	ALUM. ROOF PURLIN
E	OL-470	ALUM. RIDGE LUGS
F	5506-490R	ALUM. BACKING ANGLE
G	OL-494X	SPECIAL LENGTH NEOPRENE COVERED CABLE WITH EYE BOLT & CLAMPS
H	OL-514-22	ALUM. GABLE END CLOSERS
I	2'-6"×6'-10"	WOOD DOOR (JALOUSIE OPTIONAL)
J	2C710	12" SHUTTER EXHAUST FAN
		MISC. BOLTS, SCREWS & FIBERGLASS

Materials Needed

All materials used in the construction of this greenhouse are listed below. Aluminum structural members and some plastic parts not locally available may be ordered from Lord & Burnham, Irvington, N.Y. 10533, using the reference number which follows those items.

3 aluminum angle posts (1 1/2" × 1 1/4" × 3/16" × 3' 5 1/8" × 6 7/8") #5506-491R
3 aluminum backing angles (1 1/2" × 1 1/4" × 3/16" × 6 7/8") #5506-49OR
4 aluminum ridge lugs (2" × 3 1/2" × 1" × 3/16") #OL-470
3 curved aluminum rafters (15'4 13/16" × 1 3/4" × 2 1/2" with irregular flanges) #5181-22
1 aluminum roof angle purlin (1" × 1" × 1/8" × 8') #5500-2
3 aluminum cable sill angle lugs (3" × 2" × 1/4" × 3 3/4") #OL-511
2 neoprene-covered steel cables (30'10" × 3/8" diam., with 3/8"-eye bolts on each end) #OL-494X
12 aluminum gable end closers (4" × 5" × 2") #OL-514-22
3 corrugated fiberglass glazing panels (4' 3 1/2" × 16')
1 corrugated fiberglass glazing panel (4'3 1/2" × 14')
2 corrugated fiberglass glazing panels (4' 3 1/2" × 9'6")
5 contoured Tesafoam closers (3' × 1/2')
2 vertical Tesafoam closers (3' × 2 1/2')
1 pound of small cubes of compressible Tesafoam
2 boxes of 100 aluminum fiberglass-to-wood screw-type fastening nails with Neoprene washers, 2" long.
19 hexagonal aluminum machine bolts with nuts (3/8" × 1 1/4")
2 hexagonal aluminum machine bolts with nuts (3/8" × 1")
4 hexagonal aluminum lag screws (3/8" × 2")
4 galvanized T-head bolts with nuts (1/4" × 7/8")
36 galvanized round-head stove bolts with nuts and washers (3/16" × 2")
3 screw eyes (1/2" inner diam.)
3 cable clamps with backings and nuts (3/4" inner diam.)
1 box 1/4" machine screws with nuts
1 10' length of 2 × 4, any lumber
1 10' length of 2 × 6, any lumber
3 10' lengths of 2 × 4, rot-resistant lumber
4 12' lengths of 2 × 4, rot resistant lumber
6 80-pound bags of ready-mix concrete product
1 quart asphaltum or creosote wood sealer
1/2 pound 6d galvanized common (wire) nails
1/2 pound 10d galvanized common (wire) nails
1/4 pound 6d casing or finishing nails
24 galvanized or brass fasteners, as needed, such as screws, bolts, masonry nails, to attach greenhouse frame to existing wall.
100 lineal feet of 1 × 3, any lumber, in 8' lengths or longer
1 fan and 1 jalousie, each 12" × 12", with capacity of 600 cubic feet of air per minute (#2C710)
1 box of 1 1/2" #12 cadmium-plated wood screws
1 1650-watt automatic air-circulation heater with built-in thermostat
1 extension cord with two-outlet 3-prong box long enough to reach an electrical source
1 garden hose long enough to reach a water source
1 tube of weatherproofing caulk for use in gun
1 standard wood door (2'6" × 6'10")
3 4" × 1 3/4" brass butt hinges with screws
17 lineal feet of standard door stop molding
Door hardware, as desired

Tools Needed

16' steel tape, level, shovel, 15 1" × 2" × 6" pieces of wood to use as ground stakes, hammer, framing square, string, post-hole digger, plumb bob, 4 C-clamps, wheelbarrow or tub for mixing concrete, hoe, bucket (5-gallon capacity), crosscut saw, socket wrench set to fit variously-sized bolts, pencil, screwdriver, 10' ladder, saber saw or keyhole saw, tinsnips, caulking gun, and power drill with 9/32", 5/32" and 1/4" wood bits.

face the wall (Figure J). Set post *c* so it is 1 inch to the right of string *al*, or 1 inch inside the boundary marked by string *al*. Set post *d* in similar fashion, ¾ inch to the left of, or inside, string *bm*. Set post *e* equidistant (4 feet exactly) from the other two (Figure J). Make all three posts plumb (perfectly vertical) up to the point where the bend deflects toward the wall. To insure accuracy use the vertical gauge of your level or hold a plumb bob (a weight on a string) alongside the post. (When the weight comes to rest, the string will indicate a true vertical.)

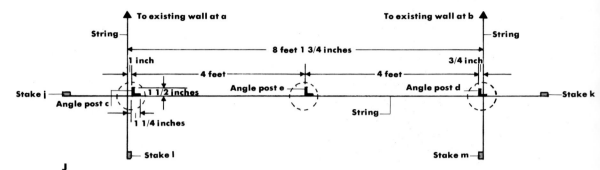

J

Figure J: To locate the angle posts, set them with their shorter (1¼-inch) faces against string *jk* and their longer (1½-inch) faces pointing toward the wall from the left-hand side of the posts as you face the wall. Set post *c* so its longer face is 1 inch to the right of string *al*. Set post *d* with its longer face ¾ inch to the left of string *bm*. Set post *e* midway between posts *c* and *d* (with its longer face exactly 4 feet from that of both of the others).

Drive each post into the bottom of its hole until the angle bend is 1 inch above ground level (Figure K), using a hammer and striking the post on its topmost edge. Protect the post from hammer blows by covering it with a rag.

When these steps have been completed, double-check to see that all three posts still line up along string *jk* (Figure J), and that the diagonals *ad* and *bc* (Figure H) are still equal, measuring from the string intersections at points *c* and *d*. Finally, secure the posts in position by attaching a 10-foot two-by-four to them with C-clamps, securing and bracing it with ground stakes (Figure L).

Now you are ready to mix the concrete for holes *c*, *d* and *e*. (Do not pour the concrete for the other post holes at this stage.) Prepare 2 or 2½ bags of ready-mix concrete, following label directions. Taking care not to dislodge the posts, pour concrete into these three holes, stopping 4 inches below the finished grade (Detail A in blueprint, page 824). Check the location of the posts again, as described above, and make adjustments, if necessary, by repositioning the C-clamps and the two-by-four brace before the concrete hardens. (You have a few hours' leeway here, so this operation need not be rushed.) Because this structure is so light, letting the concrete dry overnight is sufficient. In the morning, remove the two-by-four brace. All told, you'll need five or six 80-pound bags of ready-mix concrete for this greenhouse. Sub-zero weather should cause no problems, because the construction materials are flexible enough to adjust to any frost heaving.

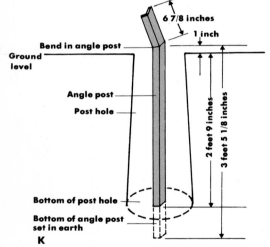

K

Figure K: To position the angle posts, drive each post into the earth at the bottom of its hole until the bend stands 1 inch above ground level. The slight angle of the post should point toward the wall, to connect later with a curved rafter.

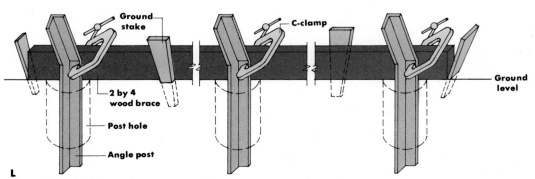

L

Figure L: To hold the angle posts securely in place while concrete is being poured and until it hardens, clamp them to a length of two-by-four wood secured and braced with ground stakes. Use as many ground stakes as are necessary to keep the two-by-four properly positioned.

Preparing to Raise the Rafters

The wood frame against which the greenhouse will fit can now be attached to the existing wall. This includes the header to which the curved aluminum rafters will be attached (Typical Section, Detail "B" on page 825, and materials list on page 825). For this frame, and all other wood in this project, use rot-resistant lumber. If possible, get wood that has been pressure-treated with a preservative. Otherwise, coat any wood that will lie near the ground with asphaltum or creosote sealer. To forestall rust, use galvanized or aluminum nails.

At the locations marked by stakes a and b (Figure H), attach two uprights to the existing wall as detailed in Figure M. These can be cut from 10-foot lengths of two-by-four lumber. Be sure to use fasteners suited to the wall material (see "Fasteners" Craftnotes, page 829 for information on this). Position the posts so that a wide side faces the wall, and check to see that the outer edges are 8 feet 1¾ inches apart at all points. The posts should be plumb and their tops level.

Cut an 8-foot 1¾-inch length from a 10-foot two-by-six to use as the header. Preparing for a later step—attaching the rafters to the header—mark a horizontal pencil line across the length of the header face 2⅛ inches in from one edge (henceforth the top edge). This 2⅛-inch margin is the distance between the top of the header and the point at which the rafters will be attached. Intersect this line at its midpoint with a perpendicular line, 4 feet ⅞ inch from each end. Put the two-by-six on the tops of posts a and b, with the pencil lines facing out and nearer the top than the bottom. Using 10-penny common galvanized nails, nail the two-by-six to the tops of the posts, making sure that the outer ends of header and posts are flush with each other. Because of the width of the two-by-six, you will need to toenail it to the posts, that is, drive the nails in at an angle. Once the two-by-six is nailed to the uprights, it can be secured to the wall in the same way as the two-by-fours were attached.

After the concrete sets, loosely bolt the backing angles to angle posts c, d and e, setting the fasteners into the pre-drilled holes. Use hexagonal ⅜-by-1¼-inch aluminum machine bolts (Figure N). Position the backing angles so the longer (1½-inch) face points toward the wall, but leave a gap of about ¼ inch between the backing angles and the angle posts, as the ends of the curved aluminum rafters have to fit into this opening. The tops of the backing angles will line up with the tops of the angle posts and the bottoms with the bends of the angle posts.

Next, mount the angled aluminum ridge lugs (Detail "B" of blueprint, page 825) on the ends of the curved aluminum rafters that will be attached to the wall. To what will become the central rafter, mount two lugs back-to-back with a single ⅜-by-1¼-inch aluminum machine bolt (Figure O). The outer face of each lug should be flush with the end of the rafter. Mount only one angled ridge lug on each of the two gable rafters (Figure P, page 828), using a ⅜-by-1-inch aluminum machine bolt to attach the lug to the interior face of the rafter.

Raising the Rafters

Insert the lower ends of the curved aluminum rafters into the gaps between the angle posts and backing angles (Detail "A" and Section "C-C" or "D-D" of blueprint, pages 824 and 825). Using a socket wrench, bolt each three-piece assembly together with two ⅜-by-1¼-inch machine bolts (Figure Q, page 828). Be sure that the center rafter is in the central position (Figure O), and that each gable rafter is positioned so that its lug faces inward (Figure P). Tighten the lower bolts that were left loose at an earlier stage. The lug ends of the rafters should now be resting against the face of the 2-by-6 header.

The rafters with lugs attached can now be used as templates. Align the outer edge of each gable rafter with the end of the header, and center the middle rafter on the intersection of the pencil lines that you have drawn. Then hold each rafter in turn up to the header so that the holes in the lugs are centered on the horizontal pencil line. Through the hole in each of the four lugs, drill holes 1½ inches into the header, using a 9/32-inch bit. To insure getting the proper depth, mark your drill bit with a piece of tape, 1½ inches in from the tip. Join the rafters to the header with ⅜-by-2-inch hexagonal lag screws (Detail "B" of blueprint, page 825). The frame is now secure in the ground and against the existing wall.

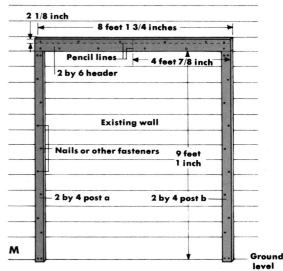

Figure M: To construct the frame that will connect the greenhouse to the existing wall, attach two two-by-four posts to the wall at the points marked by stakes a and b. These should go from ground level to a height of 9 feet 1 inch. A wide side of each post faces the wall, and outer edges are 8 feet 1¾ inches apart at all points. Attach an 8-foot-1¾-inch two-by-six header to the tops of the post and to the wall. A wide side of the two-by-six also faces the wall.

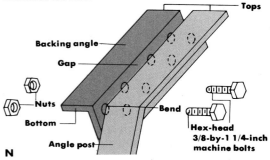

Figure N: Connect the backing angles to the angle posts by passing bolts through the two lower holes in each piece. Do not tighten nuts all the way, but leave a gap of about ¼ inch between the two pieces so the rafter can be inserted.

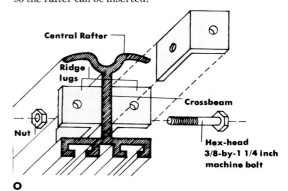

Figure O: To mount angled ridge lugs on the wall end of the middle rafter, bolt the longer legs of two lugs back-to-back on the crossbeam of the rafter, using a single bolt. Predrilled holes in the rafter and lugs will position the shorter legs of the lugs flush with the end of the rafter.

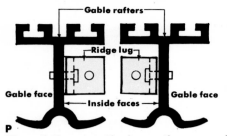

Figure P: To mount ridge lugs on the upper ends of gable rafters, proceed as in Figure O, page 827, but attach only one lug to each rafter. Put the lug for the right gable rafter (as you face the wall) on the left side of the crossbeam, and for the left rafter on the right side.

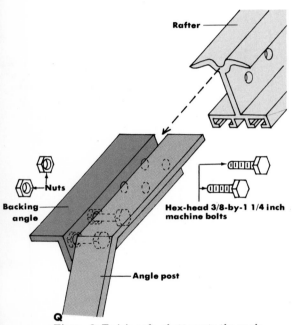

Figure Q: To join rafter bottoms to the angle post-backing angle assembly, insert each rafter into the gap between angle post and backing angle (further loosening bolts if necessary), and fasten with two bolts in the remaining predrilled holes. Then tighten the lower bolts.

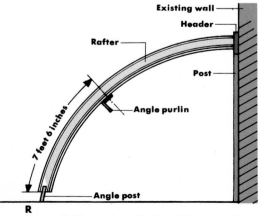

Figure R: The angle purlin is positioned vertically, by means of holes predrilled in it. Center these 7 feet 6 inches from the base of the rafters, measuring along their circumference.

828

Installing the Roof Purlin

The next step is to mount the aluminum angle purlin—a section of framing that runs horizontally across the inside of all three rafters and keeps them braced and properly positioned (Figure R; Typical Section and Detail "C" of blueprint, page 824-825). Measure along the outer circumference of the rafter, starting from its base, to a height of 7 feet 6 inches, and temporarily fasten the purlin to the rafters at that height, using C-clamps and checking for level. Note that the purlin will extend only to the center of each gable rafter (Figure S). When the purlin is in place, drill four holes, penetrating both purlin and rafters—one through each channel in the central rafter and one through the inner channel of each gable rafter, using a 9/32-inch drill bit. Secure the purlin to the rafters with ¼-by-⅞-inch galvanized T-head bolts (Detail "C", page 825).

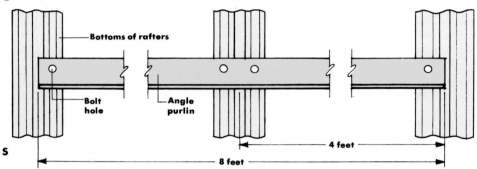

Figure S: To locate the angle purlin horizontally, position its two ends at the center of the inner flange of each gable rafter. The predrilled holes in the purlin will then fall at the openings in the inner flanges of the rafters, to which they will be bolted in the next step. The view is from below, looking up at the undersides of the rafters and purlin.

Attaching the Rafter Backings

At this juncture, a wood backing, to which the fiberglass panels will later be attached, can be installed along the underside of the gable rafters (Figure T and Section "D-D" in blueprint, page 825). Starting with four one-by-threes (available in 8-foot lengths), cut out two 7-foot-9-inch lengths and two 7-foot-4-inch lengths. These will be attached to the gable rafters, one long and one short length to each, as follows: First, run a short length from the base of each rafter up to the purlin, and a long length from the top of each rafter down to the purlin. The outer edge of each one-by-three should be flush with the outer edge of its rafter (Figure T). Use

[Text continued on page 830]

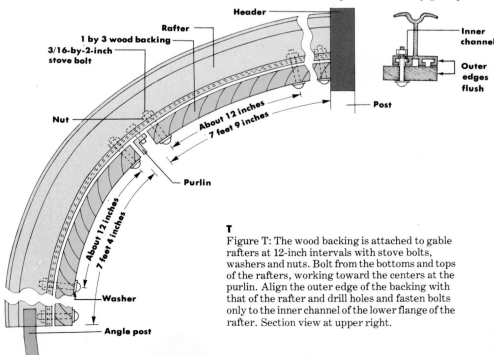

Figure T: The wood backing is attached to gable rafters at 12-inch intervals with stove bolts, washers and nuts. Bolt from the bottoms and tops of the rafters, working toward the centers at the purlin. Align the outer edge of the backing with that of the rafter and drill holes and fasten bolts only to the inner channel of the lower flange of the rafter. Section view at upper right.

CRAFTNOTES: FASTENERS

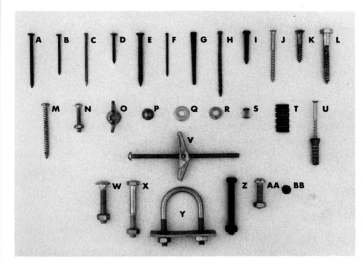

Among common types of fasteners are: A, wire or common nail; B, box nail; C, finishing nail; D, gypsum nail; E, masonry nail; F, G and H, flooring nails; I, roundhead screw; J, flathead screw; K, oval head screw; L, lag screw; M, sheet metal screw (self-tapping); N, stove bolt; O, wing nut; P, cap nut; Q, washer; R, lock washer; S, rivet; T, corrugated fastener; U, masonry screw with lead plug; V, toggle bolt; W, carriage bolt; X, machine bolt (hex-head); Y, U-bolt; Z, machine bolt (square-head); AA, machine screw; and BB, Phillips head screw viewed from above.

Different projects and materials require different types of fastening, and it pays to take the trouble to use the proper hardware and the right technique.

Nails are generally, though not always, used for joining wood. As a rule of thumb, use nails on rough work and screws for finer work. Nails are made in a wide variety of types and sizes, depending on the nature and scale of the materials.

There are three basic types of nails. Common (or wire) nails are for rough, heavy work, as in this greenhouse. They range in size from 2-penny (2d), 1 inch long, to 20d, 4 inches long. The 6d and 10d nails used in this greenhouse are 2 and 3 inches long respectively. Anything under 1 inch is called a brad or tack, and is named by its length; anything over 4 inches is usually called a spike and is specified by a penny size of up to 60d. When fastening the posts and header of this greenhouse to an existing wooden wall, use common nails, 10d or larger.

Box nails come in approximately the same lengths as common nails but are thinner and thus less likely to split the wood. However, they have less strength.

Finishing nails have small heads that can be driven into the surface of the wood and entirely out of view by means of a small tool known as a nailset. They range in size from 3d to 10d, or 1 1/4 to 3 inches. Similar to finishing nails are casing nails, which have a head that blends gradually into the shank. These range in size from 2d to 16d, or 1 to 3 1/2 inches. You will be using finishing nails or casing nails for the doorstop in this greenhouse.

Nails made of untreated steel are commonly used indoors; galvanized (zinc-coated) nails are used for exterior work, to prevent rust.

Among the more than 100 other specialized types of nails are the gypsum nail (tapered threads and a large, flat head to hold in plaster); masonry nails (made of high-carbon steel with longitudinal threads to hold in concrete and cinder block—these may be of use in fastening the greenhouse frame to an existing masonry wall; a wide variety of flooring nails; and screw-type fastening

nails with neoprene washers for attaching fiberglass to wood and weatherproofing their own hole (Figure HH, page 834).

Screws have greater holding power than nails and can be removed without damage to the wood, but they require more work. Small screws can usually be driven into soft wood by means of a screwdriver without any preparation; others require only a pilot hole, made by driving a nail and then removing it (you will be using this procedure twice in the greenhouse).

Screws are made of aluminum, brass, nickel, steel, and steel-plated metals and may be flathead (designed to be entirely set into the surface of the wood), roundhead (with a domed cap that sits above the surface), or the decorative, brass oval head designed to sit partly above and partly below the surface. Lag screws — you'll be using these to fasten your greenhouse rafters to the wood frame — have a square or hexagonal protruding head and are driven with a wrench. Most screws that require a screwdriver are made either with a regular head—a simple slot that the flat blade of the driver fits into—or a Phillips head for a driver whose tip is shaped like a cross.

Machine screws, unlike wood screws, are not tapered because they are used for the assembly of metal parts and are either driven into threaded holes or drawn tight with nuts. They differ from most bolts in that their heads are made to receive a screwdriver rather than a wrench.

Specialized types of screws include self-tapping screws (i.e. screws that drill their own holes) for use with sheet metal; masonry screws that come with lead plugs which grip both the screw and the medium it is entering; plaster screws (or toggle bolts) with special wings that spread out after they are inserted into a wall through a predrilled hole; and eye screws, which have a circle instead of a head, such as the ones through which cables are threaded in the greenhouse project (Figure Z, page 831).

Bolts also come in many shapes and sizes. Some important types are carriage bolts, tightened by turning the nut; machine bolts (unslotted) or stove bolts (slotted) which can be tightened from either end (by turning head or nut); and U-bolts, shaped like the letter U, which are fastened with nuts on both ends. The cable clamps for this greenhouse are in the shape of a U-bolt, but they have an additional fixture which grips the cables when the nuts are tightened. Unlike machine screws, bolts usually come paired with nuts that have matching threads.

Of course, nails, screws and bolts are not the only fasteners available. A few other possibilities, each having its own range of proper applications, are adhesives, glues, rivets, corrugated fasteners, wire, rope and soldering and welding, in the case of metals.

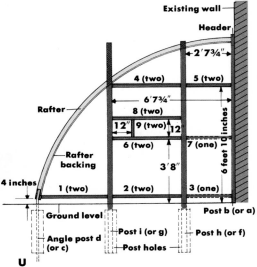

U

Figure U: To locate and cut the wood posts to size, mark the underside of the wood backing on both gable rafters at distances of 2 feet 7¾ inches and 6 feet 7¾ inches, measured out horizontally from the wall. Stand each post in its hole (at points f, g, h and i) and align its top with the mark on the rafter backing. Then scribe and cut the post at its intersection with the underside of the rafter backing. To locate the one-by-three framing pieces, set the pieces numbered 1, 2 and 3 with their bottoms 4 inches above ground level; pieces numbered 4 and 5 with bottoms 6 feet 10 inches above ground level; pieces numbered 6 and 7 with bottoms 3 feet 8 inches above ground level. Position strips numbered 8 with their bottoms 12 inches above the tops of strips numbered 6, and similarly space pieces numbered 9 from posts i and g. Dotted lines indicate pieces used only on the side with no door; the numbers in parentheses tell how many pieces of a given length are needed.

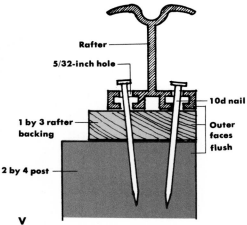

V

Figure V: To fasten posts to rafters and rafter backings, drill holes through both channels in the lower flanges of the rafters and drive nails through the rafters and backings into the tops of the posts, keeping the outer face of each post flush with that of the rafter and backing.

3/16-by-2-inch galvanized stove bolts and set them at 12-inch intervals. To do this, drill a hole through both wood and aluminum 1 inch from either the bottom or top of the rafter with a ¼-inch bit. Secure the bolt at this point, using a household flathead screw driver and wrench, before going on to drill and bolt the next hole. The bolts will do the work of permanently drawing the wood in to the curve of the rafter, so fasten one after another, working from each end, rather than attempting to drill all the holes in advance or to work from the middle out. It isn't crucial if the wood splits under this stress as it is not a structural member but merely a convenient means of attaching the fiberglass panels to the rafters. Just continue bolting from the point of the break, should one occur. The one precaution is to avoid positioning the bolts directly over the centers of post holes f, g, h and i; these areas must be kept free for later connections. You can determine these points on the rafters by using a plumb bob, but will probably be able to gauge them as well by eye. (If attaching the rafter backings in the above manner is awkward, temporarily fasten the wood backing to the aluminum rafter with C-clamps.)

Completing the Frame

Measuring horizontally from the existing wall (*not* along the circumference of the rafter) mark the underside of the one-by-three backing on each rafter twice—once at a distance of 2 feet 7¾ inches from the existing wall and again at 6 feet 7¾ inches. These measurements correspond to the distances from the wall for post holes, f, g, h and i (Figure I), minus half the space occupied by the two-by-four wood post itself (Figure U). Now stand a 12-foot length of two-by-four rot-resistant lumber at the approximate center of each of the holes, keeping its broader face parallel to the existing wall, and mark a line on the top of each post where it intersects the lower face of the one-by-three rafter backing at the distances you have just measured and marked from the wall (Figure U). Saw off the tops of the two-by-fours at this point.

Drill holes 5/32 of an inch in diameter through both channels of the lower flange of each rafter above the areas where the tops of the posts will be nailed to the rafters (Figure V). Drive 10-penny nails through rafters and backings, going into the tops of the two-by-four posts, and checking to make certain that the outer (side-wall) face of each post is flush with the outer face of the rafter backing (Figure V). When you have the two-by-four posts attached to the rafters, check that they are plumb and that they are aligned at ground level, using strings al and bm (Figure I). Then secure them in position with a two-by-four at least 6 feet long, C-clamps and ground stakes, as previously done with the angle posts (Figure L), working from post h to post i and from post f to post g. Mix and pour the concrete as before, and allow it to harden overnight. When the concrete has set, the braces, string and stakes can be removed. This completes the heavy construction.

The remainder of the frame consists of the one-by-three strips shown in Figure U, with the numbers in parentheses indicating how many lengths of a given piece are needed. Two pieces are called for when the detail on both sides of the greenhouse is the same, and only one piece when differences occur. Keep this diagram at hand while following the instructions given below, and refer to it as needed. Each strip should be measured as you go, and the easiest way to get accurate measurements is to hold the one-by-three in place and measure the distance it will span. Then scribe and cut the piece. (Note that, because there are slight variations in the distances each framing element will span, the strips cannot be cut to a standard length.) In each case, the wider surfaces of the one-by-three act as the top and bottom faces of the piece, the narrower sides as the edges. Set the outer face of each strip flush with the outer face of all the other framing elements and secure all pieces with 6-penny galvanized nails, toenailing where necessary. Locate the pieces numbered 1 on Figure U. These run from points c to g on one side wall of the greenhouse, from points d to i on the other. Nail these strips to the bottom ends of the rafters and rafter backings, 4 inches above ground level, and extend them horizontally to posts g and i. With the pieces numbered 2, continue this horizontal line from the opposite sides of posts g and i to posts f and h, and in like manner, extend the piece numbered 3 to post a, noting, however, that this is not done on the side of the greenhouse where the door will be installed. Position pieces 4 and 5 with their bottom edges 6 feet 10 inches above ground level. Be sure to measure accurately here, as piece 5 on one end will be part of the door frame.

Position the pieces numbered 6 and 7 parallel to and midway between the horizontal lines established by the pieces numbered 2 through 5 (i.e. 3 feet 8 inches above ground level). Note that piece number 7 exists only on the side of the greenhouse that will not have the door.

This completes the basic frame of the greenhouse, and at this point provision should be made for the fan and jalousie that will later be installed for ventilation. There are several options and a number of factors to consider. Your plants will require a fan that can circulate approximately 600 cubic feet of air per minute (one complete change of air every minute for this greenhouse), so be sure to check the capacity of the fan you purchase. This should be paired with a 12-by-12 inch jalousie set into the opposite wall. An alternative is to install a door with a built-in jalousie.

If your fan housing and jalousie units are indeed exactly 12 inches square, arrange the pieces numbered 8 in Figure U so that their bottoms fall exactly 12 inches above the tops of the pieces numbered 6, and similarly space the pieces numbered 9, 12 inches away from the posts g and i. Check the pieces numbered 6, 8 and 9 with a level, plumb bob and framing square. If the fan is any other size, you will have to work out your own framing aordingly at this point, adapting the spacing of strips 8 and 9 to the outer dimensions of your units.

Preparing to Install Fiberglass Panels

The fiberglass roof will be held in place by neoprene-covered cables, one along each rafter (blueprint, pages 824 and 825, and list of materials, page 825). To install these, you will first need to secure a ridge cap to the header, to be used as an anchoring point for the upper ends of the cable. Cut an 8-foot-1¾-inch section from a 10-foot, rot-resistant two-by-four (Figure W). Nail this to the top of the header with galvanized 10-penny nails spaced 8 inches apart. The cap's ends should be flush with the ends of the header and its narrower edge face the existing wall (Figure W). Bolt an aluminum cable sill angle lug (Figure X) at the lower end of each rafter, using ⅜-by-1¼-inch aluminum machine bolts in the holes predrilled between the bend in the backing angle and the lower end of rafter. Position the angle lug at the top and facing out, as shown in Figure X.

Next scribe vertical lines on the ridge cap directly above the center of the valley on top of each of the three rafters, and intersect these lines with a horizontal line midway between the upper and lower faces of the ridge cap (Figure Y). Use 6d nails to make three pilot holes in the ridge cap where these lines intersect to receive the cable-anchoring screw eyes (Detail "B" of blueprint, page 825). Drive the nails about halfway in and then remove them. The cables to be used come in lengths twice as long as those called for in these plans. Get two double lengths, 30 feet 10 inches long, and cut them in half with a wire cutter, discarding the extra length. This may seem wasteful, but it is actually less expensive than ordering pre-cut cables. Take each of the three cables, now measuring 15 feet 5 inches, slip a ½-inch screw eye onto the cut end and bend about 5 inches of the cable back on itself (this can be done by hand). Fasten the two lengths together with a cable clamp, keeping the screw eye inside the loop thus created (Figure Z). Attach the cables to the ridge cap (Figure Y and Detail "B" of blueprint, page 825) by tightening the screw eyes in the pilot holes, and let the lower ends of the cables hang free.

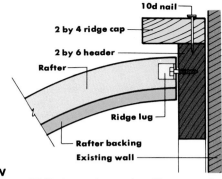

W

Figure W: To fasten the wooden ridge cap to the header, set it on top of the header with its wider side at top and bottom and one of its narrower sides butting against the wall. Nail the cap to the header as shown above.

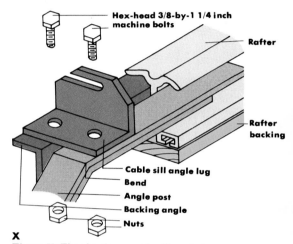

X

Figure X: The aluminum cable sill angle lugs are bolted to the angle posts and backing angles so that the notched face of each lug points upward just above the bend in the angle post.

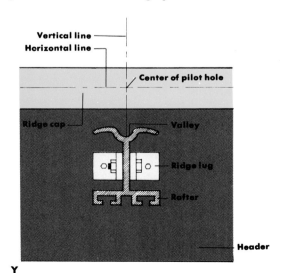

Y

Figure Y: Locate holes for the cable-anchoring screw with vertical lines that extend from the valley in the upper flange of the rafters and intersect the horizontal line that you scribed on the ridge cap earlier.

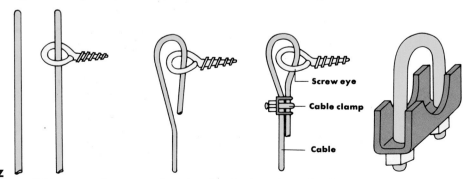

Z

Figure Z: To prepare the upper ends of the cables for fastening to the ridge cap, thread each cable through a screw eye. Double the end of the cable back on itself over a length of 5 inches and then fasten the two widths of cable together with a cable clamp.

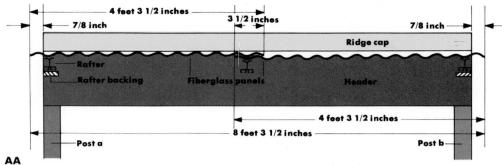

AA

Figure AA: To locate the tops of the two fiberglass roof panels, insert the panels into the gap between the upper faces of rafters and the bottom of ridge cap until they butt against the header. Putting the panels side by side, let them overlap each other by 3½ inches at the central rafter. Their combined width of 8 feet 3½ inches will extend beyond the gable rafters by ⅞ inch.

Installing the Fiberglass Roof

With the help of a friend, insert the shorter ends of two sheets of corrugated fiberglass, 4 feet 3½-inches by 16 feet (list of materials, page 825), under the cables and into the gap between the rafters and ridge cap. Have the panels overlap each other by 3½ inches, or 1½ corrugations (Figure AA and Detail "B" in blueprint, page 825). The combined width of 8 feet 3½ inches should extend beyond the gable rafters by ⅞ inch on each end. The panels themselves will jut out horizontally from the ridge and sag slightly under their own weight (Figure BB). This step should not be attempted on a gusty day as the unsecured panels could be damaged.

Weatherproof the greenhouse at the ridge with closers made of Tesafoam—a compressible foam insulation, excellent for waterproofing, which is available in corrugated strips that match the contours of the fiberglass paneling. You will need three 3-foot lengths to seal the ridge cap, tamping them between cap and fiberglass panels until they make contact with the header (Figure BB). Trim and discard any excess. Go on to the next step immediately.

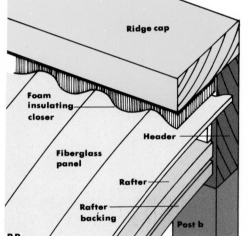

BB

Figure BB: To weatherproof the ridge, tamp corrugated insulating closers all the way back to the header, between the underside of the ridge cap and the top face of the fiberglass panels.

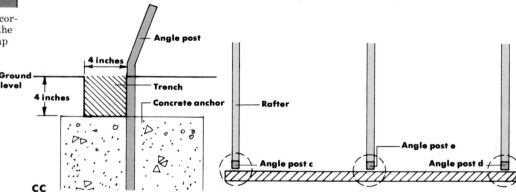

CC

Figure CC: Locate the trench for the roof fiberglass panels 4 inches out from the angle posts, digging down to the concrete anchor. It should run from end post to end post and overlap by an inch or two.

The next major step—conforming the roof panels to the curve of the rafters and anchoring them in the ground—will require some preparation and a little help from a friend. Begin by digging a trench, approximately 4 inches deep, which stops at the top of the concrete anchors. This should run from post *c* to post *d* and extend for 1 or 2 inches beyond them (Figure CC). The width should be about 4 inches so the bottoms of the panels can be fitted into place below ground level (Detail "A" of blueprint, page 824). At this point, working with your assistant, shape the panels to the rafters, handling one panel at a time and starting with the one that is at the lower position where they overlap. To curve the panel, pull down with both hands on its free end, while your assistant presses its upper end against the header. Insert the curved panel into the trench and keep it from springing back by wedging rocks or other weights against its base.

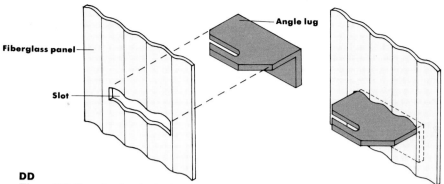

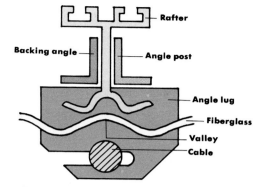

DD

Figure DD: To make slots in the fiberglass panels where they must fit around the angle lugs, scribe and cut notches in the panels just large enough to push them back beyond the groove in each lug.

EE

Figure EE: To secure bottoms of the roof fiberglass panels, slip the lower end of each steel cable into the groove in the angle lug.

After checking to see that the panels are perfectly aligned at the header, the gable ends and the overlap (Figures AA and BB), mark them at the points where the cable sill angle lugs (Figure DD and Detail "A" of blueprint, page 824) separate them from the rafters. Having your assistant hold the panels in place, scribe them with elongated rectangles, slightly larger than the outer edges of the lugs, which will be visible through the fiberglass. Remove the panel bottoms from the trench and carefully cut them with a keyhole- or saber saw, making slots just large enough to fit over the lugs (Figure DD and Detail "A" of blueprint, page 824).

Reposition the panels in the trench, fitting the slots over the lugs and slipping the lower ends of the cables into the grooves in the angle lugs. Each cable will run along a valley in the fiberglass, and pull it into the recess in the rafter (Figure EE and Detail "A" of blueprint, page 824). Secure the center cable first, tightening the eye bolt at the bottom of the cable to remove any slack. Repeat for the side cables. The cables will hug the fiberglass to the rafters along most of their length, but there will be a slight space near the angle lugs (Figure FF), leaving room to tighten the eye bolt. Refill the trench with dirt, tightly packed to secure the bottom edges of the panels. The roof is now secure.

Cutting the Fiberglass Side Walls

At this point, the fiberglass panels that form the side walls of the greenhouse can be installed. Dig 4-by-4-inch trenches along the sides of the greenhouse as before (Figure CC), omitting the section that the door will occupy. Each side will be made up of three sections of paneling. These will be mounted vertically, from rafter to ground level, and will run horizontally from post to post (Figure U). Cut the middle sections first (those that lie between posts *f* and *g* and posts *h* and *i*, Figure U), finding your cutting line by putting the panel up so its top presses against the end of the curving fiberglass roof panel. Making sure both sides of the panel extend equally (1 inch) beyond the posts, scribe a line along the fiberglass, tracing the curve of the roof. Take the panel down and cut it gently along this line, using tinsnips and zigzagging in and out of the corrugations. Avoid abrupt cutting motions as these increase the danger of shattering the fiberglass. Once the panel is cut, rest it in its proper place (bottom in trench, top fitted snugly under the roof paneling, sides parallel to and equally spaced beyond the posts). Scribe the insides of the squares (visible through the fiberglass) where the fan and jalousie will be located (Figure U and Perspective End View in blueprint, page 824). Remove the panel once more and, with the tinsnips, make cuts about ½ inch outside the lines that you have drawn so that the sides of the framing pieces will be partially exposed. This will allow you to insert insulating closers after the fan and jalousie are installed at a later stage.

Following the same general procedure, and working from a single 4-foot-3½-inch-by-14-foot sheet of fiberglass, first cut the panel so you have one 11-foot and one 3-foot section; these will become the sections that fit respectively, above the door (between posts *b* and *h*, Figure U) and opposite the door (between posts *a* and *f*, Figure U). This latter section will extend the full height of the structure and enter the ground as did the earlier pieces. Once you have cut the

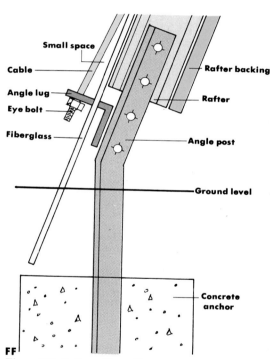

FF

Figure FF: So the cables will press the fiberglass against the rafters, tighten eye bolts at bottom of cables to take up slack.

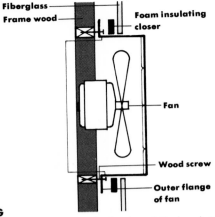

GG

Figure GG: To mount the fan, insert the housing into the frame opening and fasten the fan to the frame with screws driven through the predrilled holes in fan flanges. When you attach the fiberglass panels to the frame, insert insulating closers between fiberglass and flanges.

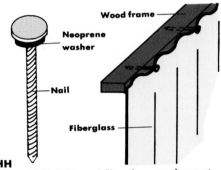

HH

Figure HH: Gable end fiberglass panels are attached to the frame with fiberglass-to-wood screw-type fastening nails with neoprene washers. Space them at 12-inch intervals along rafter backing, wood posts, and rest of frame.

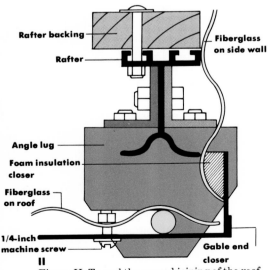

II

Figure II: To seal the curved joining of the roof and side-panels, attach gable end closers to the roof fiberglass with machine screws and insert insulating material between the closers and the gable-end fiberglass panels.

panels to the proper height, trim them along their sides, cutting from top to bottom, so their overlap with the center panels is reduced to 3½ inches (1½ corrugations). When properly cut, each should measure 2 feet 10¼ inches wide.

Finally, from a single 4-foot-3½-inch-by-16-foot sheet of fiberglass, cut the sections for the two outer corners (between angle post d and post i, and between angle post c and post g). These, too, should be cut to overlap the adjacent panels by only 3½ inches. (Where the overlaps obscure the holes you cut for the fan and jalousie, make additional cuts to restore these openings to their original size.)

Installing the Side Walls

The six panels, at this juncture, span the posts at points a-f, f-g, g-c, b-h, h-i, and i-d (Figure U), overlapping each other by 3½ inches. They are positioned in the ground, and fit snugly under the roof fiberglass. They are ready to be nailed into place (Gable End Elevation and Perspective End View in blueprint, page 824.) Before hammering, however, place the fan and jalousie units in the spaces provided in the frame. For installation, line up the outer flanges of the housings with the outside of the frame (Figure GG), and fasten them to the frame with whatever size wood screws are needed (usually 1½-inch, No. 12 screws.) The fastening flanges of most fans and jalousies come with holes predrilled at the recommended intervals.

Using 2-inch-long aluminum, fiberglass-to-wood screw-type fastening nails with neoprene washers (Figure HH), nail the panels to the one-by-three rafter backings, taking care that they are still aligned with the roof, posts, ground, fan and jalousie units, and with each other. The best place to begin is at the point where the overlapping sections meet the rafters. Use two nails on each gable end, going into the rafter backing above the tops of posts f, g, h and i (Figure U) to tentatively secure the panels. Continue nailing at 12-inch intervals along the rafter backings, down the two-by-four posts, and to all the one-by-three framing pieces, except those which enclose the fan and jalousie. Don't drive nails at these points, but seal them with insulating closers on all four sides (Figure GG). The tops and bottoms of these units should be sealed with the contoured closers used on the ridge, the side seams with vertical closers. When you are finished attaching the fiberglass, refill the side trenches, packing the earth tightly around the panels. This completes the roofing and walling of the greenhouse.

Attaching Gable End Closers

Any gaps that occur where the fiberglass roofing and side panels meet should be sealed at this time. Starting from the tops of the cable sill angle lugs at angle posts c and d (Figure U), attach 14-gauge aluminum gable-end closers (Section "DD" in blueprint, page 825, and list of materials, page 825). These are supplied in curved, 4-foot lengths, with ¼-inch machine screws and nuts, and are made to overlap both sections of fiberglass at once. The closers should be bolted to the greenhouse so that their wider faces cover the roof surface and their shorter faces cover the side surfaces (Figure II). Once these are installed, the cables running along the fiberglass will be sandwiched between the closers and the fiberglass. The closers have seven predrilled holes in each length, and act as convenient templates for making holes in the fiberglass with a ¼-inch drill bit. Overlap the closers shingle-fashion to keep the structure water-tight, by fastening the top hole of the lower closer and the bottom hole of the upper closer with a single screw.

Because the uppermost length of closer on each gable will have to cover he ridge (Figure JJ), and thus cannot overlap the side fiberglass panel at this point you will need to compensate for this by using an extra length of closer in reversed orientation before attaching the last length of closer at the ridge, as shown in Figure JJ. Position this segment so that its shorter face covers the roof and sits on top of the ridge cap, its longer face covers the side. Then fasten it to the side fiberglass, rather than the roof. Go on to attach the uppermost section of closer, working in the usual way, but putting it on top of the reversed piece (Figure JJ). If this section is too long for the space that remains, you can overlap the preceding section by more than one screw-hole, or cut the closer to size with tinsnips. To seal the gable-side faces of the closers, insert insulating cubes between the closer and the fiberglass. These, unlike the corrugated and vertical insulators, can be made to take any shape.

Hanging the Door

This plan calls for a standard 2-foot-6-inch by 6-foot-10-inch wood door of any desired thickness. As mentioned earlier, you can vary this by using a door with a jalousie, but any door used should be the size designated above. Hang the door so that it opens out from the greenhouse and does not restrict the use of space inside, and so that it moves toward the existing wall and thus does not endanger the fiberglass wall if it is swung by the wind. Use door hinges made of brass or some other rustproof material. Start by mounting three 4-inch hinges onto what will be the pivoting edge of the door, so that the pin-side of the butt is flush with the outer face of the door and the pin protrudes beyond the outer face. Pilot holes for the screw can be made with a drill or with nails, as previously described. Position the top of the uppermost hinge 4 inches from the top of the door, the bottom of the lowest hinge a foot above the ground, and the center hinge halfway between the other two. The position of the hinges does not have to be exact.

When the hinges are in place on the door, set the door into the frame and have someone move it into its open position while you trace the outlines of the hinge plates and the locations of the hinge screw-holes on the door jamb (in this case, the two-by-four post *b*). Position each butt with its pin side flush to the outer face of the frame and the pin protruding beyond the outer face. (If you do not have a helper, you can brace the door and nail it in the open position.) Remove the door, slip the pins out of the hinges, and, after drilling pilot holes, screw the hinge plates to the jamb in the positions marked. Returning the door to its place, slip the pins back into position. Finally, attach doorstop molding to the top and sides of the frame just inside the door (Figure KK), using 6-penny casing or finishing nails. This will prevent the door from being pulled in far enough to weaken the hinges and will also close any gaps between the door and the frame. Where the strips of doorstop meet at the two upper corners, miter the ends to a 45-degree angle for a tight fit. Apply weatherstripping to the doorstop to block drafts.

The Caulking

The final step in completing the greenhouse structure is to spread a bead of caulking in the few locations where water is likely to seep in—across the length of the ridge cap where it meets the existing wall (Figure LL); down the seam formed by the gable ends where they meet the existing wall; under the ridge cap where the insulating closer rests on the fiberglass; and at any points where you have cut holes in the fiberglass (Figure DD). For this, caulking compound is forced out of the tube in a steady stream. If you work at an even pace and keep the tip of the tube about ¼ inch away from the surface you are covering, you will get a neat, even strip of caulking exactly where you want it.

The Heater

The heater recommended for this greenhouse is a plug-in model with a circulation fan, built-in thermostat, and 1,650-watt capacity. It will maintain a temperature of 70 degrees Fahrenheit when it is 30 degrees Fahrenheit outdoors, and even in sub-zero weather will normally keep the greenhouse temperature at about 55 degrees Fahrenheit (warm enough for almost all plants.) Note: you will need a separate circuit for this heater, the greenhouse fan, and any lights you install.

Filling the Space

How you furnish and use your growing space will depend largely on what you want to get from it, but the following suggestions will apply in any case. The ideal bench-width is 2 feet to 2 feet 6 inches, and the bench seats should be 2 feet 6 inches above the floor. When you begin to use your greenhouse you may find that the soil floor does not absorb water quickly enough to prevent getting your shoes muddy after you water the plants. Coating the floor with bark mulch or gravel will help prevent a mud problem. In any arrangement you may use, the roof purlin can serve as an anchor for hanging planters and various gardening implements.

For related projects and entries, see "Bonsai," "Bottle Gardens," "Herbs," "Light Gardens," "Planting Pits and Seeds," "Soilless Gardening," "Sprouting," "Terrariums," "Vivariums," "Wildflowers and Weeds," and "Yard Environments" in The Family Creative Workshop.

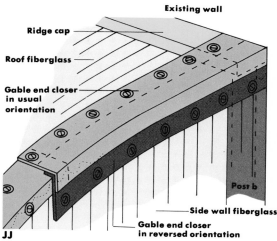

Figure JJ: To seal the gable ends where the gable end closer must rise above the roof to cover the ridge cap, use an additional length of closer, reversing its orientation so that the shorter leg is positioned on the roof and the longer leg on the side wall. Fasten this section first to the gable-end fiberglass by driving screws through predrilled holes in the closer, then proceed to attach the topmost section of closer above it in usual way.

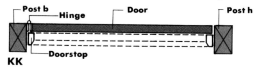

Figure KK: Doorstop molding is installed with the door held closed. The molding is scribed where it meets the sides and top of the door frame. Nail the molding along the full length of the sides and top of frame, keeping its outer edge along this line. Put the wider face of the door stop against the frame and the narrower face against the closed door.

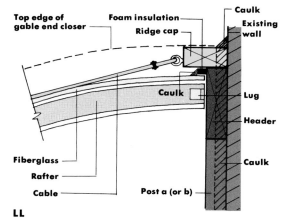

Figure LL: To completely weatherproof the greenhouse, spread beads of caulk along the entire length of the meeting of the ridge cap and existing wall, down the seams where the side walls join the existing wall, and under the ridge cap along the full length of the fiberglass panels where they meet the insulating closers.

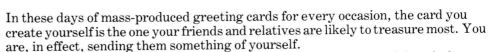

The Personal Touch

Nancy Bruning Levine studied advertising design and visual communication at Brooklyn's Pratt Institute and worked as an assistant crafts editor and designer for McCall's Needlework & Crafts. Prior to creating greeting card designs for this volume, she was busy designing her own wedding invitations and pursuing other creative crafts including needlepoint, weaving, crochet, silkscreening, and macrame.

In these days of mass-produced greeting cards for every occasion, the card you create yourself is the one your friends and relatives are likely to treasure most. You are, in effect, sending them something of yourself.

There is no end to the variety of greeting cards you can make. Although the projects that follow call for diverse techniques, they are but a limited sampling. When you make personalized greeting cards, the most important thing to remember is that the pleasure is twofold: the creator's joy in the process of making the card, and the recipient's delight in receiving it. Therefore, choose a design and technique that you will enjoy working with, and one that will appeal to the person who will be receiving it. If your friend likes flowers, why not send a pressed flower card (page 838) as a reminder of a shared excursion? If you know an avid bookworm, a ribbon bookmark (opposite) is certainly appropriate. If he or she likes stained-glass windows, the card on page 841 will be a reminder that you remember that special interest. Represent a favorite pastime, such as music or fishing, by choosing an appropriate motif for the cardboard-printed card on page 844.

Designing Your Own Greeting Cards

When you design a specialized greeting card, you needn't limit yourself to working with a sheet of paper. Perhaps you would rather use cloth, leather, wood, plastic or metal. The Florentine Stitch card on page 839 is one way of using a needlecraft skill; you can also embroider on paper, cloth, or leather (see "Embroidery" in Volume Six). Many other crafts in this *Family Creative Workshop* series—block printing, stenciling, serigraphy, cartooning, woodcuts, calligraphy, to name a few—can be readily adapted to greeting-card designs. A packet of seeds glued onto a green background paper would make an unusual but appropriate card for a gardener. Or how about sending a packet of stamps to a philatelist friend? Photographs are a popular greeting-card feature around Christmas time, but why not use them to announce the acquisition of a new house or car or pet? If the size of the photograph satisfies postal regulations (see below), you can use a photograph as you would a postcard. Simply put the stamp, the message, and the address on the back of the photograph.

Don't let size limit you in designing your card. There are postal regulations on sizes of envelopes, but they need not be restrictive. For instance, a card which the postal service considers unmailable (smaller than 3 by 4¼ inches) can be slipped into a larger envelope. If you like small work, you might draw inspiration from the smallest greeting on record: an inscribed grain of rice presented as a Christmas greeting to the Prince of Wales in 1929. At the opposite extreme, postal regulations say that the combined length, width, and thickness of an item may not exceed 100 inches if it is to be mailed first-class. Therefore, you could conceivably mail something measuring 50 by 49¾ by ¼ inches. But anything larger than a No. 10 business-size envelope (4⅛ by 9½ inches) should be reinforced with a piece of stiff paper or thin cardboard to prevent damage during handling. Poster-size greetings can be rolled and sent in a mailing tube, or folded to a more manageable size and put into a large envelope. But if you plan to use an unorthodox method of sealing a self-mailer type of card (the birth announcement on page 845 belongs in this group) check with your local postmaster concerning the acceptability of the design.

The amount of time needed to complete a greeting card varies with the technique used. You may decide to devote a considerable amount of time to a card for a close friend or relative (such as the Florentine Stitch needlepoint card on page 839 or the stained-glass-window card on page 841). In other instances, the technique chosen may be one that lends itself to rapid duplication either by yourself (such as pressed flowers, ribbon bookmark, cardboard printing), or by a professional printer (the birth announcement). Craftnotes on how to prepare materials for a printer are on pages 842 and 843.

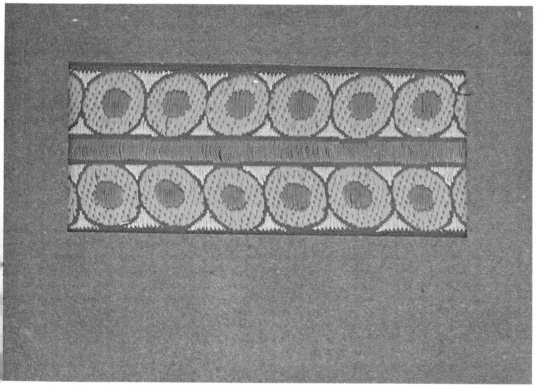

A machine-embroidered ribbon was used to make this brightly colored bookmark card. Any decorative ribbon (sold at fabric and department stores) can be used in such a practical gift.

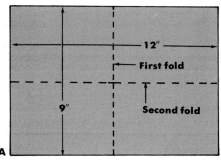

A

Figure A: Fold paper in half from left to right, matching 9-inch-long side edges. Fold in half from top to bottom, forming a 4½- by-6-inch card.

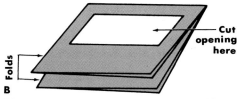

B

Figure B: Crease all folds to make sure card lies flat. Cut opening in front quadrant: for horizontal card shown, position final fold at the top; for a vertical card, position final fold at the left edge.

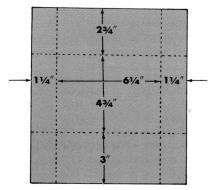

C

Figure C: To make an envelope fit a 4½-by-6-inch greeting card, start with an 8¾-by-10½-inch piece of paper. Make folds as shown (dashed lines) in any sequence. Unfold paper.

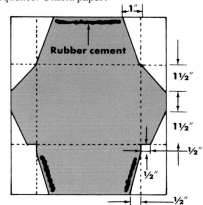

D

Figure D: Measure, mark, and cut as indicated by solid lines. Refold side flaps. Apply rubber cement as indicated to bottom flap; refold bottom flap. Insert card. Before mailing, apply rubber cement to top flap as indicated and fold it down.

Paper Folding and Cutting
Ribbon bookmark card

This card can be made easily and quickly; it is designed so the ribbon can be removed by the recipient of the card and used as a bookmark.

For each card you will need: a decorative ribbon about 2 inches wide and 5½ inches long, one 9-by-12-inch sheet of construction paper in a color that goes well with the ribbon, a pencil, a metal-edged ruler for measuring and guiding cuts, scissors, a single-edged razor blade for cutting the opening in the card, double-faced masking tape, white glue, and clean cardboard to use as a cutting surface. In addition, to make a matching envelope you will need: an 8¾-by-10½-inch piece of construction paper and rubber cement.

If you are making several cards, purchase a quantity of ribbon and cut it into 5½-inch lengths. If you are skilled in embroidery, and you'd like to individualize the card even further, consider substituting a hand-embroidered bookmark for a purchased machine-embroidered ribbon. Embroider a simple design on a small piece of fabric (see "Embroidery"). Run a thin line of white glue along the cut edges of the bookmark to seal them and prevent raveling. Set aside to dry. Meanwhile, fold the sheet of construction paper into quarters by making a French fold as shown in Figures A and B. Next cut an opening in the front quadrant. The width of the opening is 4½ inches to allow a ¾-inch margin at the ends. The height of the opening should be ¼ inch less than the width of the bookmark. Unfold the paper and place it upside down on the cardboard cutting surface. Using a pencil and ruler, mark the dimensions of the opening on the wrong side of the front quadrant. Leave a ¾-inch margin at the sides and at the top (folded) edge. Using the single-edged razor blade with the metal-edged ruler as a guide, carefully cut out the opening. Refold the paper. Insert the bookmark in the card, under the opening; hold it in place with a small piece of double-faced masking tape. Make the matching envelope by following Figures C and D.

Greeting cards made with pressed flowers are easily assembled, and the results are lovely because nature has done most of the work. Nancy Levine recommends using flat, thin flowers, but thick, pulpy flowers such as roses can be pressed, if the petals are dried separately and later glued to paper in an attractive composition.

E Figure E: Follow this chart for the needlepoint card, opposite. The arrow indicates first stitch.

Color key
- ■ black: 10 yards
- ■ red: 4 yards
- ■ blue: 5 yards
- □ beige: 3 yards

Paper Folding and Cutting
Pressed flower cards

These flower cards are made so easily (and quickly, if pressed flowers are on hand) that you could send one to just about everyone.

To make each card you'll need: one large or several small pressed flowers, one 9-by-12-inch sheet of construction paper in a color that coordinates with the flower(s), 4-by-5-inch piece of heavy white paper for the design background, pencil, metal-edged ruler for measuring and guiding cuts, single-edged razor blade for cutting the opening in the card, white glue, rubber cement, plastic spray in an aerosol can, tissue paper, cardboard for a cutting surface. For each matching envelope, you'll need an 8¾-by-10½-inch piece of construction paper.

Pick flowers, interesting weeds, leaves, and ferns. Because they dry quickly and are more easily pressed, I recommend choosing thin flowers that can be readily flattened such as buttercups, daisies and violets. Dry and press your collection by sandwiching the flowers and foliage between two layers of facial tissue (this blots up moisture). Arrange the parts so they lie flat and open, without petals or leaves overlapping. Then insert each sandwich between pages of a heavy book. Allow them to dry in the book for one to three weeks.

When a flower is ready, coat the back of it carefully with white glue and apply it to the white paper, placing it at the paper's center. When you use several small flowers, arrange them in a design that pleases you. Spray flower and paper with plastic to protect them. Fold the sheet of colored construction paper, following Figures A and B on page 837. Then cut the opening through which the flowers will be seen. To determine the size of the opening, measure the flower design's width and height; add about ¼ inch to each measurement to obtain the height and width of the opening. (If you wish to have the stems extend beyond the opening, as I did, add only ⅛ inch to the height). Unfold the card, and with pencil and ruler mark the dimensions of the opening on the wrong side of the front quadrant. The opening can be centered in the quadrant, or moved slightly above center. Place the unfolded card on the cardboard cutting surface and use the single-edged razor blade and the metal-edged ruler to cut the opening. Refold the card and insert the flower design behind the opening, making sure the design is centered. When you are satisfied with how it looks, apply rubber cement to the wrong side of the front quadrant borders and press them against the white paper. Make a matching envelope as directed in Figures C and D, page 837. After you have written your message inside the card, fold a 9-by-6-inch sheet of tissue over it, and insert it in the envelope. It is wise to mark the envelope "Please Hand Cancel."

Needlecrafts
Needlepoint cards

If you decide to make a needlepoint card, reserve it for someone really special—and allow five or six hours to complete the project. It is well worth the time, though, because it could be a gift ready for framing.

To make one card, you will need: tapestry or Persian yarn in the colors and amounts listed below the chart for the design (Figure E, left), one 7-by-7-inch piece of No. 14 mono needlepoint canvas, tapestry needle No. 20, masking tape, pencil, waterproof marking pen, household and embroidery scissors, metal-edged ruler, single-edged razor blade or draftman's knife, rubber cement, piece of matboard measuring about 7 by 16 inches (available at art-supply stores) in a color that coordinates with the yarn colors, clean cardboard for a cutting surface. A matching envelope requires a 9-by-12-inch piece of colored paper.

The needlepoint design is worked in Florentine Stitch, so refer to that entry in Volume Six for additional information on this technique. The overall design here consists of two parts—the center design and the border worked in a Gobelin stitch. The center design is worked first.

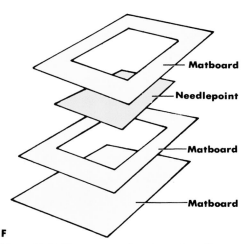

F

Figure F: Rubber-cement the trimmed needle-point between layers of matboard as shown.

Share your needlepoint skill with a special friend or relative by working this Florentine stitch design. Then finish it with matboard so it's ready for framing.

Using the waterproof marker, mark a 3⅜-by-3-inch rectangle, the size of the center design, at the center of the canvas. Following the directions on pages 678 and 679 in Volume Six, work the first row (black) of the center design, starting at the upper right corner as indicated on the chart (Figure E), and working to the left. Work remaining rows following the chart and the color key below it. Because the design is small, the chart shows the entire design. When the center design is complete, work the Gobelin stitch border all around it, using a diagonal stitch at each corner. This completes the actual stitching.

A Florentine Stitch piece this small shouldn't require blocking or reshaping, if the stitches haven't been worked so tightly that the piece is distorted. However, if you find your canvas has been pulled out of shape, you can block it as directed in "Crewelwork Sampler," pages 546 and 547, Volume Five. When the canvas is dry, trim margins to ½ inch on each side. Because the yarn adds thickness to both sides of the canvas, I used matboard to mount the needlepoint and guarantee a flat finished product. On the wrong side of the piece of matboard, mark three 5¼-by-6¼-inch rectangles. Place matboard on cardboard cutting surface, and using the metal-edged ruler and mat knife or razor blade, cut out the three rectangular pieces. On the wrong side of two of these pieces, mark a rectangle the size of the stitched area (this should be 3⅜ by 3¾ inches, but since needlepoint canvases vary slightly, check these measurements against your finished piece). Center these rectangles on the matboard pieces, or place them 1½ inches above the bottom edge as I did. Cut out marked rectangles as before, forming two frames; be careful that the cuts do not extend beyond the corners.

The needlepoint and three layers of board are assembled as in Figure F. Apply rubber cement to the back of each frame; let dry. Place right side of needlepoint on back of one frame, centering the design within the frame opening. Tape canvas corners to frame. Place wrong sides of framed needlepoint and remaining frame together; make sure edges of both pieces are even, and press together. Coat the back of the needlepoint frame and the back of the remaining piece of matboard with rubber cement. When dry, press together with edges even. Write your message on the back of the card. Make a matching envelope following Figures G and H.

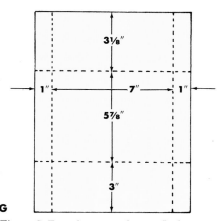

G

Figure G: To make an envelope to fit the 5¼-by-6¼-inch needlepoint greeting card, start with a 9-by-12-inch piece of colored paper. Make folds as indicated by dashed lines. Unfold paper.

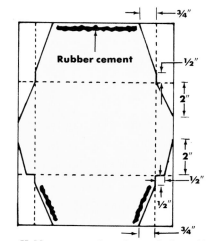

H

Figure H: Measure, mark, and cut as indicated by solid lines. Refold side flaps. Apply rubber cement as indicated to bottom flap; fold bottom flap up. Insert card. To seal, apply rubber cement to top flap and fold it down.

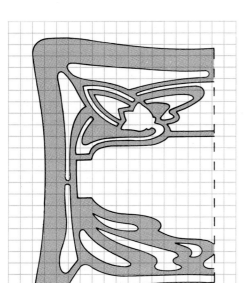

1 square = ¼ inch

Figure I: Enlarge this half-pattern for the border of the stained-glass-window card, opposite, by copying it on a ¼-inch grid as described on page 57 in Volume One. First enlarge the left half of the border design which is shown above (the dashed line indicates the center of the over-all design). Then enlarge the right half by copying the enlarged left half in a mirror image. To avoid confusion, white areas of the pattern are pieces to be cut out and removed; use a pencil to shade in areas on your enlarged pattern that will *not* be cut out, corresponding to gray areas in the pattern above.

Graphic Arts
Stained-glass-window card

The recipient of a stained-glass-window card simply hangs it in front of a window, letting light shine through translucent tissue paper to get an illusion of stained glass. Two identical cutouts of heavy black paper provide the opaque elements of the design. You glue bright tissue paper between them, sandwich-fashion, to make a card with a finished look on both sides. At the center of the design pictured, I chose to put a short salutation—the recipient's name. (It happened to have five letters; directions that follow explain how to enlarge the design to create a larger center area to accommodate a longer name or more than one word).

To make one card you need: two pieces of heavy black paper (available at art-supply stores) measuring at least 6 by 8 inches, rubber cement, white glue, small brush for applying glue, small amounts of tissue paper in a variety of colors (available in gift-wrap departments of card shops and department stores), sharp single-edged razor blades or a draftsman's knife with replaceable blades (available at art-supply stores), white paper for enlarging patterns, pencil, carbon paper, one 13-by-14-inch sheet of colored paper for the envelope, a large piece of cardboard for a cutting surface.

To begin, enlarge the pattern for the left half of the border design (Figure I) by copying it on a ¼-inch grid ruled on white paper. To obtain the right half of the border, copy the enlarged left half in a mirror image. On a separate piece of white paper, trace the required letters of the alphabet (Figure J). If this name or message is short enough to fit within the border design shown, arrange the letters within the center area, referring to the photograph opposite to see how to space them. Rubber-cement the letters into position within the border on the white paper pattern. Draw thin connecting bars between letters and border so all elements are joined (see photograph opposite).

ABCDEF
GHIJKL-
MNOPQ?
RSTUV&
WXYZ-!

Figure J: From this full-size alphabet you can trace the letters you need to compose your message for a stained-glass-window card.

J

Suspend this card in front of a window, and the light shining through will give a stained-glass effect.

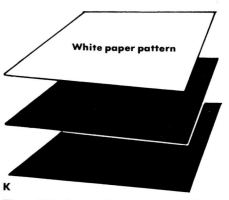

Figure K: Before you do any cutting, rubber-cement the white-paper pattern and the two pieces of black paper together in three layers, with the pattern on top as shown.

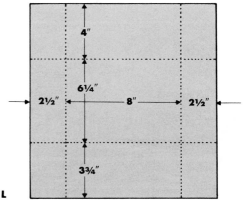

To make an envelope to fit a 6-by-8-inch stained-glass-window card, start with a 13-by-14-inch piece of colored paper. Make folds as indicated by dashed lines, then unfold paper.

If the message consists of a longer word or name, or of several words, you will need to extend the border design. After cutting the enlarged letters apart, arrange them on another piece of paper in the desired order, using a ruled line to keep them straight. Rubber-cement them to the paper. Now fold the entire enlarged border into quarters, and cut along the folds. (If you plan to make several cards with different messages, make a carbon copy of the border before cutting it apart.) Position the quarter sections at corners around your message, checking to make sure opposite edges are parallel. Rubber-cement the quarters in place. Join these border sections at sides, top and bottom by extending border lines until they meet. Then draw thin connecting bars to the letters as described above.

If you decide you want to make more than one card with the same message, or fear that you might spoil the first try, make a carbon copy of the entire pattern—border and message. For each card, you will cut the pattern apart so you will not be able to use it again to make another card.

Next, cut identical designs from two pieces of black paper. I found the best way to do this was to rubber-cement the pattern and two pieces of black paper together (see Figure K). Thus both black pieces can be cut simultaneously, using the white-paper pattern lines as a guide. This insures two perfectly matching pieces and eliminates transferring the pattern to the black paper. On the cardboard cutting surface, cut the design out with a razor blade or draftsman's knife, making several gentle cuts until all three layers have been penetrated. Easy does it—if you apply much pressure you might lose control of the knife. Cut out and remove the inside shapes first, then cut along the outside line. When finished, carefully peel apart the two black paper designs. Rub off cement with your fingertips.

Following the color photograph above, or using colors of your own choice, glue tissue paper to the face of the back piece of black paper. Cut each piece of tissue paper slightly larger than the opening it will fill. Then use the brush to apply white glue to the black paper all around the opening. Press tissue paper on the glued area and cut away any excess tissue with a razor blade. Use only one piece of tissue to fill in adjacent openings that are to be the same color. When all cutouts have been covered, rubber-cement the top black piece in place, matching edges carefully. Let dry. Make a matching envelope, following Figures L and M. If you enlarged the design, you'll need to enlarge the envelope. To do this, make a tracing paper envelope and enlarge it as you did the border.

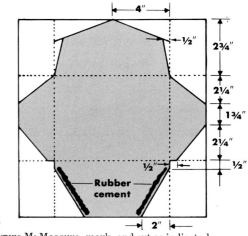

Figure M: Measure, mark, and cut as indicated. Refold the side flaps. Apply rubber cement to the bottom flap and refold it. Insert the card and write any message on the top flap. To seal the card, cut a 2-inch circle from scrap paper; fold the top flap down, apply rubber cement to the seal, and press the seal in place over the tip of the top flap.

841

The best way to reproduce an image in quantity (50 or more) is to have it printed professionally. The printing process rapidly transfers an image from one surface to another through the medium of ink. Today, most commercial printing is done by lithography, more commonly called "offset." The procedures to follow in preparing a design for such reproduction are described below.

What is a paste-up?

No matter what color ink or paper is used to produce the final printed piece, a printer first requires a "paste-up" in which all of the elements to be reproduced appear in black on stiff white paper or white board. The elements should be of reproduction size (although most printers can enlarge or reduce) and be in the position they will occupy in the final printed piece.

Preparing the paste-up

Preparing a paste-up is not difficult. However, having the right equipment and following the suggestions below should help you achieve professional-looking results. The basic supplies are: a drawing board or table with a straight edge (with no bumps or depressions), ruler, T-square, right-angled triangle, blue pencil, eraser, fine-pointed black felt-tipped pen, scissors, single-edged razor blade or mat knife, rubber cement and stiff white paper or white board at least 2 inches larger on all sides than the size of the paper on which the image is to be printed. All of these supplies are available at art-supply stores, many stationers, and the artists' supplies department of department stores.

Guidelines

All guidelines (lines that you don't want to print) should be drawn with a light blue pencil, since light blue will not register when the printer photographs your paste-up. A very light black pencil line, to be thoroughly erased later, may also be used as a guideline.

Using a T-square
To make parallel horizontal lines, or to make sure all elements of your paste-up are parallel with each other, use a T-square as pictured above. The T-square is placed on a drawing board or table with the T-square's crossbar resting against the left edge of the table or board. As the T-square's crossbar slides vertically along the table edge, all horizontal lines drawn along the base of the "T" on the board will be parallel.

Using a triangle
To mark parallel vertical lines or to line elements up vertically, use a triangle in conjunction with the T-square as pictured above. Keep the T-square's crossbar tight against the board or table edge and slide the right-angled triangle along the T-square's horizontal edge. All lines drawn using the triangle's vertical edge as a guide will be parallel; they will also be at perfect right angles to the horizontal lines.

MATERIAL FOR THE PRINTER

Step 1: Determine the size of the paper you want the design printed on, and where on the paper you want it placed. A standard, economical paper size is 8½ by 11 inches. To keep your printing cost down, the size you use probably should not exceed these measurements (larger paper requires larger, more expensive to operate presses).

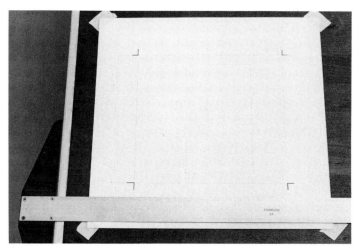

Step 2: Tape the white board or stiff paper to your drawing board or table as pictured above. Mark the size of the paper you will use on this paste-up board, leaving an even border around the edge. Use the T-square and triangle to mark these lines extending the lines beyond the corners where they meet. Using the felt-tipped pen, draw "crop marks" over these guideline extensions as pictured. Crop marks tell the printer where to cut or crop the paper in relation to the printed design.

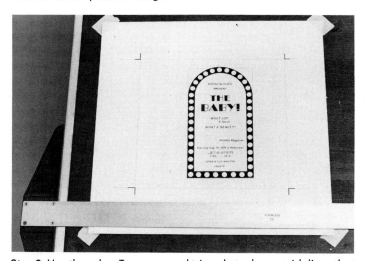

Step 3: Use the ruler, T-square and triangle to draw guidelines that will aid you in placing the artwork and type exactly where you want them to appear in the final piece. Next, rubber-cement the elements to the paste-up board; see photograph above. Prepare the artwork on a separate piece of paper to permit changes in the arrangement when it is cemented in place. The artwork must be in black, and preferably be the same size as it will be printed. If you

need to alter the size of a piece of artwork, the least expensive way to do so is to enlarge or reduce it on a grid as described on page 57, Volume One. Using the enlargement as a guide, execute the artwork in black ink or paint, using a pen or a brush. If the shapes are large, cut them from black paper and glue them in place. If you don't mind the additional expense, and if a photostat service is available (see the yellow pages of the telephone book), you can have the artwork enlarged or reduced photostatically. Request a "line" stat, which picks up only black and white, enabling you to rubber-cement the photostat directly to the board, without copying it by hand.

Step 4: If type is a part of your printed piece, it can be prepared by you (using transfer type described below), or set by a professional typesetter. Transfer type, available in many sizes and styles at art-supply stores, comes in the form of thin plastic sheets that have letters printed on them in a special ink. To use it, place the plastic sheet on a sheet of paper and position the base of a letter on a guideline. Use a dull pencil point or the tip of a ball-point pen to rub over the letter you want transferred. The letter will be released from the plastic sheet and will adhere to the paper. When the words you want have been transferred, rubber-cement the back of the paper and paste it to the board in the desired position. If you decide to use a typesetter, type or neatly print the words you want to have set. Make sure all capital letters ("uppercase" in typesetter's terminology) and small letters ("lowercase") are indicated exactly as you want them to appear. Take along a pencil sketch and discuss the type style and size you require. When you receive the type (in the form of a "reproduction proof" or "repro"), rubber-cement it on the paste-up board (see photograph below left).

Step 5: Before sending your paste-up to the printer, give it a final check. Trim away any paper edges that overlap other parts of the design. Repair any broken or cracked lines or letters. Check carefully to make sure all elements are straight, and erase all guidelines.

Color

These directions apply to images printed in only one color of ink. For each additional color the printer would have to put the paper through the press again. Printing in more than one color, therefore, becomes quite expensive. There are ways to create the illusion of more than one color. You might ask the printer to print on colored paper with a colored ink. This will increase your printing bill slightly because the printer may have to wash the usual black ink off his press before and after he prints your job. Colored paper is also harder to obtain than white, so ask the printer what colors he has on hand. Another possibility is to hand-color certain areas of the design with ink, paint, colored paper or felt-tipped pens.

Graphic Arts
Cardboard printing

Charming hand-printed greeting cards like the one pictured below do not require the costly equipment used in other printing methods. In fact, the butterfly design results from the use of a homemade cardboard printing block, used much as you would use a rubber stamp and pad, so duplicate cards can be made swiftly.

Materials needed are: tracing paper, soft and hard lead pencils, two pieces of heavy cardboard (one a 3-by-4½-inch rectangle and the other a 3-by-3-inch square) to make the printing block, one larger piece of cardboard (such as the back of a sketch book) to use as a cutting surface, two 1-inch lengths of heavy string, single-edged razor blade or mat knife (available at art-supply stores), white glue, acrylic, tempera, or tube watercolor paint, construction paper (one 9-by-12-inch sheet will make two cards), masking tape, watercolor brush No. 8, one 9-by-12-inch piece of construction paper and rubber cement for each matching envelope.

To make the printing block: Place tracing paper over the full-size pattern (Figure N) or a design of your own, and trace outlines. On the back of the tracing paper, go over the pattern lines with a soft pencil. Prepare the printing block as follows: place tracing, right side up, centered on the 3-by-4½-inch cardboard and tape in place. Using a sharp, hard pencil, go over the outlines. The soft lead on the reverse side of the pattern will act as carbon paper, transferring the outlines to the cardboard to guide you in positioning the printing design. Remove pattern and darken lines on cardboard if necessary. Re-blacken the back of the tracing and repeat the transferring process on the smaller piece of cardboard (omitting antennae, which will be string). Place this smaller cardboard piece on the cutting surface and cut out the butterfly pieces with a razor blade or mat knife. Glue the cardboard pieces and string antennae in place on the larger piece of cardboard, which will be the printing block base; let the glue dry.

Printing: I advise making a few test prints on scrap paper so you can determine the best amount of paint and the pressure needed to make good prints. Using a paintbrush, put paint on all the raised surfaces of the printing block design. Apply the paint heavily, but be careful not to flood the crevices between the pattern pieces, or you will blur the printed image. Quickly, before the paint begins to dry,

Patricia Lee, a graduate of the Fashion Institute of Technology, has also attended Parsons School of Design in New York City. She is a free-lance illustrator and designer, and is an audio-visual coordinator/director for a New York marketing firm.

N

Figure N: To make the cardboard-printed greeting card at right, trace the outlines of this full-size butterfly pattern.

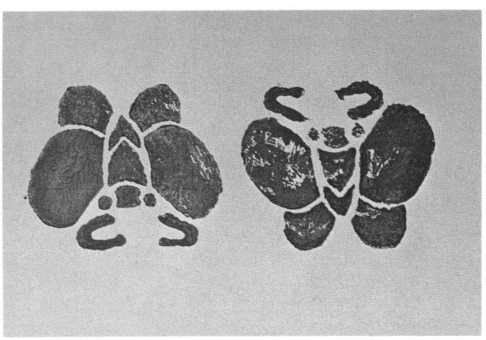

The charming, hand-painted look of this card was obtained by printing at home with a simple cardboard printing block. Pat Lee chose a butterfly to decorate her greeting card.

turn the block over and press it firmly on scrap paper, applying even pressure so all elements of the design are printed. Lift the block and check the results. Continue making test prints, adding fresh paint each time. Thin the paint with water if it is too thick or adjust the amount of paint applied until you are getting satisfactory and consistent results. Your goal shouldn't be something so perfect that it looks machine-made. When you feel you are ready, cut the 9-by-12-inch construction paper in half to form two 6-by-9-inch pieces; fold each piece in half to measure 4½ by 6 inches. Apply paint to printing block and print the design on the left half, lining up the left, top and bottom edges of the block with the left, top and bottom edges of the card. Reapply paint and print on the right half of the card (rotate the block 180 degrees if you like, as I did) matching right, top and bottom edges of block and card. After several printings, you may notice that paint is accumulating on the block. To maintain clear, sharp edges on the print, rinse by passing the block quickly under running water and rubbing the printing surface gently with fingers or paintbrush. This can be done many times without injuring the block, if you avoid actually soaking the cardboard in the water.

Make matching envelopes following Figures C and D on page 837.

Graphic Arts
Broadway birth announcement $ ⧖ 🚶 🎨

Although the birth of a baby is a momentous occasion, the cards you send out announcing the birth needn't be stuffy, as the photograph at right illustrates. Since a large quantity of announcements are usually mailed, you may want to have them printed professionally.

You may want to create your own unique design, but to make a printed birth announcement of the type shown, you will need the materials listed under "Preparing a Paste-Up" in the Craftnotes on pages 842 and 843. I also used red, gummed foil stars in ½-inch and 2-inch sizes (available at stationers and papercraft shops).

Prepare a paste-up on a board measuring at least 12½ by 13 inches. Follow the directions in the Craftnotes and in Figure P. The easiest way to duplicate the artwork shown here, if you are so inclined, is to take this volume to a photostat service and have a photostat made of the photograph above right. Cut out and remove type you don't want, rubber-cement the photostat to the paste-up board, and replace the removed type with type prepared as described in the Craftnotes.

To speed production, prepare the paste-up well in advance of the big day, leaving only the name, weight and date to be added at the last minute. When your printed cards come back from the printer, affix four ½-inch gummed stars in a row to each, as shown. Fold the paper as in Figure Q to make a self-mailer requiring no envelope. Seal the card with a single large star, and write the address on the outside.

For related crafts and projects see "Birthday Celebrations," "Block Printing," "Calligraphy," "Cartooning," "Christmas Celebrations," "Collages and Assemblages," "Serigraphy," "Stenciling," "Typography," "Valentines."

O

Figure O: If you have a photostat made of this drawing of a birth announcement, request that the focus be set at 143 per cent.

This shows how the finished card will appear, after folding as described in Figure Q, and after the stars have been adhered.

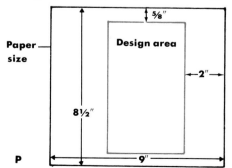

P

Figure P: To make the paste-up for the birth announcement shown, place the design (4 by 7¼ inches) as shown in relation to the sheet of paper (8½ by 9 inches) on which the design will be printed.

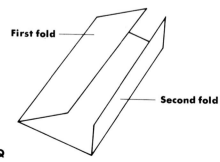

Q

Figure Q: When you receive the finished birth announcements from the printer, fold the paper along the outermost vertical lines of the design, as shown.

HAMMOCKS AND SLINGS
Swinging Suspensions

A hammock is a light, portable bed that you can roll up and tuck easily under your arm, or lash to a back pack. It can be made of string, rope or canvas. Because it is suspended—between two trees, for example, or between any two points strong enough to bear the weight—what is underneath doesn't matter. If you are ashore, the ground may be rocky, wet or sloping; a hammock will still be comfortable. If you are aboard ship, the movement of the vessel won't dump you out of bed, as it might if you were in a bunk. The hammock will swing with the motion, but it will always return to level.

When European sailors discovered the cool string hammocks used by natives of the South Pacific and West Indies, they decided to try these beds aboard ship, and were delighted with the results. But their sea-going hammocks were made of sailcloth and rope, using techniques of stitching, splicing and knot-tying known to sailors everywhere. I designed my hammock (shown opposite) while I was a merchant seaman. I slept in it on deck when my ship was in the tropics and I left it hanging there no matter what the weather. Canvas is a fine all-weather material.

You can make a hammock like mine to roll up and take on camping trips, or just to leave hanging in your backyard all summer long. But the best way to learn the techniques for making such a hammock is first to make a canvas sling that you can use to tote things. The sling shown on page 850 is a mini-version of the cargo sling used by ships at dockside to load or unload all kinds of cargo and machinery; a large sling can lift as much as half a ton. The small one I have designed can be trusted with as many books, fireplace logs, bricks, or other heavy things as you can comfortably lift by its handles. Before you make either a sling or hammock, become familiar with the equipment you will use (described below), and learn how to make a grommet, splice rope, and do flat stitching (see Craftnotes, pages 848 and 849).

Tools and Materials

To work with rope and canvas, use the sailmaker's equipment pictured in photograph 1. This may be purchased from sailmakers or marine supply shops, or obtained by mail from Alan-Clarke Co., Sailmakers, 220 Route 25A, Northport, Long Island, N.Y. 11768. Tools and equipment that may be unfamiliar to you are:

Fid: A piece of smooth hardwood, pointed at one end and rounded on the other. (Use a fid to make a grommet hole if you have no hole punch, or to stretch a stitched grommet.)

Hole punch: A piece of forged steel with a round cutting edge. (Use a ½-inch punch to start rope holes for the hammock and sling.)

Marline: Two-ply string, sometimes called marlin, that is oiled or tarred. (Use marline to make rings that will become grommets for rope.)

Marlinspike: A pointed tool made from steel and slimmer than the fid. (Use a marlinspike to separate rope strands when making a splice.)

Palm or *sailor's sewing palm:* A device made of stiff leather and fitted like a glove, with a lead-lined cup just above the heel of the hand. (Use a palm instead of a thimble to push the needle when sewing canvas. You can buy a left-handed or right-handed sewing palm.)

Rubber: A piece of smooth hardwood for rubbing or smoothing seams and making sharp creases. (You can whittle one, as I did, from an old hammer handle.)

Sail needles: Large sewing needles that are triangular near the point and cylindrical at the eye. (The wide shank of a sail needle spreads canvas weave so the twine can pass through easily; use a size 13 for the hammock and sling.)

Twine: Heavy string much thicker than sewing thread but thinner than cord. (Use 10-ply waxed rayon or linen twine or cotton tubing on the hammock and sling.

Joe Scheurer learned to splice rope, tie knots and make hammocks in the merchant marine. He was an able seaman for 3½ years, sailing on tankers and container ships to the Far East and to Gulf Coast and Caribbean ports. He perfected his design for a hammock during these voyages.

1: These sailmaker's tools and materials, reading from left to right, include: In the background, canvas and coils of ½-inch and ⅜-inch manila rope; back row, spools of rayon twine, cotton tubing and linen twine; center row, coil of marline, clasp knife, two turns of marline coiled into a grommet ring, hammer, hole punch, handmade seam rubber, marlinspike, small and large fids, shears; front row (next to hammer handle), sailor's palm, sail needles.

The only trick in hanging a hammock is to find two strong supports about 10 feet apart. Sling the hammock from these supports so that the center of the canvas, before anyone gets in, is one to two feet below the level of the rings on the harness (see color photograph on page 851).

Making a stitched grommet

Canvas hammocks and slings have ropes going through them. To keep the ropes from tearing the canvas, the edges of the holes are reinforced with stitched grommets. To make a grommet, mark the location of the center of the hole on the canvas with pencil or chalk. Place canvas on a piece of scrap hardwood. Center a ½-inch-diameter punch over the hole mark, and rap the punch sharply with a hammer. Hole edges should be clean-cut. If you have no punch, draw a ½-inch circle around the center mark, pierce center with a fid or an awl, and cut around the circle with a sharp knife or single-edge razor blade. Thread a No. 13 sailmaker's needle with a little more than 6 feet of 10-ply waxed rayon or linen twine, so the needle will be pulling a double strand about 3 feet long.

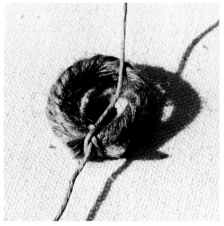

Forming the grommet: Lay two turns of marline around a grommet hole to make a ring slightly larger than the hole, and tie marline ends with twine. Place the ring over the punched hole, and use a pencil to draw a sewing-line circle on the canvas ⅛ inch outside the circumference of the marline ring.

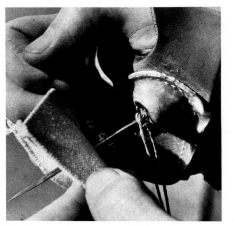

Beginning the grommet stitches: Slide a sailor's sewing palm over the top of your hand and thumb, with the strap around your palm, and begin the first stitch on the sewing line. The small lead-lined cup should be just below your thumb at the heel of your hand. Fit the eye end of the needle into this cup, and apply pressure gradually until the needle pierces the canvas. Don't move sewing palm from side to side trying to force the needle; if you do, the needle end may slip out of the cup. On the first stitch, pull all but ½ inch of twine through the canvas, and use the next two stitches to tie down the loose ½ inch of twine.

"Drawing" the radius: After each stitch, turn the canvas over and pull twine toward center of hole, as if you were "drawing" the radius of the hole; double strands of twine should lie nearly parallel and appear to radiate from center of hole. After "drawing" radius, pull twine outside of hole and begin the next stitch on penciled sewing line.

Completing the stitching: Spacing your stitches ¼ inch apart, sew all the way around the grommet until the hole edges are covered with twine.

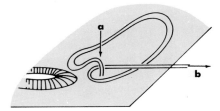

Tying off with a half hitch: With the stitching completed, tie off with a half hitch on underside of canvas. Hold loop (a) with finger and pull free end of twine (b) with other hand until the knot lies flat and tight against the canvas.

Flat stitching a canvas hem

Flat stitches for a sling or hammock hem are made with a No. 13 sailmaker's needle and waxed rayon or linen twine.

Making the crease: Fold canvas twice, so the hem is three layers thick, and use a seam rubber to make a sharp crease.

HAMMOCKS AND SLINGS

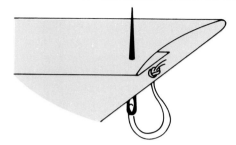

To stitch hem, pass the needle upward through the center of hem.

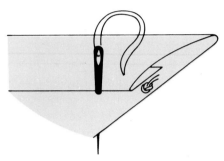

Then pass needle directly downward on the sewing line.

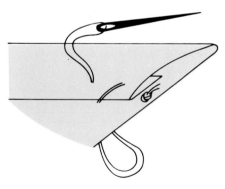

Finally, pass needle upward through center of hem so finished flat stitch lies on the front of the canvas at about a 60° angle to the crease. After each stitch, flatten out double strands of twine so that they lie parallel.

Permanent short splice

After you have marked the right length for a sling's handles with a square knot (see page 851), substitute a permanent short splice for the temporary square knot. Mark rope on each side of the square knot with chalk. Untie the square knot and cut off rope ends 3 inches above your marks. Note that each end of the rope has three strands, wound in a spiral; the direction or twist of this spiral is called

the lay of the rope. As you splice, you will weave "uphill" or against the lay or spiral of the rope. Make the splice as follows:

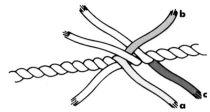

Unravel the strands for 3 inches on each end of the rope, and bring the two rope ends together, alternating the strands (a), (b) and (c) of the left-hand rope end with the strands in the right-hand rope end, as above.

Tie light twine or whipping thread around the strands of both ends of the rope, as above, to keep rope from unraveling any farther as you work.

Working "uphill"—against the lay or spiral of the rope—begin splice by weaving and tucking each strand through, as above; repeat three times, always alternating them in the same sequence. Cut the whipping and turn the rope around. Finish the splice by weaving the remaining three strands of rope, following the same pattern.

Making an eye splice

An eye splice is formed by bending an end of rope back and splicing it into the rope so that the end of the rope becomes a loop. Such splices are used on boat mooring ropes, and to attach the stretcher dowel in a hammock to the hammock's harness ropes (see page 853). For a hammock, the first eye splice is made in one of the two ropes on the outside of the harness. In weaving a splice, you hold the rope just below the splice area and twist main or standing part clockwise. This opens the main part enough to tuck a strand through. Use a marlinspike to keep strands separated during the tuck, withdrawing it when the

strand is in place. Prepare to make the eye splice by unraveling the strands at the end of the rope for 3 inches, then doubling the rope back on itself to form a small loop.

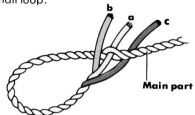

After twisting rope to open main part, tuck the first strand (a) through, uphill and against the spiral of the rope, as above. Position second and third strands (b) and (c) as shown.

Lift second strand (b) over main part of rope and tuck it into the lay of the rope, going "uphill" as before. Note that second strand (b) is inserted below first strand (a) and in a different part of the lay. At this stage the third strand (c) is underneath the main part.

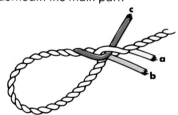

Turn loop over so that the third strand (c) now lies on top of main part, and tuck it in, doubling it under, as shown, to go against the lay. When this tuck is complete, turn loop over and begin a second three-step sequence with the first strand (a). Continue until all the loose strands of rope are woven into the main part. Trim any short ends close to rope.

Weaving, Braiding, Knotting
Making a log sling

For this project, you will need 24 inches of No. 8 (medium-weight) dyed cotton-duck canvas. It comes in many colors and may be purchased at a canvas, awning or tent store. The actual width is slightly narrower (35 inches) than the stated width (36 inches), due to shrinkage during processing. Cotton duck is weather-resistant, although some colors (notably reds) may fade in the sun. It may be washed with a mild detergent in warm water without affecting the color. In addition to the tools listed on page 847, you will need the following from an awning store, sailmaker or marine supply store: 50 feet of 10-ply waxed rayon or linen twine; about 5 feet of marline; and 15 feet of 3-strand ½-inch manila rope. Note in Figure A that the selvage—the woven edge that resists raveling—is at each narrow end.

Pin the canvas to a flat working surface with weights or tacks. Then, with a yardstick, T-square and chalk, lay out and mark the cutting lines, the fold lines, the sewing lines, and the center lines for the grommet holes. Mark the sewing lines on both sides of the canvas. Trim the canvas along the cutting lines with a large pair of shears. Crease the edges along the fold lines on each end for the hems, using the seam rubber to make sharp creases.

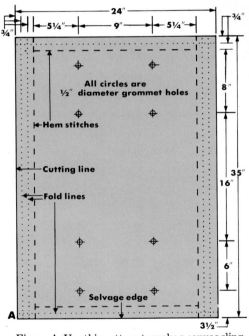

Figure A: Use this pattern to make a canvas sling. Fold lines are shown by dots, sewing lines by dashes. All circles are grommet holes. Stitch grommets after canvas has been cut and hemmed.

A canvas sling makes a handy, comfortable tote for hauling fireplace logs into the house; you might even want two so you could hold one in each hand. When not in use, the bright blue canvas with contrasting white grommets and stitches is attractive enough to be hung on your den or playroom wall.

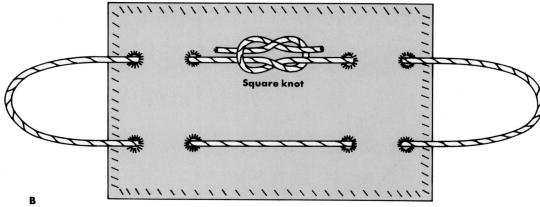

Square knot

B

Figure B: To adjust the sling's handles to your height, run rope through completed grommets and tie the temporary square knot shown. If the sling hangs too low or too high when you lift it, adjust the knot. When length feels right, substitute a permanent short splice (page 849) for the knot.

Use a flat stitch along sewing lines to each corner and finish with a half-hitch (Craftnotes, page 848). Then make hems in both sides, overlapping at the corners (photograph 2). With a hammer and a ½-inch canvas punch, cut the eight grommet holes at the positions marked in Figure A. Stitch grommet rings around each hole (Craftnotes, page 848.)

Adjust the handles of the log sling to suit your own height. When the grommets are finished, run the length of rope through the grommet holes, as shown in Figure B, so the ends meet in the middle. Tie the ends in a square knot and bring together the two handles. The sling, even with a log in it, should hang comfortably at your side. If it drags on the ground, shorten the handles and retie the square knot. When the handles are the right length, substitute a permanent short splice (Craftnotes, page 849) for the temporary square knot.

2: At each corner of the sling, overlap the two hems and stitch inside edges together. Tie a half hitch to finish stitch and trim loose ends.

Weaving, Braiding, Knotting
Making a naval hammock $\$ \boxtimes \text{\textdagger} \text{\textsection}$

To make a rope-and-canvas hammock, you will need heavy No. 4 cotton duck, a good bit thicker than the medium-weight No. 8 canvas suggested for the log sling. Eight feet of 36-inch No. 4 duck will do for the hammock; an awning or tent store or a sailmaker can supply it dyed or undyed. As noted earlier, the actual width will be 35 inches, due to processing shrinkage. In addition to the tools shown on page 847, you will need 70 feet of ⅜-inch manila rope; two oak dowels 40½ inches long and 1¼

Aboard ship there are usually plenty of strong supports that will hold a hammock. On land, use trees or posts spaced about 10 feet apart for your hammock supports.

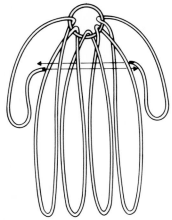

D
Figure D: To make the large clew (knot) in the harness ropes, turn four 3-foot-long loops over the brass ring. Twist ropes so the back and the front of the loops are reversed, then weave free ends of rope through as shown.

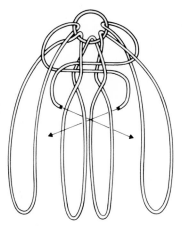

E
Figure E: As the second step in making the clew, by-pass the two outside loops and weave the free rope ends through two center loops that you have twisted again in order to bring the rear of each center loop forward.

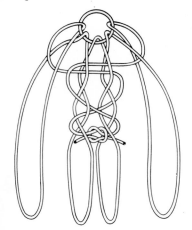

F
Figure F: As the final step in making the clew, reverse direction of free rope ends as before and, again by-passing outer loops, weave through twisted inner loops once more. Tie off rope ends with the square knot shown.

inches in diameter; two brass rings with 3-inch outside diameters; a 100-foot spool of 10-ply waxed rayon or linen twine; and about 20 feet of marline for stitching the 16 grommet holes and for lashing the outer harness ropes. Most large hardware stores stock manila rope and twine; the marline and the brass rings can be obtained from marine supply stores.

Follow the pattern (Figure C) to measure, mark and cut the canvas. Mark fold lines, binding and hem stitches, and grommet hole centers, using chalk of a color that contrasts with the canvas. Mark the sewing lines on both sides of the canvas to help you keep the stitches aligned. Cut along the cutting line with large shears. Fold the canvas along the fold lines for the hems and use a seam rubber to press sharp creases. Sew both hems with flat stitches (Craftnotes, page 848) spaced at ¼-inch intervals. Seal the hems with flat stitches at all four corners (photograph 2, page 851). Use the canvas punch to make holes for the 16 grommets, punching through the two layers of canvas in the hemmed areas. Sew grommets for all 16 holes (Craftnotes, page 848), stitching through both layers of canvas.

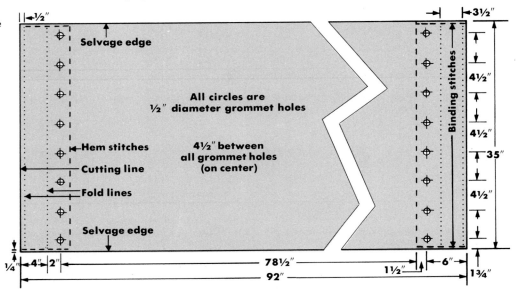

Figure C: On this pattern for the hammock, the fold lines are shown by dots, the sewing lines by dashes. Hems are flat-stitched through three thicknesses made by the two folds.

The Harness and Clew

For each end of the hammock, you must prepare a set of ropes called a harness. As illustrated at the left, these ropes are braided into a large knot called the clew, which is fastened to a brass ring (see the color photograph opposite and on pages 846 and 851).

To make the harness, hang a brass ring from a post and cut off a 30-foot length of ⅜-inch manila rope. Hold one end of the rope with your foot (or have someone hold it for you) as you feed the other end through and around the ring five times; this will give you four loops of rope and two ends hanging from the ring (Figure D). Adjust the ropes so that each loop and the two free ends of rope hang about 3 feet below the brass ring.

In turn, twist each of the loops to bring the back of the loop forward, weaving the free ends of rope through the loops (Figure D). Next, reversing the direction with both ends of rope and twisting the loops again, repeat the weaving pattern, but this time by-pass the outside loop on each side (Figure E). Make a third identical weave (Figure F), again by-passing the outside loops. Tighten the knot or clew you have just woven so that there is no slack in the weave, tie the two free ends with a square knot, and trim off the rope ends.

Near the bottom of each loop, cut the rope so the front piece will be slightly shorter than the back piece. Spread the ropes in a fan shape, with the longest sections on the outside, and the longer piece of each loop you have cut outside the shorter piece of the same loop.

A 40½-inch-long oak dowel across each end keeps the hammock from folding over you like a cocoon when you lie on it. Saw a notch about ⅛ inch deep in each end of each dowel, and make a pencil mark every 4½ inches along each dowel length.

Make a single eye-splice loop on one of longest outside ropes (Craftnotes, page 849). Then lay harness and dowel on the floor, inserting one end of the dowel into the loop of the eye splice. In sequence, nail harness ropes to each pencil mark on the dowel (Figure G); these nails will be removed later, so drive them only part-way in. When all the ropes are stretched evenly, lift the harness by the metal ring. The dowel should hang horizontally, with no slack in any of the ropes. If any ropes are slack, remove temporary nails and make necessary adjustments. Repeat the procedure for the other harness.

The clew is a large knot braided into each set of harness ropes just below the brass rings from which the harness hangs. The two clews—one on each end—keep the harness ropes from snarling or chafing when the hammock swings.

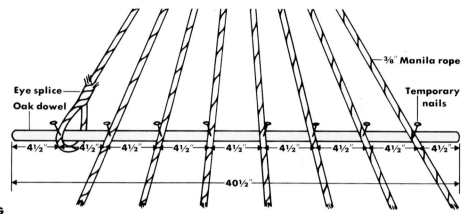

G

Figure G: With one end of the dowel inserted through an eye splice (page 849), lay out remaining seven ropes as shown and drive a 1½-inch nail through each rope to hold it temporarily.

Each nail now marks the point where an eye-splice loop will be located. With the dowels still in place, double back the ends of the ropes and make eye splices (Craftnotes, page 849). Trim loose strands from the splice close to the main part of each rope. Remove all nails and set the spreader dowels aside. In sequence, insert the loops of the eye splices through each of the grommet holes in the canvas. Slide the dowels through the loops again (Figure H). To keep the hammock spread, lash the outside ropes of the harness to the ends of the dowels with marline, using the technique shown in photograph 3.

Now you are ready to hang your hammock. Tie the rings to posts or trees that are about 10 feet apart. Leave plenty of slack in the middle; the center of the canvas should hang a foot or two below the level of the rings on the harness. To use the hammock, sit sideways in the center; then swing your feet up and over carefully until your weight is centered in the hammock. When you first try a hammock, the canvas may feel stiff; with use, it will loosen and conform to the shape of your body. You can speed this process by soaking it overnight in water. To clean your hammock, untie the lashings, remove harnesses and spreaders, wash the canvas in warm water with a mild detergent, then rinse and dry.

For related projects and entries, see "Carryalls," "Macrame," "Netting."

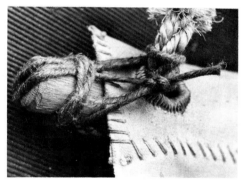

3: To keep ends of hammock spread, use a piece of marline, tying a square knot around the outer rope and lashing it to the end of the dowel as pictured. Then wrap a second piece of marline around the dowel over the first piece of marline and knot it in place.

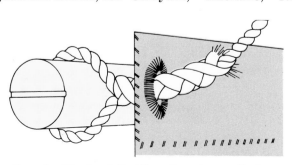

H

Figure H: After notching the ends of the dowel, feed them through eye-splice loops underneath the canvas hem at both ends of the hammock. The splices will fit snugly in the grommet holes.

HARDANGER EMBROIDERY
Scandinavian Handwork

Hardanger, also known as Scandinavian embroidery, is characterized by geometric patterns formed with open squares and embroidered blocks. These effects are achieved by stitching over some fabric threads while other threads are cut and withdrawn, as they are in other forms of drawn-thread embroidery. The photograph opposite, a detail of hardanger embroidery, shows the embroidered blocks that surround the cut-out squares.

Hardanger is named for a district in southwestern Norway, where people use this form of embroidery to decorate both household and personal linens. Embroidery artist Rita Tubbs' painstaking re-creation of an heirloom Norwegian costume is pictured below; it was copied from a costume left to her by her mother, a native of

Marion Scoular, a graduate of London's Royal School of Needlework, is a nationally known lecturer. Marion teaches hand embroidery in Clemson, South Carolina, where she maintains her Robin Hood Wool Shop.

This Norwegian costume is a replica of an authentic heirloom. The apron border, collar and cuffs have been worked in a particularly intricate design of classic white-on-white hardanger embroidery which gives a lace-like appearance to the even-weave linen.

Namdalseid, Norway. Rita worked hardanger embroidery on the collar and cuffs of the blouse and the border of the apron. Hardanger is traditionally worked in white thread on white even-weave linen as shown in the costume, in contrast to the silk on gauze used in an ancient form of hardanger work done by the Persians. Although white thread on white fabric is still considered classic hardanger, colorful threads and fabrics began to be used in the early nineteenth century.

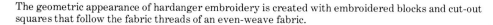

The geometric appearance of hardanger embroidery is created with embroidered blocks and cut-out squares that follow the fabric threads of an even-weave fabric.

Stitch key

|||| Satin stitch

 Woven bar

Vertical lace filling

O Picot

Materials and Basic Preparation

Hardanger fabric with an even weave (having the same number of threads per inch horizontally and vertically) may be used for hardanger embroidery. In fact, you can order an even-weave cotton fabric called hardanger cloth from mail order needlework shops such as Lee Wards, 1200 St. Charles St., Elgin, Ill. 60120, and Meribee, 2904 W. Lancaster, Fort Worth, Tex. 76107. I used it for all of the projects that follow. In addition to the hardanger cloth, you need: a blunt size 22 tapestry needle; one ball No. 5 pearl cotton thread for the satin stitch blocks, and one ball No. 8 pearl cotton thread for the filling; and sharp-pointed embroidery scissors. For instructions in basic embroidery techniques and information about the preparation of the work, see Embroidery Craftnotes, page 540, Volume 5.

Three-Step Procedure

The geometric pattern of hardanger embroidery is accomplished in three separate steps (Craftnotes opposite). The first step is to embroider the satin stitch blocks. Photograph 1 (below) shows satin stitch blocks worked in a diamond shape. These blocks must be worked first because they are not only decorative but they also serve as a reinforcement for the ends of the threads that are, in the second step, cut out and withdrawn. Photograph 2 shows the same diamond motif with the threads cut out. The third step is to decorate the exposed threads with a needlewoven bar (photograph 3) and to decorate the holes with lace filling (photographs 4 and 5).

1: The first step in hardanger is to work the kloster or satin stitch blocks, 5 stitches over 4 threads each, placed here to form a diamond.

2: The second step is to cut and withdraw fabric threads, where they are supported by kloster blocks, creating holes and exposed threads.

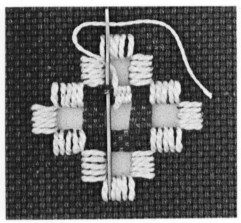

3: The third step is to decorate the exposed horizontal or vertical threads by weaving each group into a bar using the needleweaving stitch.

4: When you have woven to the middle of the fourth bar, pierce the center of the previous bar to start a stitch called vertical lace filling.

5: This diamond motif has woven bars with vertical lace filling and picots, small loops made with the embroidery thread.

CRAFTNOTES: STITCHES

Hardanger embroidery is worked in three steps. The first step is to stitch the satin stitch blocks (Embroidery Craftnotes, page 542, Volume Five), called kloster blocks, which outline the squares to be cut out, securing the ends of the cut thread. The blocks are stitched over an even number of fabric threads and are made up of the number of fabric threads plus one (usually 5 stitches over 4 threads). The second step is to cut the fabric threads. If vertical threads, called warp, are protected by a kloster block, then warp threads are cut leaving only horizontal threads called weft. If weft threads are protected, then weft threads are cut leaving only warp. If both warp and weft are cut, a hole is created. The third step is to decorate the threads exposed after cutting with woven bars, picots, and lace filling.

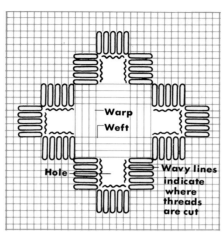

All threads to be withdrawn are cut before any are pulled out. On wrong side with embroidery scissors, snip threads at right angles to the kloster block supporting them (as shown above, along zigzag line). When all cut threads are withdrawn from the diamond motif, five holes are created. The hole in the center is created by removing the warp threads from top to bottom and the weft from right to left.

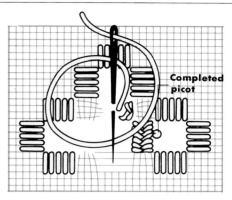

To make a picot, a small loop made with the embroidery thread, on a woven bar; needleweave to the center of the exposed threads, then bring the thread around to the front and under the needle (above), and pull the needle through. Continue needleweaving to the end of the bar.

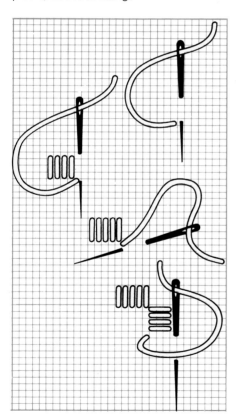

To stitch a kloster block, work 5 stitches over 4 threads (above). Make the stitches along the warp, if warp threads are to be cut and withdrawn. If weft threads are to be cut and withdrawn, make stitches along weft. Complete all kloster blocks before cutting any threads.

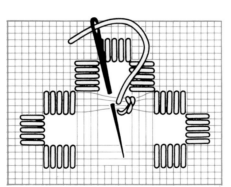

To decorate exposed fabric threads with a woven bar, use the needleweaving stitch. Place the needle under two fabric threads, then over two threads (above). See photograph 3, opposite.

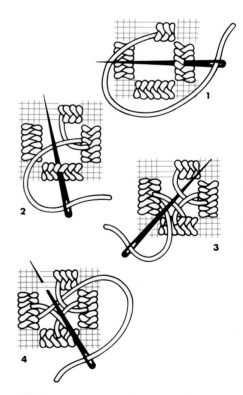

To fill the open areas with vertical lace, work to the middle of the fourth bar and make a stitch piercing the center of the last bar completed (1 above). Continue around the four bars piercing the center of each (2 and 3 above). Continue weaving the fourth bar (4 above). See photographs 4 and 5, opposite.

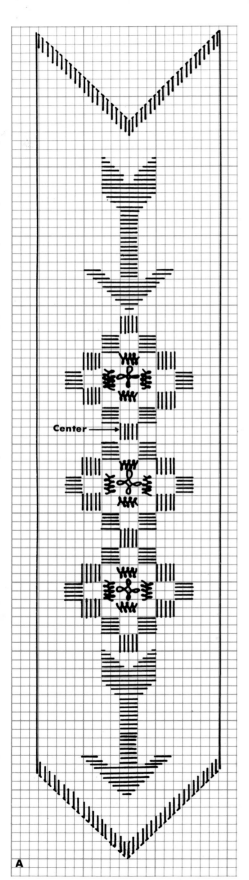

Center

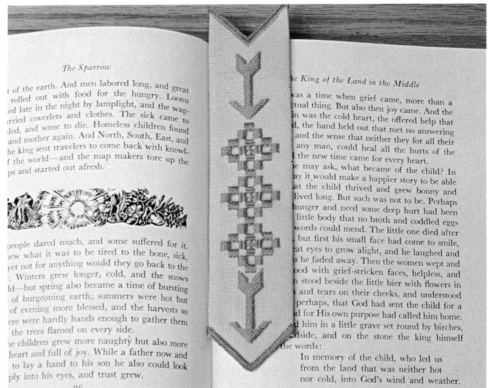

The center three motifs of this bookmark are outlined with kloster blocks whose open spaces are worked with woven bars and lace filling; the arrows are worked in satin stitches.

Needlecrafts
A bookmark

To make the bookmark pictured above, you need two pieces of hardanger cloth 3 by 10 inches. I chose pale yellow cloth and gold thread, but the color combination is optional. On one piece of fabric find and mark the center. Following the diagram (left), and using No. 5 pearl cotton thread, start stitching the first kloster block in the center and work from the center of the design down and then back up (Figure A). All blocks are five stitches over four threads. Complete all the kloster blocks (Craftnotes, page 857) for the three diamond-shaped motifs. The next step is to work the arrows in satin stitch also (see Embroidery Craftnotes, Volume Five, page 542). The placement of the arrow is shown in Figure A. When all the satin stitching is completed, cut and draw the threads (page 857). Using No. 8 pearl cotton thread, work four woven bars with a vertical lace stitch (page 857) in the center cut-out space of each motif.

To finish, place the embroidered fabric face down on the second piece of hardanger cloth. Baste the two pieces of fabric right sides together and machine stitch approximately six threads away from the widest part of the design along the two long sides, thus forming a long tube. Trim the seams to ¼ inch and turn the tube right side out. Press it lightly with a steam iron set on "cotton," laying the embroidery side face down on a towel. To finish each end, start at left edge and work a row of buttonhole stitches (Embroidery Craftnotes, Volume Five, page 544) picking up four horizontal threads of the fabric for the first stitch. Then, working left to right, descend one thread of the fabric with each stitch until the center, then begin ascending one thread until the edge is reached. Trim the fabric close to the buttonhole stitch.

Figure A: The hardanger embroidery bookmark shown at left, is started at the center kloster or satin stitch block, as indicated on this pattern, near the center of the fabric.

A

Needlecrafts
A cocktail mat

In the Scandinavian countries, small mats embroidered with hardanger are used between china plates to protect them when they are stacked in a cupboard. Such craftsmanship is seldom seen, but to work hardanger into a cocktail mat, as illustrated below, cut a piece of hardanger cloth 9 inches square. I like the contrast of the white stitches on bright red cloth, but the choice of colors is optional. Measure 4½ inches in from the side to find the center of the top edge of the fabric, and then from the center, measure down 2 inches (Figure B, page 860). At this point, begin the satin stitch blocks (5 stitches over 4 fabric threads) that form the large diamond motif. Using No. 5 pearl cotton thread, stitch the first block in vertical stitches, then a block of horizontal stitches; alternating blocks are worked clockwise to form a diamond (Figure B). The bottom stitch of the horizontal block and the first stitch of the vertical block share a hole.

The use of color in hardanger embroidery creates a very striking effect, as shown in this red cocktail mat embroidered in white thread. The circles, stars and diamonds in the design, all made with straight stitches, show up vividly against the red background.

Figure B: The satin stitches in this cocktail mat are varied in length so that the sides of four of them appear circular. Some of the circles are filled with stars made of 8 running stitches.

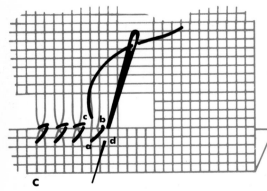

Figure C: To hemstitch, bring needle up about 2 threads below the openwork section (a). Bring needle from right to left (b to c) under 2 vertical threads and pull to front. Insert needle into hem from the back and emerge on front 2 threads below openwork section (d). Repeat across hem.

Start the star-like motif in the exact center of the mat. Make 8 running stitches (see Embroidery Craftnotes, Volume Five, page 542) from the center point, each 5 threads long, to form a star. The satin stitches that surround the star are graduated lengths on either side of a long center stitch to make the points shown. The center stitch of each of these blocks is over 6 threads, the two stitches on either side of it are over 4 threads and the end stitches of each side are over 2 threads. To place the satin stitch blocks evenly around the star, count 8 threads from the center point of the star and begin the longest stitch (over 6 threads) here. Follow diagram (above) for the placement of the remaining stars and satin stitch blocks. When the embroidery is complete, carefully cut the threads inside the small squares formed by the graduated satin stitches.

To finish the edges with a hemstitched hem (an openwork finish), turn the raw edge to the wrong side of the fabric making the fold ¼ inch from the raw edge. Baste the hem following the exact thread of the fabric. For an openwork of 2 threads, cut ends of 2 threads on each of the four sides directly above the folded raw edge and carefully pull them out. Hemstitching can be worked from left to right or right to left, whichever is more comfortable for you. Figure C shows hemstitch being worked from left to right. To fasten end of thread, after last hemstitch, hide the end of the thread in the hem and fasten with a few small stitches.

Needlecrafts
Wine place mat and napkin $ ● ⚹ ⛛

The dark red fabric provides an interesting background for the hardanger embroidery shown below. A detail of this place mat is shown on page 854. This type of embroidery is practical for a place mat and napkin set because, although it looks delicate, it withstands both machine washing and tumble drying on gentle cycles. To iron, place the dampened mat embroidery side face down on a towel, then press with iron set on "cotton."

To make the place mat, cut a piece of hardanger cloth 13 by 18½ inches. Using No. 5 pearl cotton thread, begin the satin stitch blocks 1¼ inches in from the edge of the center of the shorter side (Figure D, page 862). The last stitch of one block and the first stitch of the next block share a hole. The satin stitch bars in each of the four corners are 13 stitches over 4 threads. Work the kloster blocks along each of the four sides following the pattern (Figure D, page 862). There are 55 satin stitch blocks on each short side (not counting the corner bars), and 87 satin stitch blocks along each long side. When the outer row is completed and you have met the starting block, work the decorative inside row using a double running stitch ("Embroidery," Volume Six, page 654). There are 8 fabric threads between the row of satin stitch blocks and the row of double running stitches.

This attractive place mat and napkin are coordinated with the same hardanger embroidery border design; the corner motif is more elaborate on the place mat.

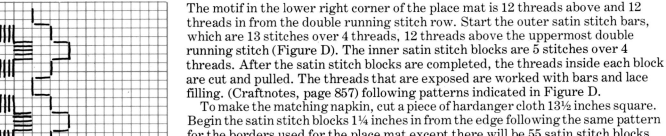

The motif in the lower right corner of the place mat is 12 threads above and 12 threads in from the double running stitch row. Start the outer satin stitch bars, which are 13 stitches over 4 threads, 12 threads above the uppermost double running stitch (Figure D). The inner satin stitch blocks are 5 stitches over 4 threads. After the satin stitch blocks are completed, the threads inside each block are cut and pulled. The threads that are exposed are worked with bars and lace filling. (Craftnotes, page 857) following patterns indicated in Figure D.

To make the matching napkin, cut a piece of hardanger cloth 13½ inches square. Begin the satin stitch blocks 1¼ inches in from the edge following the same pattern for the borders used for the place mat except there will be 55 satin stitch blocks between the corner bars. A decorative row of double running stitch is placed 8 threads in from the satin stitch row. The corner motif (Figure E) is 12 threads in and 12 threads above the uppermost stitch of the double running stitch row. The motif is made up of five groups of 4 satin stitch blocks. The threads are cut from the center of each of the five squares formed and only the middle square is worked with lace filling. To finish place mat and napkin, turn raw edges under ⅛ inch and fold again so that the fold lies along same thread as the outermost satin stitches and hem.

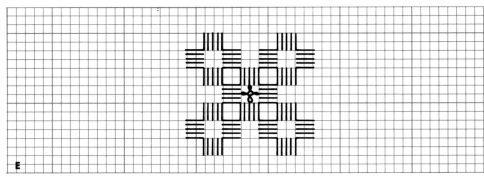

Figure E: The corner motif for the napkin, a simpler version of the one for the place mat, is placed 12 threads in from the row of double running stitches.

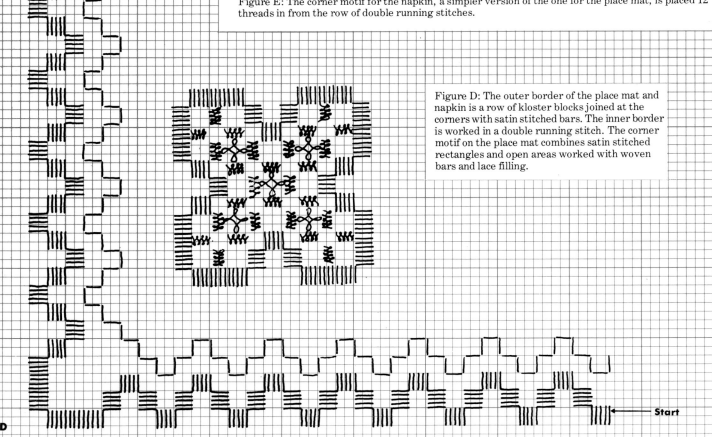

Figure D: The outer border of the place mat and napkin is a row of kloster blocks joined at the corners with satin stitched bars. The inner border is worked in a double running stitch. The corner motif on the place mat combines satin stitched rectangles and open areas worked with woven bars and lace filling.

Start

D

Needlecrafts
White place mat and napkin $ ● ✦ ✦

This lovely place mat and napkin have been worked in the traditional hardanger of white stitching on white fabric. The edging of Italian hemstitching, a decorative openwork hem, and fringe, complement the hardanger embroidery. The openwork for the hemstitching is cut and withdrawn first, the hemstitching is worked next, and then the hardanger embroidery is worked.

Rita Tubbs became interested in traditional hardanger embroidery because she was intrigued by her mother's Norwegian costume. In her search for hardanger information, she consulted a Norwegian friend in Atlanta, Georgia; found a book on hardanger embroidery in a Danish shop in Solvang, California; and had a woman from the Hardanger area of Norway work a sampler of the embroidery to use as a reference. After she successfully copied the costume shown on page 855, Rita then designed this place mat and napkin set in traditional white-on-white hardanger.

To make the place mat, cut a piece of hardanger cloth 14 by 18 inches. Since the hemstitching is part of the design, it is easier to do it first but the fringe is left to last. Starting at the lower right corner, measure 1 inch in from the edge to allow for

Rita Allgood Tubbs, born in China of missionary parents, graduated from the University of Alabama with a degree in clothing, textiles and related arts. A member of the Georgia and Dogwood Chapters of the Embroiderers' Guild of America, she teaches hardanger embroidery in Atlanta and Marietta, Georgia. Her embroidery has won many awards.

The delicate beauty of traditional white hardanger embroidery worked on white even-weave fabric is illustrated by this place mat and matching napkin.

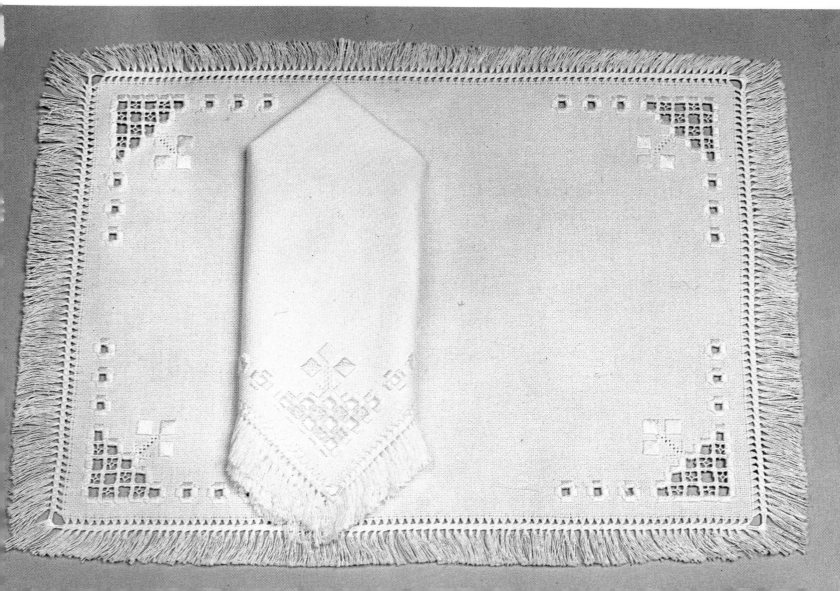

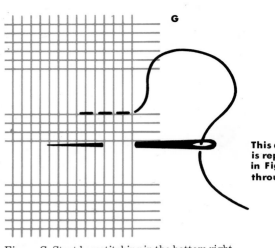

Figure G: Start hemstitching in the bottom right corner of the open mesh. Secure the thread with several running stitches, then take a stitch under the first 4 vertical fabric threads.

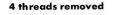
4 threads removed

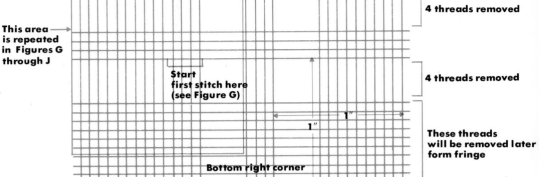

This area is repeated in Figures G through J

Start first stitch here (see Figure G)

Bottom right corner

4 threads removed

4 threads removed

These threads will be removed later form fringe

1"

1"

F

Figure F: To begin the hemstitching pictured on page 863, an open mesh 1 inch from the edge along each of the four sides is formed by withdrawing 4 threads from each side of a 4-thread group.

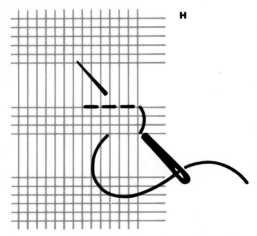

Figure H: To bind the four threads together at the bottom open mesh, take a stitch across them and bring the needle up at the upper edge of the horizontal 4-thread group.

fringe and pull out 1 thread (Figure F). Count 4 threads toward center and pull out the next thread. Now remove 3 threads on each side of this group of 4 threads. Repeat this procedure on each of the sides of the place mat, leaving an open mesh (Figure F). To begin hemstitching, fasten thread by taking a few running stitches in the fabric between the two spaces where the threads were withdrawn (Figure G). Insert the needle, right to left, under the first 4 threads in the lower space. Bind these 4 threads together by taking a stitch back over them, bringing the needle out in the upper space at the left of the same 4 threads (Figure H). Then bind them together in the upper space by taking a stitch back over them (Figure I) and bring the needle out again at the left of the same 4 threads in the upper space. Repeat the process, inserting the needle from right to left under the next 4 threads of the lower space (Figure J) and proceed as before, binding 4 stitches together first at the bottom and then at the top. At the corner (Figure K), weave a bar over the 4 horizontal threads (Craftnotes, page 857), and then buttonhole stitch (see Embroidery Craftnotes, page 544, Volume Five) around small woven square to turn corner. Next, turn the place mat so that the left side becomes the bottom and

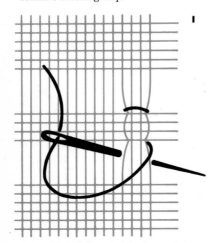

Figure I: Take a stitch in front of the same 4 threads (as in Figures G and H). Bring the needle out again at the top to the left of the threads to bind them together.

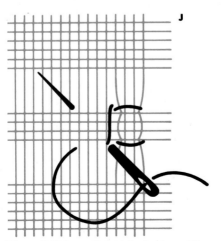

Figure J: Take a stitch at the bottom of the next group of 4 vertical threads to bind them together after bringing down the thread from the top of the previous group of 4 threads.

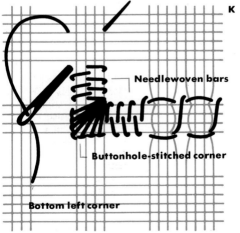
Needlewoven bars

Buttonhole-stitched corner

Bottom left corner

Figure K: To bridge the corner, work a needlewoven bar between hemstitching and corner, buttonhole stitch in corner, a needlewoven bar; then take a stitch over first 4 threads of left side.

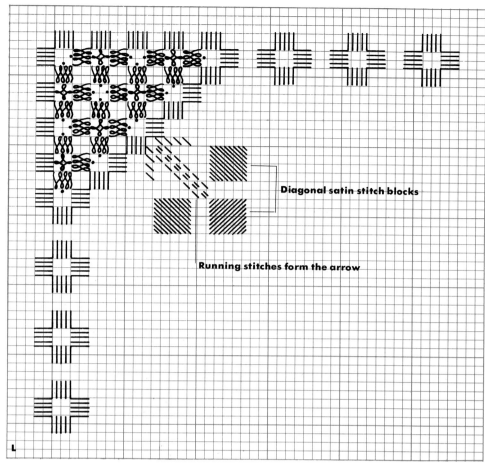

Diagonal satin stitch blocks

Running stitches form the arrow

Figure L: This corner motif is repeated in each of the four corners of the white place mat but in only one corner of the matching napkin. The 3 diagonal satin stitch blocks and the arrow are worked after the kloster blocks, cutting, and lace filling are completed.

weave another bar (Figure K). Continue the hemstitching along each side. Do not pull remaining threads from hemstitching to edge of fabric (to make fringe) until the embroidery is completed.

The place mat is now ready for the hardanger embroidery. Work the kloster blocks starting in the corner 8 threads up from the hemstitching. Make 5 satin-stitched blocks, 4 threads apart. Repeat this vertically, starting in 8 threads from the hemstitching on the left side and leaving 4 threads between blocks. To complete the third side of the triangle and the 3 squares on either side of the triangle, follow the klosters as indicated in Figure L. When all the kloster blocks are completed, carefully cut the threads from the 3 squares on either side of the triangle. Then cut the threads from the squares that form the triangular motif.

To finish the embroidery, make woven bars of all the exposed threads in the triangle (Figure L), and stitch the picots shown (Craftnotes, page 857). Then work vertical lace filling in the squares as indicated. To complete the motif, make small diagonal running stitches over 2 threads in the shape of an arrow. The center row of stitches is worked with a double thread. Work the three blocks shown in diagonal satin stitch. Repeat this motif in each corner of the place mat.

To make the matching napkin, cut a piece of hardanger cloth 18 inches square. Hemstitch as you did the edge of the place mat (page 864). Make the same triangular corner design as for the place mat, but in one corner only. Finish both place mat and napkin by pulling out remaining threads of the marked-off inch on each side between hemstitching and edge (Figure F). This will form the fringe.

For related crafts and projects see "Crewelwork Sampler," "Embroidery," "Florentine Stitch," and "Needlepoint."

HERALDRY
A Medieval Legacy

William Metzig is internationally known as a graphic artist with a special knowledge of heraldry and heraldic design. Born in 1893 in Hanover, Germany, he has been creating distinctive commercial designs for more than 60 years. He is the author of Heraldry for the Designer. *He and his wife Erica live in Forest Hills, New York.*

Armorial bearings, the distinguishing marks born by a medieval knight on his shield, were all that kept him from total anonymity within the heavy and cumbersome armor that covered him from head to toe. In battle, such anonymity could be fatal, since no one could know for sure if he were friend or foe and could hardly wait for an introduction. In tournaments, where he risked life and limb for glory, he needed quick and sure identification marks in much the same way as does a modern professional football player.

The knight was not a legendary figure, of course, but a very real person who fought valiantly in the service of his king. He was usually of noble birth, probably a landowner, and a commander of troops. To let the world know at a glance who he was, he first adopted insignia to mark his shield. Then, to add color and dash to tournaments, he had his insignia embroidered on the coat, called a tabard or surcoat, that he wore over his armor to keep it from rusting in the rain and to keep himself cool in the sun. This flowing coat of decorated fabric was the original "coat of arms," and the insignia became known as a "coat of arms" as well.

Such symbols chosen by knights might demonstrate a simple color and pattern preference, they might symbolize virtues and attributes, or they might even make a rebus—a word-picture of his name. But as more and more knights assumed armorial bearings, great confusion arose as colors and patterns were duplicated.

Medieval knights engage in battle, resplendent in armor, protected by a fabric surcoat. This original "coat of arms" at a later time would be decorated with the insignia here used only on the shields.

Enter the Heralds

The dilemma was solved by the heralds, those messengers of kings who also graced the medieval scene as arrangers of tournaments, where the nobility displayed battle skills. By assuming responsibility for systematizing the design and execution of armorial bearings, so important to those trying to identify the participants in a tournament, they created the art and science that bears their name: Heraldry. In many cultures since the beginnings of civilization, men have had symbols, badges and emblems to represent name, family or rank. Many of these symbols

The style of a coat of arms reflects its age. At top left, a shield is shown as it might have been decorated for a Crusade in the Early Gothic period, when the design was needed for instant recognition in battle. The shield design evolved through the Renaissance as a symbol of rank, reaching a peak of elaboration during the Baroque period. The twentieth century transformed it back to a device for quick recognition.

About 1350

Late Gothic About 1450

Early Gothic About 1300

Early Renaissance About 1500

Late Renaissance About 1650

Baroque About 1700

Rococo About 1750

TWENTIETH CENTURY

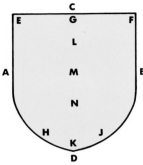

A

Figure A: The heraldic points on a shield are indicated by letters; they are described in heraldic terminology as follows:

A: Dexter side (shield carrier's right).
B: Sinister side (shield carrier's left).
C: Chief (top of the shield).
D: Base (bottom of the shield).
E: Dexter chief (top left).
F: Sinister chief (top right).
G: Middle chief (top center).

H: Dexter base (bottom left).
J: Sinister base (bottom right).
K: Middle base (bottom center).
L: Honor point (one-quarter down center line).
M: Fess point (halfway down center line).
N: Nombril point (three-quarters down center line).

Per pale

Per fess

Per bend

Per bend sinister

Per chevron

Gyronny

Per saltire

Per cross, or quarterly

B

Figure B: The shield is referred to as the field—the area on which the design is drawn. Medieval field divisions are shown with their heraldic designations. Patterns that can be derived from these divisions are shown opposite in Figure C.

868

were incorporated into heraldic design. The eagle is a good example: It has been used by empires, monarchies, and republics. What distinguishes heraldry from ancient custom is, first, its systematization under heralds; and second, the custom that evolved whereby fathers bequeathed arms to their sons.

The College of Arms in England, established in 1484 by Richard III, exists to this day and still carries the prestige of former times, deciding who is entitled to wear what coat of arms. Shakespeare's "Enter the heralds with trumpets" is a stage direction that probably gave rise to the popular belief that heralds were trumpeters. Perhaps it was an economy measure in Elizabethan times to have actors double as heralds and trumpeters, but in fact the original heralds might have led in the trumpeters but never actually blew the trumpets. As kings' ambassadors, they were many ranks above that.

The Language of Heraldry

The old French word for trumpet is *blazon;* and it was the blazon that announced the knights in their colors, bearing and wearing their coat of arms and ready to enter the tournament games. From this is derived the terms *emblazon,* meaning to depict an armorial design graphically, and *blazon,* to describe the design verbally. Blazonry is the language of medieval heraldry. A glossary on page 870 defines heraldic terms, giving a small sampling of a medieval vocabulary.

From Shield to Trade Mark

I have no doubt that a knight visiting the twentieth century in a time machine would be puzzled to see the wealth of commercial objects that bear coats of arms. What possible connection could he make between his medieval peers and a bottle of ginger ale or a pack of cigarettes or an automobile? Remnants of heraldry would surround him in frivolous proliferation. Today coats of arms are used by states, churches, associations, universities and corporations. Sometimes such insignia were originally granted by royal charter, but in the world of commerce, they usually are designed and used purely as decorative devices; if they can be made memorable, they become effective sales tools.

The granting of arms was, and in some places still is, a serious custom. In England, the right to have such insignia has been controlled by the College of Arms for hundreds of years. In raids during the sixteenth and seventeenth centuries, heralds were actually sent on missions to find and destroy insignia held by those not entitled to them. The heraldic scene has cooled considerably since then. Heraldry, outside of England, is no longer under such rigid controls. But a study of its medieval origins offers insights into a remarkable culture that was destroyed by the invention of gunpowder.

Medieval Heraldic Design

The shield was the field upon which the original armorial bearings were designed. For this reason, the shield remains the focal point today and is the only essential part of a coat of arms in contemporary designs. To understand the heraldic system, look first at the shield itself on which specific points are designated (Figure A). The dexter side corresponds to the right side of the shield carrier and the observer's left (hence the word dextrous). Figure B, left, illustrates the ways in which a field could be divided. At first glance, the medieval expressions for these divisions seem like pure jibberish to us; and in fact, it is a kind of medieval jargon; but the meanings are simple and merely indicate direction. Anyone who becomes seriously interested in heraldry would have to learn these words and expressions since they are used to describe, or blazon, coats of arms in a particular way. But the terms can also be read and savored as evocations of a gallant, if barbarous civilization of long ago and far away. The heraldic language defined on this and the following pages will also be useful to crossword puzzle enthusiasts who have been stumped by these terms.

The Honorable Ordinaries

The geometric patterns opposite (Figure C) were called "honorable ordinaries" because they were used frequently, but with distinction. They are the oldest, simplest, and most basic patterns in heraldry. A glance at Figure B, left, shows how these patterns emerged when the shield was divided.

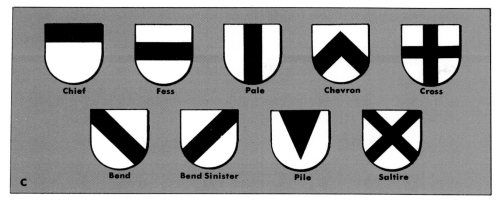

Figure C: These medieval shield patterns are called the honorable ordinaries in heraldic parlance.

The Subordinaries

Scholars of heraldry dispute the actual number of subordinaries, a more intricate group of patterns that evolved to give distinction to coats of arms. Some say there are fourteen, others count more than twenty with all the variations. Illustrated at the right (Figure D) are major subordinary patterns that all agree upon.

Representational Patterns

Mythological beasts, animals, birds, plants, planets, the sun, tools, sailing ships, musical instruments, in short almost anything with a significant meaning for an individual, a family, or a nation may be considered a suitable design—called a charge—for a shield, so long as it retains a certain amount of dignity. Some of the oldest charges are shown below, but there are many more. Some of the varied positions assumed by heraldic animals are demonstrated by the six lions; English, Norwegian, Danish, Finnish, Spanish and Flemish royal families all adopted the lion as their emblem, so variety was in order. Hereditary aspects of heraldry are indicated by the marks (Figure F) that sons placed upon a father's shield to make it their own. The labels in these charts are defined in the glossary on page 870.

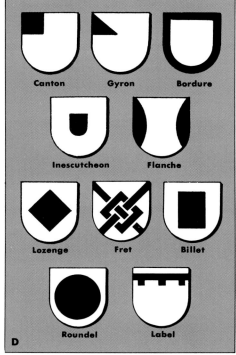

Figure D: The subordinaries are shield patterns, more complex and varied than the ordinaries illustrated at the left. They are equally esteemed in traditional heraldry.

Figure E: These are but a few of the many possible representational patterns, the pictorial designs called "charges" in heraldry. Unfamiliar heraldic terms used in the designations, many in Norman French, are defined in the glossary on page 870.

Figure F: Distinguishing marks assigned to sons to indicate birth rank in a family are called marks of cadency. Each son placed one on his father's shield to make it his own.

Glossary of Heraldic Terms

Achievement: A fully emblazoned coat of arms including shield, helmet, crest, mantling and motto (see Figure I).

Affrontée: Position displaying full face or front.

Annulet: A ring, symbol of the fifth son.

Armigerous: Arms-bearing.

Caboshed or Cabossed: Beast's head shown affrontée (see above) with no part of the neck included.

Cadency: Symbols for the first nine sons of a family, shown in Figure F.

Caduceus: Two snakes entwined on a staff, an ancient sign of a physician.

Caltrap: Medieval spur-like weapon having four spikes.

Charge: Medieval term for a pattern or symbol on a shield.

Clarion: A symbol of music.

Cockatrice: Mythical beast with the head of a cock and a dragon's tail, wings and feet.

Compartment: Area below the shield on which the supporters (see below) stand.

Couchant: An animal position, lying down, breast to earth and head raised.

Crescent: Crescent moon, horns turned inward; symbol for a second son (see Figure F).

Crest: Any decoration borne on the helm, like a plume or an animal.

Cross Moliné: Symbol for the eighth son.

Displayed: Bird viewed from the front with wings and legs outspread.

Dragon: Mythical creature, part bird, part beast, part reptile.

Embowed: Bent, or curved, like a bow.

Escutcheon: Another word for a shield, sometimes used to express an entire coat of arms.

Fleur-de-lis: Literally, flower of the lily, also called "flower of Louis" (XIV), the symbol of France, also the symbol of a sixth son.

Griffon: Mythical beast, half eagle, half lion.

Garb: A sheaf of corn or wheat.

Gaze: "At gaze," applied to an animal standing still and looking earnestly outward.

Hatchment: The arms of a widow displayed with her husband's on a diamond-shaped lozenge (see page 875).

Helm: The knight's helmet.

Knight: Title of honor conferred for services performed in war (medieval).

Label: Mark of the first son and heir.

Mantling: Drapery flowing from beneath the wreath, covering the armor.

Martlet: Mythical, sometimes legless bird, symbol of the fourth son because he inherits no land to light on.

Mullet: Five-pointed star; symbol of the third son.

Naiant: Fish in swimming position.

Octofoil: An eight-leaved flower; symbol of the ninth son.

Passant: An animal in a walking position.

Pennon: Small flag borne on the end of a lance.

Plenitude: Full, as "moon in plenitude."

Proper: Said of a charge (see above) appearing on the shield in its natural colors.

Rampant: An animal position—erect with hind paw on ground, three paws and tail raised.

Reguardant: An animal looking toward the sinister (right) side of the shield.

Rose: Symbol often associated with England; also symbol of the seventh son.

Salient: Animal's position, springing forward.

Séjant: Seated positon.

Semée: Sprinkled, as "semée of fleur-de-lis" meaning that a shield is covered with that design.

Sol: The sun in its splendor, said of the sun when depicted with a human face surrounded with rays.

Supporters: Figures flanking a shield, either animal or human,

Tierced: A shield when divided into three equal portions.

Torse: Another word for wreath.

Trefoil: Three-leaved clover—a shamrock.

Unicorn: Mythical beast, like a horse, with cloven hoofs, a goatee and one horn in the center of his forehead.

Volant: flying.

Winged: Said of a beast whose wings are colored differently than its body.

Wivern: Mythical beast resembling a dragon with a knotted tail.

Wreath: A circlet of two-colored silk placed on the helm and around the crest.

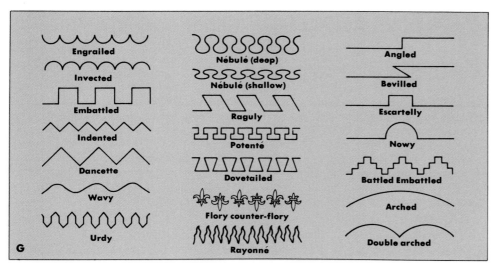

Figure G: Decorative lines of partition may be used to divide or outline any area of the shield.

The coat of arms of the King of France in the seventeenth century displays the ermine of royalty. The two shields, side by side, show the golden fleur-de-lis of Louis XIV, left, and the symbol of the Bourbon dynasty.

Lines of Partition

Areas of heraldic design may be defined graphically by straight lines or by decorative lines like those shown above (Figure G). Some have symbolic meaning. For example, a wavy line may signify water, as in the coat of arms of the City of Paris (right), while the nebule, an old French word for "cloudy," is often used to indicate an uncertain past.

Tinctures: Colors, Metals and Furs

Heraldic colors—clear, strong and brilliant—were originally chosen to give instant recognition on the battlefield (Figure H, below). Pastel colors are almost never used, even today. Other colors are used only when something is "rendered proper," that is, in its actual colors. The system of indicating color by means of black-and-white dots and cross-hatching was invented by an Italian in the seventeenth century. Knowing the system, if you look at an old engraving of a coat of arms, you will be able to read its colors from these patterns.

Furs, now rarely used, often indicated royalty as in the seventeenth-century arms of the King of France (above right). Some folktale scholars think that in the original story of Cinderella, her slippers were actually of vair—squirrel fur—but the word was misread as *verre*, the French word for glass, giving rise to the legend.

In medieval times, one simple rule governed the use of all these tinctures: color never lay on color, nor metal on metal, nor fur on fur. Even today, when this rule is observed, clarity of the design is ensured.

The City of Paris added the cap on the staff to its coat of arms after the French Revolution. The arms of cities and towns in France that retained the fleur-de-lis did so on a grant from the Republic to connote a good city.

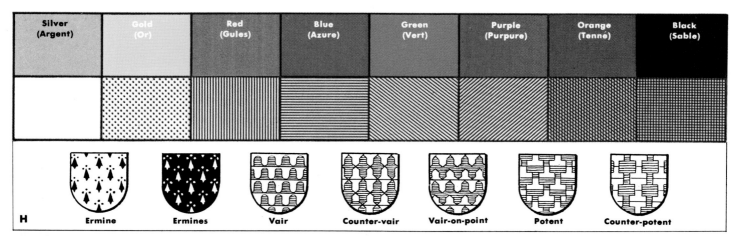

Figure H: In heraldic language, tinctures include furs (bottom row) as well as colors and metals (top row). The French word for each color is given in parentheses. The black-and-white graphic equivalent below each color block (dots or lines in the middle row) is used to represent that color in an engraving.

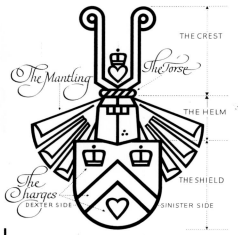

I

Figure I: A coat of arms is referred to as a "full achievement" when it has all the elements identified above. To this may also be added a motto and supporters—figures flanking the shield, as the lion and unicorn shown at right in the British Royal coat of arms.

European Heraldic Agencies

Austria: Heraldisch-Genealogische Gesellschaft
Adler, Vienna II, Haarhof 4a.
Oesterreichische Staatsarchiv, Wien 1, Minoritenplatz 1, Austria

Denmark: Dansk Genealogisk Institut
Peblinge Dossering 26B, Copenhagen N

England: College of Arms
Queen Victoria Street, London E.C. 4

France: Président de la Société Française d'Héraldique et de Sigillographie,
113 rue Courcelles, Paris 17e.

Germany: Zentralstelle für Deutsche Personen und Familiengeschichte, Abteilung Internationale Genealogische Forschung, Berline-Zehlendorf West, Goethestrasse 39.

Holland: Centraal Bureau voor Genealogie, Nassaulaan 18, The Hague

Ireland: Chief Herald and Genealogical Officer,
Office of Arms, Dublin Castle, Dublin

Luxembourg: Délégué aux Relations Extérieures du Conseil Héraldique,
25 Rue Bertholet, Luxembourg

Norway: Head Archivist, Riksarkivet, Bankplassen 3, Oslo

Poland: Archuwirum Glownym Akt Dawnych, Warsaw ul. Dluga 7

Portugal: Conselho de Nobrezza,
Praça Luis de Camoes 46, Lisbon 2

Scotland: Court of the Lord Lyon, H.M. Register House, Princes Street, Edinburgh

Sweden: Riksarkivet, Arkivgatan 3, Stockholm 2

The Parts of a Coat of Arms

Figure I (left) shows how a coat of arms is assembled with its customary components. As I have mentioned, the shield is the only element that is essential. All the rest, though significant, is decorative and may be altered at the whim of the designer. The helm, of course, is the medieval helmet, and though it has little relevance to modern times it is retained as a traditional design element. The crest is borne on the helm, sometimes as a plume or as an heraldic bird or animal. As you will see on pages 874 and 875, the crest can be designed to suit an individual. The wreath or torse is a circlet representing two colored silks, traditionally the principal colors of the shield; it tops the helm and encircles the base of the crest. Knights wore them to cover the joint between crest and mantling. The mantling is the drapery flowing from beneath the wreath symbolizing the knight's surcoat. Supporters are usually heraldic animals flanking the shield, but they may also be human figures. They stand on a ground called a compartment. The motto, originally a war cry, may express any dignified sentiment, any belief or goal.

The British Royal insignia is properly displayed only by the Queen. The shield at center is quartered to show (top left and bottom right) the golden lions of Richard the Lionhearted and symbols for Scotland (top right) and Ireland (bottom left) held together with a blue garter signifying the Knights of the Garter, England's highest order of knighthood.

How Heraldic Designs Develop

In 1198, Richard I the Lionhearted assumed a striking coat of arms of three golden lions on a red shield. When Scotland and Ireland were added to the British realm, the shield was quartered and the emblems of these nations added. Richard's lions now occupy the first and third quarters of the British Royal Arms pictured above. The encircling garter bearing the words *Honi soit qui mal y pense* (Shamed be the one who thinks evil of it) was added as the result of a capricious incident in British history. At a celebration following the capture of Calais, the Countess of Salisbury dropped her blue garter. In a gesture of gallantry, Edward III wrapped it around his left knee and responded with the now famous phrase. He founded the Order of the Garter in 1348 and took this emblem as its symbol.

Today the Queen's coat of arms bears the lion and the unicorn as supporters and the motto *Dieu et Mon Droit* (God and my right) which proclaims the divine right of kings. In English heraldry, only nobility and certain orders of knights are permitted to have supporters on their insignia. Outside of England, however, supporters holding the shield are used freely, often even whimsically.

Heraldic customs developed and spread over Western Europe, so that by the sixteenth century a coat of arms could be granted only by a sovereign. Pictured opposite is part of a seventeenth-century board game whose purpose was to teach children of the Neopolitan nobility the coats of arms of their royal houses, vivid proof of the importance attached to heraldry at that time.

Coats of arms of seventeenth-century Neopolitan nobility spiral from the center of this antique board game, once intended as an enjoyable means of instructing children about the glories and splendors of noble birth.

Heraldry in America

Every American citizen has the right to display the seal of the United States as his own coat of arms. Though it is engraved on every one-dollar bill, millions of people who trade with it every day know little of its interesting history.

The seal is the first instance of original heraldry in America. After the signing of the Constitution on July 4, 1776, the Continental Congress resolved that a seal of the United States of North America should be prepared. They elected a committee —Benjamin Franklin, John Adams and Thomas Jefferson—to design it. When faced with the problem of creating a design to symbolize the new country, these illustrious forefathers met the fate of many a committee. It was duly recorded that "the device of this committee did not meet with favorable reception." It was not until three years and several committees later that a design was finally approved and the seal cut in brass.

The focal point of the accepted design is the shield or escutcheon placed on the breast of an American bald-headed eagle, holding in his beak a scroll inscribed with the motto *E Pluribus Unum* (meaning "one from many" and borrowed from the *Gentleman's Magazine*, a publication familiar to the colonists). In his right talons he holds an olive branch, in his left a bundle of thirteen arrows. The crest appears over the eagle's head as a constellation of thirteen stars radiating through a cloud.

Know Your Heraldic Rights

There is surely something satisfying, if not exciting, in knowing that you have an historical past, and the discovery that you are entitled to bear the coat of arms of an ancestor is stimulating proof. However, it is not easy proof to establish. Companies that offer to send a family coat of arms for a few dollars mislead many people into believing that the insignia they receive in the mail are actually their own. The standard texts on heraldry that these companies consult list thousands of family coats of arms dating back hundreds of years. Your name may be among them, but that is not proof that you are descended from that particular branch of that particular family. Should you bear the aristocratic old English name of Howard, for example, you are not necessarily entitled to assume the insignia of the Duke of Norfolk, the Howard progenitor. The Howard family tree had many branches, some with its own insignia and many without any, so it is a family, rather than a name, that one must be sure of. There are numerous heraldic agencies in Europe (see listing opposite) but they cannot really assure you of your right to a coat of arms unless you supply them with a detailed genealogy proving your lineage. "Genealogy" in Volume Six will help you trace your ancestry if you wish to do so.

The Roll of Arms of the New England Historic and Genealogical Society bears fewer than 1,000 names of American immigrants (with ancestors now living throughout the country) for whom the right to a coat of arms has been established. If you think that your ancestors may have registered such insignia, you can check with the Society (101 Newbury Street, Boston, Mass. 02116).

The coat of arms of the United States is called the Great Seal of the United States of North America. It is described in the records of the Continental Congress in heraldic language: "The escutcheon (*shield*) is composed of the Chief (*top of shield*) and Pale (*bottom of shield*) . . . The latter represents the several states all joined in one solid compact entire, supporting a Chief, which unites the whole and represents Congress; the Motto alludes to this union. The Colours or tinctures of the Pale are those used in the flag of the United States; White signifies purity and innocence; Red, hardiness and valor. The Chief denotes Congress— Blue is the ground of the American uniform and this colour signifies Vigilance, Perseverance and Justice . . . The escutcheon being placed on the Breast of the eagle displayed is a very ancient mode of bearing and is truly imperial . . ."

Can You Start Anew?

If your past seems to elude you, or you would rather not go to the trouble of tracing your genealogy, yes, there is no reason why you should not start afresh like a young knight of the twelfth century. Since heraldry in America has no official status, any citizen can create and assume an original coat of arms without feeling constrained by rules from the past. If you doubt this, be assured by the words of a proper Bostonian, who declared in the 1880s, "We Americans set its rules (British Heraldry) at defiance and do as we choose."

The designing of the Great Seal of the U.S. might be taken as a model by Americans who wish to design their own coat of arms. As symbols and a motto were chosen to express the spirit of the new nation, an individual can choose tinctures, patterns and crests that best express his name, occupation, origin, or an important event in his life. An immigrant who has achieved distinction in his new country should be justly proud of a new coat of arms that expresses his achievement.

How Do You Begin?

A coat of arms should convey meaning with a sense of dignity, and so when I design arms, I prefer to choose symbols from the host of traditional possibilities. For example, I would prefer to represent music with a clarion, rather than an electric guitar. Anyone can select elements and colors that please him and sketch his ideas, even if he thinks he has no particular artistic talent. The arms pictured on this and the opposite page are among the many that I have designed for individuals from widely varying backgrounds and occupations, both in America and in Europe.

This coat of arms was designed for a printer whose name, Schoenberg, means beautiful mountain. The name is depicted in the crest at the top as a mountain covered with flowers. The shield describes the printer's trade by the ancient symbol of the mythical griffon holding two printer's tools over an open book.

An azure glove, appliqued in red and trimmed in ermine, is prominent on the coat of arms of a glove maker. Four blue circles, called roundels, are decorated with golden mullets — five-pointed stars.

The family name Fantasia is rendered in this coat of arms as a golden bird of Paradise, or a fantasy. The family's Italian origin is represented by the Italian flag in the center of the crest.

The city of Noto on the coast of Sicily is depicted in this coat of arms for a physician named DiNoto. The caduceus, symbol of the medical profession, is drawn on the ship's sail in the crest.

This coat of arms was designed for a man named Zak, which means young student in Russian. The shield gives the name pictorially by showing a young student standing between two saplings and holding an open book in each hand.

The coat of arms of this husband and wife combines occupations of both families. The husband's family, once wheel-makers, now manufactures gears and tires, shown by the half-wheel in the shield. The sheaf of wheat symbolizes the wife's ancestors, who were farmers.

The name Shaeffer means shepherd and is indicated on this shield by the sprinkling of golden sheep on a green field. The silver shepherd's shears further symbolize the occupation.

Arms for a Husband and Wife

The bearing of armorial insignia by women has been governed by heraldic rules since medieval times. Customarily, unmarried women are allowed to bear their father's coat of arms on a lozenge (a diamond-shaped field) or on an oval instead of on a shield. When a woman marries, she can combine her insignia with her husband's in one of several ways. The simplest is by *impalement* in which the shield is divided *per pale* (that is vertically) with the husband's insignia borne on the left half and the wife's on the right half. If the wife is an heiress, however, the husband may choose to bear her insignia on the center of his shield; this is appropriately called an "escutcheon of pretense." Or the shield can be quartered, as was done with the British Royal coat of arms. The insignia of a widow (right) are always displayed on a right half of a diamond-shaped lozenge.

It is also acceptable and traditional to display insignia side by side, as in the Zahn-Narr coat of arms below. In a time when women are inclined to assert their independence and identities, this seems a most acceptable and reasonable method to choose. However, the Kloke-Engel coat of arms (right, center) shows how impalement can create an original design that owes nothing to the past. By playing with the name, a composite of Kloke (bell in German) and Engel (angel in German), I was able to give equal importance to both partners.

The coat of arms of a widow are displayed in a diamond-shaped lozenge, divided vertically (impaled), with the husband's coat of arms on the viewer's left and the wife's on the right.

A husband and wife named Zahn-Narr are represented in this coat of arms by two shields conjoined. The profession of the husband, Zahn, a pharmacist, is represented in the crest at left by a caduceus in a mortar. The wife's crest, a jester, is "narr" in German. Her shield is decorated with a lyre, a musical symbol relevant to her background.

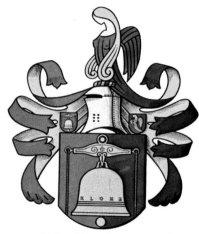

Kloke means bell and Engel means angel, so the name portrayed is Kloke-Engel. Both are given equal prominence in this design created for a husband and wife.

Display your Coat of Arms

Once you have settled on a design, you may have an artist do the final rendering, or you can do it yourself. I suggest using white illustration board and tempera paints for finished artwork. Framing and hanging a coat of arms is the first thing that comes to mind, but your design can be used in many ways. You might have your insignia glazed on a ceramic tile which can then be set into a mantelpiece or a mosaic table top. A coat of arms is also an excellent subject for needlepoint, weaving, tapestry or embroidery. It can be engraved professionally on signet rings, silverware, christening bowls and goblets, any of which would surely become family heirlooms. Insignia printed or engraved on stationery display your mark in an elegant and distinctive way. But if you treasure books, as I do, you may prefer to use your coat of arms on bookplates, perhaps the most traditional and distinguished way of personalizing your library. In whatever form you bequeath your insignia, you will be fulfilling a medieval legacy.

George Washington's coat of arms may have inspired the design of the U.S. flag. Here it is adapted to serve as the design of his bookplate.

HERBS
For Flavor, Fragrance and Fun

Herbs have always been prized for their many uses, ranging as far as the magic of witches' brews, but today it is the culinary and fragrant properties of herbs that we particularly appreciate. Gardeners and non-gardeners alike use such culinary herbs as sage and thyme to add flavor and texture to food. Fragrant herbs like lavender are used in aromatic bouquets, potpourris, sachets, herbal shampoos, perfumes and oils. A number of herbs, such as the artemesias, are valued simply for their decorative appearance, while still others are used to make dyes and medicines. In ancient times, most medicines came from herbs, which originated largely in hot, dry lands with rather poor soil. Today, some are still credited with medicinal value but much of the old advice seems fanciful in light of modern knowledge. A Victorian cure for asthma, we are told, was to "mince garlic, spread it on thin bread and butter, and eat before going to bed." Many such examples fill pages of old herbals, early books detailing the practical uses of plants.

Many people first become interested in growing herbs for their food flavoring value. Then they may turn to the growing herbs for fragrance or just because of their beauty, or to use them for something specific like dyeing. The herbs growing in Mrs. DeCiantis' kitchen garden, detailed in the plan shown on page 878, are those she has found are the most useful to her, as food flavoring or for fragrance. Such herbs are the most fun for beginners, too.

What Is an Herb?

There is no precise way of defining an herb. To a botanist, an herb is any herbaceous plant—one whose stem dies down to the root when winter comes. Herbaceous plants can be annual, biennial, or perennial; they include not only mint, parsley and anise, but peonies and potatoes. (By contrast, shrubs and trees are called woody plants because they have stems and branches that live on year after year.) To an herb enthusiast, however, herbs are all those plants—woody as well as herbaceous—whose leaves, flowers, seeds and other parts are especially valued for flavor, fragrance, dyeing or medicinal use.

Herbs are among the easiest plants to grow so this hobby can be enjoyed on many levels. If you are a beginner, you can start with one or two plants or a tiny garden, indoors or outdoors, and discover the taste and appearance of culinary herbs and the different ways one herb may be used. Sweet woodruff, for example, can flavor May wine or be dried for use in fragrant potpourris and wreaths. Parsley and basil go into pesto sauce for pasta (recipe on page 886). Fresh rosemary is known as the herb of remembrance, so it is particularly appropriate for use in gift baskets (page 884); it is a treat for the eye as well as for the taste buds, and if you like, you can grow it indoors in a hanging basket (page 882).

Experienced gardeners might choose to cultivate herbs of historical significance. Specialized herbs such as those used by the American Indians or those described by Shakespeare provide source material. In designing an herb garden, examples from the past can be inspiring if one wants a lovely formal garden filled with paths and geometric shapes. One type is the sixteenth-century English knot garden which has a central knot of clipped herbs interlaced with one another, resembling a knotted rope. Another popular design is a cottage or Colonial garden where the herbs are arranged close at hand for the convenience of the housewife. There is no need to have a formal garden unless you want to give it a lot of your time. You may prefer a simple and practical garden, requiring minimum care.

The following projects will acquaint you with a variety of herbs and ways to use them. Keep in mind that growing and enjoying herbs doesn't have to be time-consuming and complicated but fun.

Mrs. A. Frank DeCiantis, whose lovely herb garden is pictured at the left, served as the consultant for this article, written by Marilyn Ratner. Mrs. DeCiantis has had a keen interest in herbs since she exchanged apartment living for the joys of a 1790 country farmhouse with spacious grounds in North Stonington, Connecticut, 25 years ago. Several of Mrs. DeCiantis' treasured herb recipes are on page 886.

Herb or Erb?

The word **herb** is derived from the Latin word **herba**, meaning grass. In England it was spelled **erb** until 1475 but even after the h was added, it was not pronounced until the nineteenth century. Today, **herb** is preferred in England. In New England we say **erb** but everywhere else one hears **herb**. Either pronunciation is correct.

Mrs. A. Frank DeCiantis placed her kitchen garden conveniently at her back door so that she can snip culinary herbs quickly for any meal. Fragrant and dye herbs occupy a separate bed nearby.

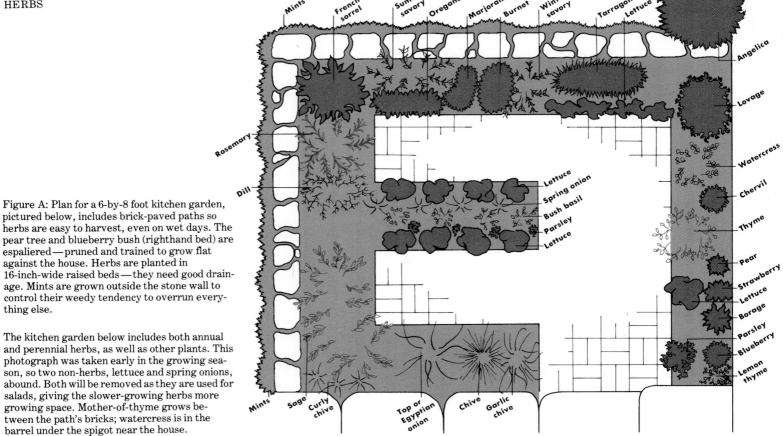

Mints · French sorrel · Summer savory · Oregano · Marjoram · Burnet · Winter savory · Tarragon · Lettuce · Angelica · Lovage · Watercress · Chervil · Thyme · Pear · Strawberry · Lettuce · Borage · Parsley · Blueberry · Lemon thyme · Rosemary · Dill · Lettuce · Spring onion · Bush basil · Parsley · Lettuce · Mints · Sage · Curly chive · Top or Egyptian onion · Chive · Garlic chive

Figure A: Plan for a 6-by-8 foot kitchen garden, pictured below, includes brick-paved paths so herbs are easy to harvest, even on wet days. The pear tree and blueberry bush (righthand bed) are espaliered—pruned and trained to grow flat against the house. Herbs are planted in 16-inch-wide raised beds—they need good drainage. Mints are grown outside the stone wall to control their weedy tendency to overrun everything else.

The kitchen garden below includes both annual and perennial herbs, as well as other plants. This photograph was taken early in the growing season, so two non-herbs, lettuce and spring onions, abound. Both will be removed as they are used for salads, giving the slower-growing herbs more growing space. Mother-of-thyme grows between the path's bricks; watercress is in the barrel under the spigot near the house.

Planning Your First Herb Garden

You can have a delightful herb garden the first season, but if you are a beginner, keep it small and simple. It will probably take three years before you are satisfied. There is no limit to the herbs you might include and the ways you could design your garden. What you grow should be determined by what you are going to use. For instance, if you like French food you might grow chervil and shallots. Italian food enthusiasts would include basil and oregano. Your local library has reference books with simple garden plans and many of the books in the bibliography on page 887 include garden designs as well as step-by-step growing information.

Just don't begin on too large a scale. You can have a productive outdoor herb garden in a space no larger than one square foot. Start with a small variety of plants, repeat those you like best next year and add a few more, and so on. If you don't like something, don't grow it again. The chart on pages 888 and 889 has suggestions for beginners, but it is by no means complete. Consult other sources of horticultural information, such as your local garden club, for more information. An excellent starter kit for beginners, "Herb-Garden-By-Number," is available by mail from *Off the Beaten Path*, Box 324, Southport, Connecticut 06490.

A garden like the one pictured opposite, located just outside the kitchen door, is often called a salad garden. To make a salad, you just pull some greens, snip some salad burnet (which has a fresh cucumber taste), cut a few culinary herbs, and you are nearly ready to eat. When you fix breakfast, you can snip some chives or chervil to give a gourmet touch to a simple omelette.

Herbs don't have to be planted in a separate garden. It's fine to mix vegetables and herbs in the same area. In fact, herbs are often planted among vegetables, since their aroma seems to repel insects. (This fact accounts for the success of the all-purpose non-toxic garden spray described on page 881.) Herbs can also occupy a sunny corner of a flower garden or edge a path leading across a lawn. In Mrs. DeCiantis' garden, fragrant herbs, which she uses in potpourris, and dye herbs grow separately in a corner of her yard behind the house. They are planted in front of a stone wall that forms a natural border (photograph below). She also has a separate garden in which her scented geraniums grow; her theory is that it is less difficult to keep a small space in good order than a large space.

Fragrant and dye herbs grow separately in their own garden where their gray, green, and silver shades intermingle. Included are foxglove, lemon balm, bedstraw, weld, woad, sweet cicely and artemisia. Brushing against many of these plants is enough to release their sweet odors.

Herbs Popular in Shakespeare's Day, and Their Latin Names

Bay
Laurus nobilis

Box
Buxus

Broom
Cytisus scoparius

Burnet
Sanguisorba minor

Flax
Linum grandiflorum

Heartsease
Viola tricolor

Hyssop
Hyssopus officinalis

Lavender
Lavandula vera

Lemon balm
Melissa officinalis

Marigold
Calendula officinalis

Roman camomile
Anthemis nibilis

Rue
Ruta graveolens

Samphire
Crithmum martimum

Summer savory
Satureia hortensis

Tansy
Tanacetum vulgare

Thyme
Thymus serpyllum

Getting to Know Herbs

First you must decide the size and location of your herb garden. Most herbs need three conditions: sun, compatible soil chemistry, and good drainage—herbs, usually native to the Mediterranean coast, will not grow well if their roots are constantly moist (except mints). Most but not all herbs are sun lovers. Chervil and tarragon will grow in partial shade; sweet woodruff grows best in shade. As for soil chemistry, most herbs prefer alkaline (or sweet) soil. Sweet woodruff is about the only herb that grows in acid soil. You can tell what your chemistry is by having a sample tested by your country agricultural agent or a professional service.

What to grow is really a matter of personal taste but you should know the characteristics of each herb you choose. Is it an annual, biennial, or perennial? Annuals, as the word implies, grow for one year, set seed, and die. Biennials, of which parsley is one, take two years to reach maturity, but leaves are often more flavorful the first year. (Hence parsley is often treated as an annual in herb listings.) Perennials continue to grow year after year, coming up each spring from the old roots.

Annual and perennial herbs make perfectly good companions in a garden; a few annuals give you a chance to vary your menus. How many plants of each variety to grow depends on how you plan to use them. You might have one rosemary plant for day-to-day cooking, for example, and one to pot as a winter house plant.

Consider whether the plants you want to grow can be started from seed or are better bought as seedlings from a nursery. Some must start as seedlings unless you are skilled at plant propagation. Tarragon, for example, can't be grown from seed. And some herbs such as rosemary and parsley grow so slowly that it seems you are waiting forever. It is less expensive to start herbs from seed and fun for those who like it, but if you have limited time or patience, you might buy healthy seedlings.

Herbs, like other plants, have various growing habits. Some are sprawling, others erect. Some, like mint, spread rapidly from their roots and will take over your garden if you let them. Rather than fight the sprawling tendencies of mint, some gardeners plant it at the back of the garden, more or less out of sight and in a place where it is welcome to sprawl if it likes. (Mint comes in many flavors— spearmint, peppermint, orange mint, etc.) Some gardeners use a metal edging strip sunk into the ground around the mint bed to forestall spreading.

Also consider plant heights. Tall plants may block sunlight and air from smaller ones and are better placed along the garden's edges. There are exceptions here, too, and experience is often the best guide. You might want a single tall plant to accent to a low bed; you can use angelica, a staturesque plant, that way, and candy its stems to decorate cookies and cakes or flavor rhubarb pie. The chart on pages 888 and 889 gives the heights of various herbs.

"Gathering Herbs" is the title of this illustration from a 16th century herbal, the *Grete Herball*.

Easy-to-Care-for-Herbs

It is a good idea to have a path to walk on when you harvest herbs. In the kitchen garden, pictured (page 876), the path is made of bricks, and borders are of fieldstone. Large, immovable rocks made steppingstones in the fragrant garden.

Be sure to choose a sunny spot for your garden. If you don't have four hours or more of direct sunlight each day, you can still grow herbs, but they may not look like the seed package. Good drainage is really the most important requirement.

Herbs do not need a rich soil; in fact, with most it is better not to add fertilizer unless growth seems weak and straggly. In the spring when you plant, add a layer of mulch. This is helpful because few weeds grow through it, and it helps retain moisture during dry spells. Buckwheat hulls, available by the bag at garden centers, do a good job. Add mulch once about the middle of the growing season.

You will learn the particular growing requirements of each herb with experience. Basil, for instance, comes up very quickly; it is sometimes joked that when you sow basil seeds, you just stamp on them and when you turn around, they are up. With experience, you will gradually acquire a timetable of growth in your head, but if you are a beginner, it is helpful to keep a journal that you can refer to each year. Mrs. DeCiantis plants lettuce and spring onions in her herb garden very early, so she can harvest them when the nearby basil needs more room to grow. If you are starting herbs from seed, it is wise to plant the perennials indoors in late winter, since they take longer than annuals to come up.

A newly-planted garden should be watered well initially but after herbs are well started, they should be kept relatively dry. Herbs repel most insects, so there is no need to spray them. In fact, a non-toxic insect spray can be made from herbs, as described above right, to protect flowers and vegetables growing elsewhere in your garden. This is especially useful if you have an organic garden.

Planting Seeds and Seedlings

When you plant seeds, follow the instructions on the back of the packet. Mark rows so you will know what each herb is. Wooden ice cream spoons make unobtrusive markers; write each herb's name on a spoon with waterproof ink.

A small plant, either started indoors in late winter or purchased at a nursery, is planted in the garden by tapping it out of its container and placing it in spaded soil so the seedling is growing at the same soil level as it was in the pot. The loose soil should be firmed around the plant's soil ball so the tender seedling is well anchored and will not be blown over by wind. Soil should be kept moist but never soggy until the plant is established.

Indoor Gardening

Some of the herbs that grow best indoors are those frequently used in cooking. A pot garden is a way for apartment dwellers and people who don't have gardens to have herbs at their fingertips in any season. Herbs can be placed in individual pots or several herbs can be planted together in one large container such as the hanging basket on the next page. As with the outdoor garden, indoor herbs are easy to care for, needing mainly sun, air, water, good drainage and occasional fertilizing. Using them will automatically prune them. Indoor plants can be started from seeds or seedlings, or can be dug up from your outdoor garden and brought indoors at the end of the outdoor growing season.

For a pot herb garden use clay pots. Plant one kind of herb in each pot. A good size pot is about 4 inches in diameter, measured across the top. Use pieces of broken pot or small stones to cover the drainage hole in the bottom of the pot. Then fill pots with sterile potting soil.

If you are planting seeds, follow planting directions on the back of the packet. After planting, keep the pots out of direct sunlight until the seeds germinate and sprouts show. (The time period varies from herb to herb.) When seedlings have grown a few leaves, thin them out, leaving the three strongest well-spaced plants. The sprouts you remove are flavorful and can be used in cooking at that tender age.

Water herbs when the soil feels dry, usually about every two days. Do not let the pots sit in saucers of water. Herbs will thrive on a sunny window sill or on a table where they will get sunlight each day and fresh air if possible.

Non-Toxic All-Purpose Garden Spray

In an electric blender blend:
   1 cup slightly soapy water
   3 large onions, peeled and cut in sections
   1 entire garlic bulb, peeled
   3 hot peppers or 1/2 cup dried hot pepper.

Pour the mixture into a covered container and let it stand for 24 hours. Strain into a large bowl or container and add enough water to make 1 gallon.

This spray can be used to repel insects in your vegetable and flower garden and is not poisonous. Bury the strained pulp under one of your favorite rose bushes.

Some Herbs to Grow in an Indoor Garden

Annuals

Chervil
Anthriscus cerefolium

Coriander
Coriandrum sativum

Dill
Anethum graveolens

Parsley
Petroselinum crispum

Summer savory
Satureia hortensis

Sweet basil
Ocimum basilicum

Perennials

Chives
Allium schoenoprasum

Mint
Mentha species

Oregano
Origanum vulgare

Rosemary
Rosmarinus officinalis

Sage
Salvia officinalis

Sweet marjoram
Majorana hortensis

Tarragon
Artemisia dracunculus

Thyme
Thymus vulgaris and Thymus citriodorus

Winter savory
Satureia montana

An indoor hanging herb garden of garlic chives, oregano, lemon thyme, marjoram, parsley, winter savory, rosemary, sage and basil has been planted in a wire basket lined with sphagnum moss. As the garden grows it will fill out and trailing herbs will hide most of the moss.

Greenery and Growing Things
Hanging garden

The hanging basket of herbs in the photograph at left is a more unusual indoor herb garden. It was planted as an experiment—to see whether the plants would yield enough to be practical. They have. You need a 12-inch wire hanging basket, 1 bag of shredded sphagnum moss and 1 bag (1½ quarts) of potting soil mix. These are available at garden centers and nurseries. In this hanging garden are garlic chives, oregano, lemon thyme, marjoram, parsley, winter savory, rosemary, sage and basil (bush and purple varieties), all of which were bought as small plants for this project. You could make such an indoor garden from rooted cuttings if you do not wish to buy small plants.

To make the hanging garden, soak the sphagnum moss in water (the sink is a good place to do this) then squeeze out the excess water. Line the wire basket with this moss, filling the spaces between the wires with bits of moss and trying to hide the wire as much as possible. Fill the lined basket with potting soil mix. Press the plants firmly into the soil, allowing 1 to 2 inches of growing space between plants.

After the basket is planted, water gently but thoroughly. The moss absorbs moisture like a sponge. Hang the basket where it will receive direct sunlight and where air can circulate freely around it. Water daily. An easy way is to throw on a few ice cubes. Every two weeks or so take the basket down and give it a good soaking in the sink or outdoors. Drain thoroughly before rehanging. You will need to fertilize your hanging garden. Use an all-purpose, water soluble fertilizer, following directions for use on the container.

The basket at left was planted only a few weeks before the photograph was taken. As the herbs grow, they will be pinched back, by taking sprigs from the ends of stems. Pinching stimulates branching and the garden will then fill out more.

Greenery and Growing Things
Harvesting and drying

Once your herbs are growing, outdoors or indoors, they can be used for flavoring and fragrance. All you need to do is harvest them. Some herbs, such as mints, are grown only for their leaves; others, like dill and fennel for seeds as well as leaves; still others for the stem or root, like angelica or horseradish.

Harvesting of most culinary herbs can start as soon as the plant is large enough not to miss a few leaves. Pinch off the top leaves and ends of the stems with your thumb and index finger, just as you would pinch back a house plant.

Though fresh herbs are a joy to use in cooking and many recipes call for fresh herbs, you can also dry herbs to cook with in winter and for such gifts as sachets, herb-lined pot holders and to press for note paper.

Herbs gathered for drying can be harvested any time during the growing season. Herbs tend to lose some of their flavor during the drying process so they should be picked during the blooming period. The best time to harvest for flavor comes when the plants are just starting to bloom. That's when the aromatic oils are most concentrated in the leaves. Pick herbs in the morning, just after the dew has dried and before the sun is hot.

Herbs harvested for seeds, such as coriander and dill, should be cut when the seed heads turn brown but before they fully ripen. If you wait too long, the seeds will drop to the ground and be lost or you'll have volunteers next year. Cut the whole seed head from the stem with garden scissors.

Drying Lemon Balm
In drying herbs, the objective is to remove moisture from the leaves as quickly as possible, in order to preserve the color and flavor or fragrance. Drying time varies from herb to herb and also depends on the humidity of the air. Lemon balm, for example, takes about a week to dry; then it can be used for tea (see page 883) or stored in an airtight container until needed for potpourris or other projects.

To dry lemon balm or any other herb, strip the leaves off the stems and spread them in a thin layer on a screen tray. Leaves should not touch one another because air must reach all of them evenly. A multilayered tray accommodates several herbs at the same time.

One way to dry herbs is on a screen tray. The tray pictured has three tiers; you could dry rose petals on one and a different herb on each of the other two but a single-layer tray is adequate. In fact, if you don't have a screen tray, just prop up an old window screen so that air can circulate under and over it.

Strip the leaves off the harvested stems and spread them in a single layer on the screen. Small herbs such as thyme and savory can be left on their stems for drying. After laying the leaves on the screen, keep it in a warm, dry, airy but not sunny place such as an attic. When one side is dry—with lemon balm after three days— turn the leaves and let the other side dry. Drying herbs usually takes a week or less. The time is shortened in dry weather. If you dry herbs outside, bring them inside each evening so dew won't dampen them.

The leaves are dry when they are crisp and then it is time to remove them from the screen tray. Seed heads are dried the same way as leaves.

Another method of drying suitable for herbs with long stems such as marjoram, sage, mint, and rosemary is to fasten the stems together in a bunch with a rubber band and hang them in a warm, dry, airy place. They are decorative in a country kitchen. Many people hang bunches upside down and may even put them in paper bags to keep light from discoloring the leaves, but herbs dry just as well right side up and make a pretty bouquet. Check the bunches every two days or so until you find the leaves are crackly dry and ready for storage.

Storing

When herbs on the screen tray or hanging in bunches are dry, you will need to store them if you are not using them right away. Many people use jars and bottles to store herbs but they will lose flavor or fragrance if kept this way any length of time unless the containers have airtight stoppers. As soon as herbs are dry, remove the leaves from the stems and pack leaves in airtight containers or plastic bags. Whole leaves are better than those that are broken or crumbled because they keep their flavor longer. Store seeds, too, in airtight containers. Keep all dried herbs in a dark, cool place. For best flavor, replace each year.

Tarragon, chives, and parsley can be preserved by freezing. Cut herb tips in the morning, wash them and pat them dry. Freeze small amounts in tightly-sealed plastic bags. You'll soon learn the amount you usually use in a recipe so none will be wasted. (Frozen herbs do not refreeze well.)

Herb Tea or Tisanes

Lemon balm is one of the many herbs that can be used to make a tasty tea. Others are lemon verbena, mint, rosemary, sage, and thyme; in fact, almost any of the culinary herbs can be used. A heaping teaspoon of the dried herb is needed for each cup of boiling water. Fresh herbs can also be used, but use about 2 heaping teaspoons of fresh leaves per cup. To make herb tea, put the herb in a warm teapot and add the right amount of boiling water. Let the mixture steep for 10 minutes. It will be light-colored. If you want a stronger flavor, add more of the herb. Never use milk but do use honey to sweeten.

Introduce a friend to herb gardening with this tiny flower basket of thyme, lavender, marjoram, and other herbs. The herbs can root in a special soil mix. The purple flower is heartsease.

Cornell Mix

This formula makes 1 bushel of Cornell Mix to use for rooting cuttings; it will keep indefinitely. All ingredients are available at nurseries and garden centers.
1/2 bushel agricultural vermiculite
1/2 bushel shredded sphagnum moss
4 tablespoons powdered superphosphate
8 tablespoons ground limestone
1 cup all-purpose fertilizer (the kind with the 5-10-5 formula on the bag)

Blank note cards randomly decorated with pressed herbs include blue flax (top card) and rosemary and heartsease (bottom).

Greenery and Growing Things
Gift basket

A good way to get a friend started as an herb gardener is to give a basket of living herbs. You can make such baskets for friends who are ill, for hostess presents or for party favors, using whatever herbs are available at the moment. The rooting soil is a potting mixture that is good to have on hand all the time. It was developed at Cornell University and herbs root in it in about one week. (The Cornell Mix can be used to root other house plants, too.)

You can use miniature market baskets available in card or party shops or a spray can top for a container. The basket can be any size—those 2 or 3 inches square work well. In addition to the basket and herbs, you need a container or containers to hold the soil—or florist's Oasis, if you do not want to root the herbs—paper cups will do, or small plastic containers such as individual ice cube holders, or you can make a liner of aluminum foil with joints tightly creased. The basket liner should be trimmed if necessary, so that it does not show over the top of the basket.

The day before you want to assemble the basket, use a sharp knife to cut herbs 3 to 4 inches long, making the cut at an angle just below a leaf or leaf node. Put cuttings in a glass of water overnight so they will be turgid when placed in the soil.

To assemble the basket, fill the container with soil mix and wet it. Arrange the plants in an attractive way in the basket (see photograph at left). Another method is first to dip the ends of the herbs in hormone rooting powder, available at plant stores, and then insert them in the soil.

The basket is then ready to present. Culinary herbs that will root easily are thyme, marjoram, oregano, lavender, and rosemary, savory mints and fragrant geranium leaves. But you can use any herb for such a basket and this depends on what you have available and what you think the person will appreciate.

Designs and Decorations
Herb note cards

A box of original note cards can be made with herbs and flowers that you have pressed in an old telephone book until they are dry. Some attractive herbs to use include sweet woodruff, rosemary, flax, thyme, bedstraw, heartsease, rue, sweet cicely, lavender, lady's-mantle, and scented geranium leaves.

In addition to a box of folded note paper, either white or pastel shades, you will need: sheets of Japanese rice paper cut the same size as the note card front or slightly larger (rice paper is available at craft shops); box of Glutoline wallpaper paste; and a sponge. If you wish to spray the note cards to show silhouettes of leaves as in the bottom card in the photograph at left, you will also need a can of green floral spray paint, available from florists.

First make the paste by mixing 3 tablespoons of wallpaper paste with 1 pint of water. Then apply the paste evenly to a note card front, using a sponge or pastry brush. Arrange the pressed herb or herbs to your liking. It's best to use only one or two pressed leaves per card to avoid a cluttered look.

Carefully place a piece of rice paper over the arranged herbs and wet with more of the paste solution. Use a sponge and be careful to eliminate any air bubbles so that the rice paper lies flat. While it is wet, trim any extra rice paper from the edges with your thumb and index finger or with a scissors.

Let the card dry and begin working on the next card. When dry, it may be necessary to press the card back lightly with a warm (not hot) iron to achieve an even flatter look. It's fine, however, to leave the cards looking slightly irregular.

Additional dried leaves can be silhouetted with floral spray paint to produce a shadow effect. If you wish to do this, place a leaf atop the rice paper where you want the leaf impression and carefully spray over the leaf. When you remove the leaf, its silhouette will show in white.

The card is now finished and when completely dry the message can be written inside. Directions for pressed-flower cards are in the entry, "Greeting Cards."

Tarragon mixed with minced clams provides a savory filling for hors d'oeuvres. Here white bread is carefully rolled to encase filling before baking. Baked clam rolls sit in bowl at right.

Kitchen Favorites and Celebrations

Come into the kitchen

More than any other room, the kitchen of Mrs. DeCiantis' 1790 Connecticut farmhouse reflects her interest in raising herbs and using them to liven up her favorite recipes. A shelf of green and brown wine bottles holds herbal oils and vinegars for salad dressing and a variety of other culinary treats. Glass jars of herb mustard, jellies and dried herbs surround her workspace. A collection of potholders hangs conveniently near the stove. These, made of herbal print fabric, are stuffed with dried rosemary in addition to the padding. When touched to a warm pan they fill the room with fragrance.

She uses herbs every day in cooking and has found that they transform many run-of-the-mill recipes into unusual and tempting fare. A few, simple "rules of herbal thumb" are all you need to get started with cooking with herbs. First, use herbs sparingly; they should accent, not disguise, the flavor of the food. Second, for a recipe serving four, start with ¼ teaspoon powdered, ½ teaspoon dried, or 1 tablespoon of a fresh herb. Finally, try herbs with old stand-by recipes in the beginning. For example, you might prepare a chicken the way you normally do, but add an accent of rosemary and see if your family likes it. This is especially effective if you have young children who are reluctant to try new foods.

Herbs can make a fine substitute for a basting brush, especially at barbecues. Pick a small bunch of herbs—rosemary, lovage, oregano, savory, mint, or marjoram, and use the herbs to brush the marinade on the meat as it cooks. A simple marinade of lemon juice and olive oil is suitable for any meat. (After a barbecue throw some mugwort on the grill to ward off mosquitos.)

On the following page is a sampling of Mrs. DeCiantis' herb recipes and at right is *Cook's Guide to Herbs*, which may be a helpful reference when experimenting with combinations of your own. With herbs, there are no hard and fast rules; you can improvise to your heart's content. The only criteria of success is that the result tastes good!

For related entries detailing herb uses, see "Perfumes," "Potpourris," "Vegetable Dyes," and "Wildflowers and Weeds."

Cook's Guide to Herbs

Soups:
Basil, bay, chives, dill, oregano, parsley, tarragon

Eggs:
Basil, coriander, cress, dill, parsley, tarragon, thyme

Breads:
Caraway, chives, dill, garlic, marjoram, parsley, rosemary, tarragon

Fish:
Chives, dill, fennel, parsley, tarragon

Meats:
Basil, dill, marjoram, mint, oregano, rosemary, sage, summer savory, thyme

Poultry:
Basil, dill, lemon balm, lovage, sage, tarragon, thyme

Salad and salad dressings:
Basil, chives, cress, dill, garlic, marjoram, oregano, parsley, savory, tarragon

Drinks:
Dandelion, lemon balm, lemon verbena, mint, sweet woodruff

885

Tarragon Clam Rolls

These excellent hors d'oeuvres (shown on the previous page) may be frozen and simply baked when company drops in unexpectedly.

1½ tablespoons chopped shallots	1 8-ounce can minced clams
1 tablespoon butter	¼ teaspoon Worcestershire sauce
1 tablespoon chopped fresh tarragon	pinch of mace
(or ½ teaspoon dried tarragon)	14 slices white bread with crusts removed
2 tablespoons flour	½ stick butter

To make filling: Saute shallots and tarragon in 1 tablespoon butter in a frying pan. Blend in flour, Worcestershire sauce and mace. Add clams and clam liquid and cook slowly over medium heat until thick. Let cool.

Melt ½ stick of butter over low heat. Flatten each slice of white bread with a rolling pin until thin. Brush with melted butter and spread with a small amount (about 1 tablespoon) of the clam mixture. Roll the bread tightly (see photograph on previous page) and cut each roll into three sections. Brush the tops with melted butter and sprinkle each with a dash of paprika.

Bake on baking sheets for 10 minutes at 425 degrees Fahrenheit. Serve. If the clam rolls were frozen, bake for 15 minutes at 425 degrees Fahrenheit.

Pesto Sauce for Pasta

Mrs. DeCiantis makes this with equal amounts of fresh basil and parsley though some versions of this recipe call for just basil. It is also possible to make pesto with dill or marjoram. In summer or fall harvest basil and parsley and make your winter supply of pesto sauce. However, if it doesn't last, substitute ⅓ cup of dried basil for each cup of fresh basil, but do use fresh parsley for this recipe.

Pesto sauce can be put in jars and refrigerated or frozen. If you plan to refrigerate it for any length of time, spread a few drops of oil on the top of the sauce in the jar to prevent mold. This recipe makes about one pint of sauce.

1 cup oil (olive oil, corn oil or ½ cup of each, well mixed)	1 cup firmly packed parsley
	4 cloves garlic
1 cup firmly packed fresh basil	½ cup pine nuts or walnuts

Put all ingredients in a blender and blend until smooth. Store sauce in the refrigerator, removing it and letting it stand at room temperature ½ hour before it is to be used.

To serve: Prepare 1 pound of fettucini according to package directions. While the pasta is cooking, saute ¼ pound of sliced mushrooms in butter in a frying pan. Drain the pasta and pour into a warmed serving dish. Top with mushrooms and about 4 heaping tablespoons of pesto sauce. Toss until well mixed.

Serve the pasta and pass freshly grated parmesan cheese in a separate dish. Additional pesto sauce might also be passed.

Mint Syrup

Fresh mint leaves can be used in a surprising array of recipes and Mrs. DeCiantis has developed an unusual mint syrup which can be used in juleps, as a sweetener for punch, or to flavor iced or hot tea. She grows several varieties of mint to make the syrup: apple, spearmint, orange mint and peppermint, but the syrup can be made of spearmint alone.

This recipe makes about 1 quart of mint syrup which can be kept in the refrigerator or frozen in cubes in an ice cube tray or frozen in a plastic bag.

Preparation: Strip and pack 3 cupfuls of fresh mint leaves. Squeeze 1 cup of lemon juice (seeds and pulp, too) and save the rind from 3 lemons. Squeeze 1 cup of orange juice, again including the seeds and pulp. Save the rind from 1 orange.

Boil 3 cups of water with 2 cups of sugar for 3 minutes. Add the lemon juice and rind and boil 3 minutes more. Add the orange juice and rind and boil for another three minutes. Add the mint leaves; boil 3 minutes more.

Pour the mixture through a colander or strainer, mashing well with a wooden pestle or a spoon. Cool.

Pour into a bottle or plastic refrigerator container for convenient storage.

A pesto sauce of basil and parsley enhances any pasta. Here it is used with fettucini, graciously serve in a pewter dish and accompanied by a separate bowl of grated cheese.

Pointed-leaved spearmint and round-leaved apple mint are two varieties that can be combined for mint syrup, a drink sweetener.

Mint juleps with a tangy twist are made by pouring 1 part of mint syrup and 1 part of bourbon over crushed ice. Garnish with fresh mint.

HERB CRAFTNOTES

Bibliography

Buchman, Diane, **The Complete Herbal Guide to Natural Health and Beauty.** Doubleday & Company, Inc., 1973.

Brooklyn Botanic Garden, **Handbook on Herbs,** and **Handbook on Herbs and Their Ornamental Uses.** Write directly to the Brooklyn Botanic Garden, Brooklyn, New York 11225.

Campbell, Mary Mason, **Betty Crocker's Kitchen Gardens.** Universal Publishing, Inc., 1971.

Claiborne, Craig, **An Herb and Spice Cook Book.** Bantam Books, Inc., 1963.

Clarkson, Rosetta E., **Herbs: Their Culture and Uses.** The Macmillan Company, 1942.

Collins, Mary, **Everyday Cooking With Herbs.** Doubleday & Company, Inc., 1974.

Foster, Gertrude B., **Herbs for Every Garden.** E. P. Dutton & Company, Inc., 1966.

Fox, Helen M., **Gardening with Herbs for Flavor and Fragrance.** Sterling Publishing Company, Inc., 1970.

Herb Grower Magazine, Falls Village, Connecticut 06031. Subscription quarterly.

Herb Society of America, **A Primer for Herb Growing** and other publications. Write for prices and a publications list to The Herb Society of America, Horticultural Hall, 300 Massachusetts Avenue, Boston, Massachusetts 02115.

Hogner, Dorothy C., **A Fresh Herb Platter.** Doubleday & Company, Inc., 1961; **Herbs: From the Garden to the Table.** Oxford University Press, 1953.

Hylton, William H., Ed., **The Rodale Herb Book.** Rodale Press, 1974.

Miloradovich, Milo, **The Art of Cooking with Herbs and Spices,** Doubleday & Company, Inc. 1950.

Simmons, Adelma G., **Herb Gardening in Five Seasons.** Hawthorn Books, Inc., 1964. **Herbs to Grow Indoors.** Hawthorn Books, Inc., 1969. **The Illustrated Herbal Handbook,** Hawthorn Books, Inc., 1972.

Schafer, Violet, **Herbcraft.** Yerba Buena Press, 1971.

Sunset Books, **How to Grow Herbs.** Lane Books, 1972.

The Time-Life Encyclopedia of Gardening, Vegetables and Fruits. Time Inc., 1972.

Webster, Helen N., **Herbs — How to Grow Them and How to Use Them.** Charles T. Branford Company, 1942.

Williams, Katherine B., **Herbs: The Spice of a Gardener's Life.** Diversity Books, Kansas City, Missouri, 1965.

Sources of Herbs

Seeds and plants are sold at nurseries and garden centers and there are also many mail order suppliers. Some require a minimum order so it is best to write mail order houses first and request a catalogue.

Barn Herbery, Inc.
14 East Germantown Pike
Plymouth Meeting, Pennsylvania 19462

Black Forest Botanicals
Route 1, Box 34
Yuba, Wisconsin 54672

Caprilands Herb Garden
Coventry, Connecticut 06238

Carroll Gardens
Box 310
Westminster, Maryland 21157

Cedarbrook Herb Farm
Route 1, Box 1047
Sequim, Washington 98382

Gilbertie of Westport
7 Sylvan Lane
Westport, Connecticut 06880

The Herb Cottage
Washington National Cathedral
Washington, D.C. 20016

The Herb Farm and Country Store
380 North Granbee Road
Route 109
Granbee, Connecticut 06060

Hilltop Herb Farm
Box 866
Cleveland, Texas 77327

Logee's Greenhouses
55 North Street
Danielson, Connecticut 06239

Meadowbrook Herb Garden
Wyoming, Rhode Island 02898

Merry Gardens
Camden, Maine 04843

Rocky Hollow Herb Farm
RD 2, Box 215
Lake Wallkill Road
Sussex, New Jersey 07461

Sunnybrook Herb Farm Nursery
Mayfield Road
Chesterfield, Ohio 44026

Taylor's Garden
2549 Stingle Avenue
Rosemead, California 91770

The Tool Shed Nursery
Turkey Hill Road
Salem Center, Purdy's Station, New York 12865

Wayside Gardens
9470 Mentor Avenue
Mentor, Ohio 44060

White Flower Farm
Route 63
Litchfield, Connecticut 06759

Where to See Herb Gardens

California
Los Angeles State & Country Arboretum
Arcadia

Illinois
Botanic Garden of the Chicago Horticultural Society
Glencoe

Massachusetts
Plimouth Plantation
Plymouth

Berkshire Garden Center
Stockbridge

Michigan
Beal-Garfield Gardens
Michigan State University
East Lansing

New Jersey
Wick House Herb Garden
Morristown National Historical Park
Morristown

New York
Brooklyn Botanic Garden
Brooklyn

New York Botanical Garden
Bronx

The Cloisters, Fort Tryon Park
Manhattan

Ohio
The Garden Center of Greater Cleveland
Wade Oval
Cleveland

Pennsylvania
Morris Arboretum
Chestnut Hill

Virginia
Mount Vernon Kitchen Garden
Mount Vernon

Wisconsin
Alfred E. Boerner Botanical Garden
Hale's Corner

Popular and Useful Herbs

These herbs are arranged according to their common names. At the right of each herb's illustration is its botanical name, description, and useful growing information.

Balm, lemon

Melissa officinalis
Perennial
Uses: culinary, fragrance

Crinkly, green leaves about 2 to 3 inches long with scalloped borders. Plant grows 1 to 2 feet tall and bears tiny, bushy, white flowers during summer.

Strong lemon-scented leaves. Flourishes in full sun or partial shade, and has a tendency to spread. Use leaves from early spring to late fall.

Basil, sweet

Ocimum basilicum
Annual
Use: culinary

Light green plant that grows 1 to 2 feet tall. Small, shiny leaves 1 to 2 inches long. Small white flowers grow in spikes at the ends of the stems.

Grows in full sun and seed is quick to germinate. Green leaves can be picked after approximately 6 weeks. Bush basil is a decorative variety that is more insect free.

Burnet, salad

Sanguisorba minor
Perennial
Use: culinary

Bushy plant 1 to 2 feet tall bearing feathery, fern-like notched leaves. Grows in clumps. Rose-colored flowers top tall stems arising from the center of the bush.

Grows well in sunlight in well-drained soil. Easy to start from seed. Tastes like cucumber. Add fresh leaves to salads, drinks, and cheese. Cutting off flower stems encourages leaf growth.

Chives

Allium schoenoprasum
Perennial
Use: culinary

Hollow, onion-like leaves growing in clumps that reach about 10 inches in height. Clusters of lavender flowers appear a few inches above the leaves in spring. Garlic chives have flat leaves.

Grows in sun. Usually bought as small plants but can be started from seeds though this takes about a year to yield usable plants. Delicate onion-like flavor; used fresh or frozen to season many dishes.

Dill

Anethum graveolens
Annual
Use: culinary

Grows about 3 feet tall. Feathery light green, many branched leaves grow on bluish-green stems. In mid-summer, yellow flowers appear and ripen into small brown seeds.

Cultivated for the pungent flavor of seeds; used for making pickles, and in a variety of other cookery. Grows quickly in full sun. Seeds should be planted in spring. Harvest the entire plant in early fall or seeds will self-sow.

Garlic

Allium sativum
Perennial
Use: culinary

Grows from bulbs that break into small sections called cloves; flat, narrow leaves grow approximately 2 feet long and are topped by globes of white flowers.

Bulb multiplies into 8 to 12 cloves during the growing season. These are dug up for use and replanting. Harvest when leaves die after flowering.

Marjoram, sweet

Majorana hortensis
Perennial
Use: culinary

Low, spreading, bushy plant some 8 to 12 inches high. Velvety, oval, gray-green leaves; small white flowers grow from knot-like leaf clusters at the end of stems.

Easily grown from seeds in spring. Cutting off the leafy stems stimulates growth of new stems and leaves. Treated as an annual in the North or as a pot plant during winter.

Mint

Mentha species
Perennial
Uses: culinary, fragrance

Growth varies with species from 1 to 3 feet. Most common is spearmint which has crisp, dark green crinkly leaves about 2 inches long. Plant grows 1 to 2 feet tall and spreads rampantly.

Cultivated for fruit-scented leaves. Will grow in sun or partial shade. Spreads rapidly by means of underground stems. Leaves can be picked any time, stimulating new growth.

Savory, summer

Satureia hortensis
Annual
Use: culinary

Narrow, dark green leaves, upright stems, often branching; 1 to 2 feet tall. Pink flowers appear about 2 months after sowing.

Grows in full sun. Leaves can be picked any time for fresh use. Delicate pepper flavor. Used with meats and vegetables.

Oregano

Origanum vulgare
Perennial
Use: culinary

Grows 2 to 2 1/2 feet tall; gray-green oval leaves that come to a blunt point. White, pink and purple flowers.

Also known as wild marjoram. Grows in sun and spreads rapidly. Flowers should be cut back. Makes a good container plant. Use fresh leaves or dried.

Savory, winter

Satureia montana
Perennial
Use: culinary

Lower, more spreading growth than summer savory. Dark green, shiny leaves. Grows 1 to 2 feet tall with light green stems at the upper ends of a woody base.

A good border plant; woody stems should be trimmed back to 4 inches in spring. Dried leaves excellent with beans and eggs.

Parsley

Petroselinum crispum
Biennial treated as an annual
Use: culinary

Grows about 1 foot tall in clumps. Curly parsley, the most popular species, has bright green serrated edges and crinkled leaves. Italian parsley has coarse flat leaves, but has more flavor. Chervil is the French parsley.

Slow to germinate; most gardeners prefer to put in new plants each spring. Grows best in full sun.

Tarragon (French)

Artemisia dracunculus
Perennial
Use: culinary

Thin bush with inch-long slender green leaves; grows 1 to 2 1/2 feet tall.

Needs well-drained soil and full or partial sun. Will not produce seeds; grows from cuttings or divisions. Should not be confused with Russian tarragon which does seed. A single plant will produce 1 to 2 cups of licorice-flavored leaves; can be used to flavor vinegar.

Rosemary

Rosmarinus officinalis
Perennial
Use: culinary

Evergreen shrub with needle-like leaves that grows 2 to 3 feet tall. Produces bluish-purple flowers.

Needs full sun and grows best in soil containing lime. In cold climates, it is brought indoors in winter. Leaves have a pine-like aroma and are especially good with meats.

Thyme

Thymus vulgaris
Perennial
Use: culinary

Small bush 1/2 to 1 foot tall; can spread 1 1/2 feet or more. Tiny, oval, evergreen leaves and small purple flowers.

Grows in well-drained soil that is fairly dry. Used sparingly as it has a strong flavor. Attracts bees.

HIBACHI AND HOT-POT COOKERY
Creative Cooking at the Table

The preparation of Japanese foods, like so many of that country's elegant arts, is a stylized ritual designed as much to create a feeling of harmony as to nourish the body. This ritual begins in the kitchen, where foods are diced or sliced with great grace and dexterity. It is then continued at the dining table, where the actual cooking takes place. Each member of the dinner party often selects those morsels that tempt him most, then does his own cooking.

Sauces with subtle flavors, freshly harvested foods in season, even artfully selected table settings add to the pleasure of the meal. These pose little burden for the host and hostess, since the main dishes are so easily prepared. Once the techniques of cutting and arranging the ingredients of the meal are mastered, the actual cooking is simplicity itself.

One of the great charms of learning to cook in a new language is the fact that a cuisine mirrors so much of the lifestyle and history of a people. Japan is no exception, and some of her most pleasing culinary customs can be linked very directly to that nation's historical past.

Hibachi and hot-pot cookery were originally rooted in the need for extra warmth in winter. Fuel has nearly always been in short supply in Japan, so at one time almost all the cooking was done over a charcoal fire housed in a tiny cast-iron hibachi grill, with the fuel warming both the food and the diners. But in a tightly built modern home, the carbon monoxide fumes given off by burning charcoal are hazardous, so today's hibachi cooking should be reserved for patios or porches.

The choice of foods as well as the mode of cooking mirrors the way things were in the past. As a densely populated series of volcanic islands, Japan had little land available for grazing, so fish, rather than beef or fowl, was the mainstay of many meals. Vegetables were consumed in great quantities, but they could only be obtained during the harvest season. To this day they are always served fresh, and often in a form that underlines the season. In fall, for example, thin slices of raw carrot might be sculpted to resemble orange maple leaves.

The Basics

The two types of Japanese cooking explored here, hot-pot and hibachi, are ideally suited for entertaining, but either can be fun at family meals too. The hibachi is a charcoal grill in which temperatures can be regulated to some extent, but hibachi recipes can be used with any kind of oven broiler or barbecue grill. For hot-pot cooking, an electric skillet or any kind of a casserole or chafing dish with a built-in heating element is suitable.

Japanese meals usually involve more preparation time than actual cooking time. The food is usually served in bite-sized pieces, mandating some skill in the kitchen with knife or cleaver. Japanese techniques for slicing, dicing and chopping are indeed an art, but once learned, they can be applied to any cooking you do. The ability to eat gracefully with chopsticks is also an art, but one you will be able to manage with a little practice: techniques are detailed on page 896.

Rice, served with every Japanese meal, is prepared in advance so it will be ready with the rest of the meal; most other Japanese foods require only a short cooking time. Bowls and cups are set out for each diner; when possible, they are selected to harmonize with the foods they will hold.

When you have mastered the techniques explained on these pages, do not be afraid to experiment. Many ingredients are interchangeable, and you can try a wealth of seasonings, both subtle and pungent. Try these basic recipes, then modify them to suit your own tastes and the occasion. With a little care you will be sure to hear, "*Gochiso-sama*—I enjoyed it," as the meal ends.

Chieko and Yasuhide Kobashi enjoy a *shabu shabu* feast of beef and vegetables that are cut into bite-sized pieces, cooked at the dining table in a pot of simmering broth, then dipped into various sauces and condiments. Rice and tea round out the menu for this delightful dinner.

Chieko Kobashi was born in Kitakami, Japan, and came to the United States to study voice at the Juilliard School of Music. While she was a student, she taught cooking at New York's Japan Society. Her husband, Yasuhide, is a sculptor. They have two sons.

A mini-glossary

Kushi: slim bamboo skewers on which pieces of food are threaded for cooking.

Kushiyaki: skewer-broiled foods.

Mirin: a sweet Japanese wine made from steamed rice and used to flavor foods.

Nabemono: one-pot, do-it-yourself cooking in simmering broth at the dining table.

Ponzu: a dipping sauce for **nabemono**, made of lemon juice, soy sauce and other seasonings.

Sake: Japanese rice wine, used in cooking and as a beverage (usually served warm).

Sashimi: slices of raw fish.

Shabu shabu: a hot-pot dish of beef and vegetables.

Shoyu: soy sauce, the single most important seasoning in Japanese cuisine; a pungent brown liquid made of soy beans, barley, yeast and salt.

Sukiyaki: a sauteed beef dish.

Sushi: vinegared rice and raw fish dishes.

Tempura: deep-fried foods.

Teriyaki: foods broiled with a glaze..

Tofu: a soybean curd that absorbs flavors from other foods.

Yakimono: foods that have been broiled or grilled, often on a hibachi.

Yakitori: grilled chicken on skewers.

Useful kitchen utensils include, left to right: An all-purpose cleaver, a fish-and-meat knife, kitchen chopsticks, a grater, a bamboo strainer, and a mortar-and-pestle for grinding seeds, nuts and other hard foods.

Equipment

Although hibachi-style cooking does not have to be done on a hibachi, the food does taste better and is more authentic if it is cooked over a charcoal fire. I use the term "hibachi cooking" to include grilling, roasting, or broiling any food over a charcoal fire. Any grill that will burn charcoal can be used to cook the skewered ingredients and many of my cooking-school students use a barbecue grill. If you want an authentic hibachi, you can buy one at a hardware or department store. It will be made of heavy cast iron and will have a removable grate on top and a small door at the bottom to use in regulating the heat of the fire. (The wider the door opening, the hotter the coals).

Although the Japanese tradition has been to use hibachis indoors, most modern homes do not provide the easy cross-ventilation characteristic of Japanese homes with sliding screens. You should not cook on a charcoal-burning hibachi indoors, even with the windows open. The incomplete combustion of the charcoal gives off a large amount of carbon monoxide, so much, in fact, that labels on bags of charcoal warn against indoor burning.

You will also need skewers, either metal ones or the slim bamboo skewers known as *kushi*. If you use bamboo, soak them in water first so they will not burn.

Since ceremony is such an important part of a Japanese meal, set your table with chopsticks as well as forks, and encourage your guests to learn to use them. Whether or not food eaten this way tastes better, the meal will last longer.

Japanese kitchens are kept well-stocked with knives, skillets, pots and pans, and certain special utensils like a rice pot. You probably already own most of the equipment you need, but you might want to invest in an extremely good knife and cleaver. These are essential for chopping foods and making thin slices and are useful for any cooking you do.

Kitchen Favorites and Celebrations
Hibachi cooking

Skewers holding either flank steak, mushrooms, onions and peppers or a combination of shrimp, scallops, mushrooms and scallions are placed on a hibachi (top). Near at hand are more filled skewers ready for cooking as appetites demand, and a bowl of marinade ready for basting.

There are several broiling variations, hence a number of terms are used to describe hibachi-cooked dishes. *Yakimono* is a general term for broiled foods, *yaki* meaning broiled. *Kushiyaki* refers to meat that is strung on skewers *(kushi)* and grilled. *Yakitori*, on the other hand, is grilled chicken *(tori)*. *Teriyaki*, the term for food that is glazed and broiled, applies to any food that has been soaked in a marinade containing soy sauce so, when it is broiled, it gets shiny *(teri)*. Usually *teriyaki* refers to fish cooked this way, but any food can be used instead.

Broiled foods are popular throughout Japan and many restaurants specialize in one or more kinds. Diners sit at a table that has a small firepot in the center. A grate of flat metal bars over the firepot serves as the cooking surface. Food is cooked directly on these bars, which have been oiled to prevent sticking.

For cooking Japanese-style at home, the easiest method is to skewer ingredients in any combination of meat, vegetables and/or fish that appeals to you, then lay the skewer directly on top of the hot hibachi. Fruits, or combinations of fruits and vegetables, can also be cooked in this way.

Skewered Dinner

The recipe on the opposite page is intended to serve as a basic introduction to the art of preparing a hibachi-broiled dinner. It is, of course, subject to an infinite number of variations. So adjust the ingredients to suit your own taste and use any combination of foods that pleases you. Remember to start a large pot of white rice cooking about half-an-hour before mealtime; instructions for cooking rice the Japanese way (which helps keep it on the chopsticks) are on page 893. A typical dinner menu might also include clear soup and, for dessert, fresh fruit.

This recipe serves as a main course for four to six people, or as an appetizer for ten or more. Be sure to include seasonal ingredients, as the Japanese do. And instead of flank steak, you might try chicken, shrimp, scallops, lamb, or a different cut of beef. If you use shrimp, leave the tails on as this makes them easier to thread on skewers.

Ingredients
2-pound flank steak
1 pound fresh mushrooms
2 bunches scallions
1 large yellow onion
3 green peppers

Marinade
½ cup Japanese soy sauce
¼ cup mirin or cooking sherry
¼ cup sake or dry white wine

Milder marinade
½ cup soy sauce
½ cup sake
4 tablespoons sugar

Slicing the Flank Steak

Before you slice a flank steak, freeze it for about an hour or until it is fairly firm. This will make it easier to slice. Cut with a sharp knife or cleaver, holding it with your fingers close to the blade and curled as though you were shaking hands with the knife. Hold the meat steady with your other hand. Slice against the grain of the meat, drawing the blade away from you with a smooth motion. Try to make each slice no more than ⅛-inch thick (photograph 1). Between slices, push the meat toward the blade with your other hand. Be sure to curl these fingertips under, as if making a loose fist, in order to keep them well removed from the sharp cutting edge of the slicing tool.

Preparing Ingredients for Skewering

Marinate the meat slices for at least one hour in either of the suggested marinades. If you like, you can marinate the meat overnight, keeping it refrigerated and covered with a piece of plastic wrap.

Wash the mushrooms and remove stems of any that are large; cut into quarters.

Wash the scallions and cut them into 2-inch lengths, using both white and green parts and making all pieces the same size (photograph 2).

Peel the onion and cut it into 1-inch chunks or divide it into sections.

Cut the green peppers into inch-square pieces, first making long strips and then cutting the strips crosswise.

Roll the steak slices into small logs and thread them onto the skewers, alternating them with the vegetables. (The photograph on the opposite page shows how this combination of food looks.)

Save any leftover marinade to use for basting the food as it cooks.

Broiling

Prepare a charcoal fire in your hibachi, allowing about 20 minutes for the coals to reach cooking temperature. They will maintain this temperature for about an hour. Experiment with your hibachi to determine how the draft opening should be set to hold the right cooking temperature.

Place the threaded skewers on the hibachi and baste them with marinade, using a pastry brush or a spoon. Broil for five minutes on one side, then turn the skewers over, using pot holders to take hold of the skewer ends. Broil for three minutes more, basting frequently.

Marinade tends to make foods burn easily, so remove the skewers as soon as the meat is done. It will be charcoal black on the outside, but pink inside. If the fire seems too hot, adjust the draft or raise the grate.

Dining Japanese-style

Each diner's place should be set with a small bowl of rice, a pair of chopsticks, and a plate. As your food-filled skewer is ready, remove it from the grill and put it on your plate. Slide one chunk of food off the skewer at a time, using the chopsticks as pushers as you lift one end of the skewer. To eat the morsel, hold the rice bowl off the table near your mouth to catch tasty drips, pick up the piece of meat or vegetable with chopsticks, and convey it to your mouth. Alternate bites of meat, vegetables and rice.

Green tea is served before and after a Japanese meal, as well as at numerous other times of the day. You may also wish to serve sake, the Japanese rice wine, with the meal. Sake should first be warmed in a pot of hot water, then served warm in small cups. Sake is sipped slowly as it is potent.

1: Knuckles of the left hand are used to guide the slicing knife as a flank steak is cut into pieces ⅛-inch thick. Mrs. Kobashi is using a sharp, triangular knife of Japanese make, designed to cut cleanly through meat and fish.

2: A cleaver is used to cut scallions in 2-inch pieces, as nearly uniform in length as possible. Try to develop a rhythmic slicing motion, positioning uncut portions with the left hand without putting fingers dangerously near the blade.

Rice the Japanese way

The Japanese traditionally prepare rice so that it has a sticky consistency and can be easily handled with chopsticks. The rice is washed, soaked, cooked and steamed. An electric rice cooker is commonly used today in Japan, and individual manufacturer's instructions should be followed. Otherwise, top-of-the-stove cooking is fine, so long as a heavy pot with a tight-fitting lid is used. The standard ratio, if you wish to increase or decrease the amount of rice cooked, is 1 cup of uncooked rice to 1¼ cups of water. If Japanese rice is unavailable, use unconverted short-grain rice.

Pour the rice into a sieve and wash it under cold running water. When clean, the rice should be left to soak in a saucepan for 30 minutes to one hour. Change the water several times until it remains clear. Drain the rice well. Then put it into the cooking pot with 1¼ cups of fresh water. Cover tightly and quickly bring the water to a boil over a high flame. Then lower the flame and let the rice simmer for 5 minutes, or until all the water is absorbed. Turn off the heat, and steam the rice by letting it stand covered for about 15 minutes.

To serve, fluff and serve the rice with a wooden spoon.

Kitchen Favorites and Celebrations
Meal-in-a-pot

$ X 🧍 🦟

Ingredients for Japanese dishes

Daikon: Japanese white radish much larger than the American variety and often called horseradish. White turnip can be substituted. **Daikon** is peeled and grated when being added to **ponzu** sauce.

Hakusai: Chinese cabbage with taste and texture somewhere between those of crisp lettuce and white cabbage. The flavor is unique.

Harusame: transparent cellophane noodles often called "spring rain." They are soaked and cut into 4-inch lengths when soft.

Kombu: dried Japanese seaweed (kelp) sold in sheets.

Shitake: dried Japanese mushrooms that can be stored indefinitely in plastic bags. When needed, they can be reconstituted by being soaked in water for about 20 minutes. Chinese dried mushrooms are a substitute.

Shoga: fresh ginger root sold in small pieces by weight. Unused portions can be wrapped in plastic and stored in the refrigerator. The root is generally peeled and grated or cut into fine slices. It has such a strong taste that it is used in small amounts. Ground ginger is not a satisfactory substitute.

Shicimi: seven-spices powder, flavoring made of white and black sesame seeds, roasted sesame seeds, Japanese powdered peppers, chili powder, dried seaweed and orange peel. It is used to flavor **ponzu**.

Tofu: bean curd cake, a custard-like cube about 3 by 5 inches in size, made from pressed soybeans. It is an excellent source of protein and a staple of the Japanese kitchen. The taste is bland, but the cake readily takes on the flavor of foods it is mixed with. Fresh cakes, covered with water, can be kept in the refrigerator for several days; water should be changed daily. Bean curd is also available canned. There is no substitute.

Nabemono is one-pot cooking that is done right at the dining table, as pictured on page 890. The pre-cut raw food is attractively arranged on a large platter and each diner, using chopsticks, picks up a tidbit and dips it briefly in the pot of bubbling water or broth. A beguiling version of this cooking is called *shabu shabu*, so named because pieces of beef being swirled through the water make a swishing sound—*shabu shabu*. Other *nabemono* dishes call for ingredients to be dropped into the broth. Diners then pluck pieces from the communal broth. The broth is usually eaten as a soup at the end of the meal with salt or soy sauce added.

A hot pot can be either an electrical appliance that is self-heating or a pot that is set on a burner, is used for *nabemono*. The heat is kept high until the broth comes to a boil, then is adjusted so the liquid is kept simmering throughout the meal. Though this is usually a long and leisurely affair, the edge can be taken off a whetted appetite quickly; it takes only a minute or two for the first few bites to be cooked to perfection. After all the pieces of meat and vegetable and fish have been cooked and consumed, the simmering broth, now richly flavored, can be sipped as a delightful close to the meal. It is considered mannerly to leave a clean table and an empty pot, indicating that the meal was delicious and properly frugal.

Any utensil that can serve as a caldron—a fondue pot, electric skillet, or shallow casserole, for example—is most effective for this type of cooking. Set the cooking pot in the center of the dining table and adjust the heat so that the cooking liquid is kept simmering, but not boiling, throughout the meal.

The *shabu shabu* recipe on the opposite page, a good introduction to the use of Japanese vegetables and dipping sauces, will give you an elegant and abundant main course for six when it is served with rice. As with hibachi cooking, be sure to start the rice well before mealtime so it will be ready when you sit down to eat. Set bowls of rice, plates and chopsticks at each place and put the beef-and-vegetable platter within easy reach of all diners.

This *shabu shabu* platter groups ingredients by kind, using a circular arrangement with *tofu* (soybean curd cake) at the center. Included, clockwise from the top, are *harusame* (cellophane noodles), sliced flank steak, *shitake* (mushrooms), *hakusai* (Chinese cabbage) and scallions. Condiments in the background to flavor dipping sauce are white and black sesame seeds, seven-spices powder and grated ginger.

The description of some Japanese foodstuffs on the opposite page will help you understand how they are used, thus helping you make substitutions if necessary. Many cities have Oriental food stores and specialty food departments that sell these products, but if you have difficulty in locating any ingredient, the Japan Food Corporation (page 896) will direct you to the nearest source of supply.

Hearty Hot Pot

Any foods that have short cooking times are suitable for hot-pot cooking. Selecting ingredients that provide both contrast and harmony in taste, color and texture assures a successful meal. Crunchy, soft and textured foods should be combined as in the suggested recipe below. This, with rice, will serve six.

Ingredients

2-pound flank steak
1 head *hakusai* (Chinese cabbage)
2 cakes *tofu* (bean curd cake)
1 sheet *kombu* (dried seaweed)
1 bag *harusame* (cellophane noodles)
12 *shitake* (dried mushrooms)
1 bunch scallions

6 cups water

For dipping sauce:

½ cup Japanese soy sauce
½ cup lemon juice
3 tablespoons *daikon* (radish), grated
1 tablespoon fresh ginger, peeled and grated

Freeze the flank steak until firm and cut into ⅛-inch slices (page 893).

Rinse and slice the *hakusai* into 1-inch pieces (photograph 3).

Wash the scallions and cut them into short pieces with diagonal slices (photograph 4). Using a cleaver or sharp knife, make a diagonal cut one or two inches from the end of the scallion. After each cut, roll the scallion a quarter-turn around and make another diagonal cut two inches from the last. Use your left hand for turning, if you are right-handed, making sure you keep your fingers curved and out of danger. This is termed a roll cut.

Cut the *tofu* into 1-inch squares. Because the cake is so fragile, it must be handled with great care or it will break apart. Place it gently on your cutting board and slice it gently as well.

Cut a sheet of *kombu* into strips and soak in water until soft.

Soak the *harusame* in hot water for 15 minutes then cut into 4-inch lengths.

Soak the *shitake* in water to cover for 20 minutes or until they are puffy, slice them in half or quarter them (photograph 5), and remove the hard stems.

3: A cleaver is used to slice Chinese cabbage into inch-wide sections. The unsliced portion is pushed toward the blade with the other hand.

4: The roll cut involves cutting a vegetable on the diagonal and turning the uncut portion one-quarter turn after each slice is made.

5: Dried mushrooms, puffed up and soft after being soaked in water, are quartered. The stems, usually too hard to eat, have been removed.

Ponzu sauce is a basic dip made from lemon juice and soy sauce. It can be flavored to taste with grated *daikon* or grated fresh ginger, ground sesame seeds, ground peanuts, *shichimi* (the seven-spices powder), chopped scallions or other condiments. Each diner should get his own bowl of dipping sauce to flavor as he chooses. Judicious experimenting should lead to a pleasing combination. All the host or hostess can do is provide a variety of condiments and garnishes that guests can add to the basic *ponzu* sauce at will.

About Chopsticks

There are several ways to use chopsticks and you will have to experiment to find the one that feels most comfortable—and works. Basically, the sticks are held in the right hand and positioned to the left. Once the chopsticks are properly placed, the bottom stick will be stationary while the top one acts as a lever, moving up and down to grasp or release food. As indicated in the photographs below, the moving top stick is held much as a pencil is. After you learn to eat with chopsticks you'll find them a useful cooking utensil as well.

6: The upper chopstick is firmly held between the thumb and first finger, pencil-fashion.

7: Slide the lower chopstick into the crook of the thumb and let it rest on the fourth finger.

8: The lower chopstick is stationary while the upper one is used as a lever to grasp the food.

Enjoying a Hot-Pot Meal

When you serve a hearty hot-pot dinner (page 895), place all of the condiments and the dipping sauce in small bowls on the table. Set the platter of prepared ingredients where all of the diners can reach it comfortably.

Put the water into the cooking pot and bring the water to a boil. You may have to do this in the kitchen, depending on the heat source you have at the dining table. But once the water is boiling, adjust the table heat so it will keep the liquid simmering through the meal.

Each diner selects a morsel from the large platter, using chopsticks, a fondue fork, or long-handled heat-proof tongs, and holds the food in the bubbling water until it is cooked. Mushrooms and tofu take the longest to cook of the ingredients suggested here, but their cooking time is only a few minutes. The meat, because it is so thinly sliced, will be done on the outside and be pink and tender on the inside in about a minute.

When a chosen morsel is done, the diner dips it into his bowl of *ponzu* sauce, seasoned to his own liking. As he lifts the bite, he raises the bowl of rice with the other hand to catch any drippings.

When all of the foods have been cooked and eaten, the water remaining in the pot has become a rich, tasty stock that may be ladled into bowls for drinking.

Once these basic forms of Japanese cooking have been tried, improvise to determine what other ingredients, sauces and seasonings appeal to you. Apply the chopping and slicing techniques to any cooking you do. Oriental cuisine is further explored in the entry, "Wok Cookery."

Where to Buy Ingredients

Ingredients for Japanese cooking can be obtained from shops in Oriental neighborhoods and in gourmet departments of many supermarkets. If you cannot locate the ingredients you need in your city, the regional offices of Japan Food Corporation can supply you with the names of the nearest retailers.

Addresses of Japan Food Corporation offices are:

Baltimore area: 95-25 Berger Road, Columbia, Md. 21046.
Chicago: 1850 West 43 Street, Chicago, Ill. 60609.
Houston: 3305 Sulrose Street, Houston, Tex. 77006.
Los Angeles: 920 South Mateo Street, Los Angeles, Cal. 90021.
New York: 11-31 31st Avenue, Long Island City, N.Y. 11106.
Sacramento: 1515 North C Street, Sacramento, Cal. 95814.
San Francisco: 900 Marin Street, San Francisco, Cal. 94119.
Toronto: 25-6 Connel Court, Toronto, Ontario, Canada.